1876.

PROCEEDINGS

OF THE

REPUBLICAN NATIONAL CONVENTION,

HELD AT

CINCINNATI, OHIO,

WEDNESDAY, THURSDAY, AND FRIDAY,

June 14, 15, and 16, 1876,

Resulting in the nomination for President and Vice-President of

RUTHERFORD B. HAYES

AND

WILLIAM A. WHEELER.

Officially reported by M. A. Clancy, of Washington, D. C., assisted by Wm. Nelson, of Paterson, N. J.

CONCORD, N. H.:
PRINTED BY THE REPUBLICAN PRESS ASSOCIATION.
1876.

REPUBLICAN NATIONAL CONVENTION,

1876.

PROCEEDINGS.

FIRST DAY—WEDNESDAY, JUNE 14, 1876.

Pursuant to the following call of the Republican National Committee,—

The next Union Republican National Convention, for the nomination of candidates for President and Vice-President of the United States, will be held in the city of Cincinnati, on Wednesday, the fourteenth day of June, 1876, at 12 o'clock, noon, and will consist of delegates from each state equal to twice the number of its senators and representatives in congress, and of two delegates from each organized territory and the district of Columbia.

In calling the conventions for the election of delegates, the committees of the several states are recommended to invite all Republican electors, and all other voters, without regard to past political differences or previous party affiliations, who are opposed to reviving sectional issues, and desire to promote friendly feeling and permanent harmony throughout the country by maintaining and enforcing all the constitutional rights of every citizen, including the full and free exercise of the right of suffrage without intimidation and without fraud; who are in favor of the continued prosecution and punishment of all official dishonesty, and of an economical administration of the government by honest, faithful, and capable officers; who are in favor of making such reforms in government as experience may from time to time suggest; who are opposed to impairing the credit of the nation by depreciating any of its obligations, and in favor of sustaining in every way the national faith and financial honor; who hold that the common-school system is the nursery of American liberty, and should be maintained absolutely free from sectarian control; who believe that, for promotion of these ends, the direction of the government should continue to be confided to those who adhere to the principles of 1776, and support them as incorporated in the constitution and the laws; and who are in favor of recognizing and strengthening the fundamental principle of national unity in this centennial anniversary of the birth of the republic.

E. D. MORGAN,
Chairman,
WM. E. CHANDLER,
Secretary,
REPUBLICAN NATIONAL COMMITTEE.

WASHINGTON, January 13, 1876,—

the Republican National Convention met at noon this day in Exposition Hall, on Elm, Fourteenth, and Plum streets, in the city of Cincinnati, Ohio, and promptly at the hour was called to order by Ex-Governor Edwin D. Morgan, of New York, chairman of the Republican National Committee, who thereupon announced that the proceedings would be opened with prayer by the Rev. D. H. Muller, D. D., of Covington, Ky.

Dr. Muller offered the following

PRAYER.

O God, whose throne is the universe, by whom kings reign and princes decree justice, in whose hands are the hearts of men, we acknowledge thee as the ruler of the nations, the author of every good and perfect gift. We come before thee with thanksgiving, for thou art a great God, and a great King above all gods. We acknowledge thee to be the giver of all national prosperity, and as our helper in past disasters; and we declare this morning, that "If it had not been that the Lord was on our side when men rose up against us, then had we been swallowed up quickly, when their wrath was kindled against us." Because thou hast blessed and helped us, therefore under the shadow of thy wing may we rejoice. Because thou hast heard our voice, therefore may we call upon thee as long as we live, and make thee our refuge and our portion.

In behalf of thy servants here assembled, we invoke thy blessing and aid. Bless them with health of body and mind. Preserve them from harm during their deliberations, and by thy providence return them in safety to their homes. By thy grace give to them the spirit of concord, that harmony may prevail in their counsels; a spirit of wisdom, that the right means may be discerned and used to promote the end for which they are convened; a spirit of patriotism, that the prosperity of the nation may overshadow all personal or sectional desires; a spirit of integrity, that they may be faithful to the deepest convictions of duty. Give grace, and wisdom, and strength to the presiding officers. For the work which thou hast wrought, for the Republic and humanity through the organized agency represented here, we give thee thanks; and we earnestly pray that its future record may be more glorious than its past one, and that the issue of the consultations and acts of thy servants here may be ruled by thee to thy glory, to the good of this country, and to the prosperity, and welfare, and honor, and safety of thy people. Guide, we beseech thee, therefore, their efforts in the choice of the men who may be commended or presented to the confidence and suffrages of the people, to the conception and declaration of right principles; and, invoking such results, we pray thee that national peace, governmental purity, truth, justice, and liberty may be established among us for all generations. We pray thee that thou mayest uphold and bless thy servant the president of the United States, and all others in authority. By the help of thy Spirit may they be inclined to thy will and walk in thy way. Grant them health, and prosperity, and long life. For the mercies which thou hast given us as a nation, we praise thee. We pray, this morning, that thy work may appear unto thy servants, and thy glory unto their children, and that the beauty of the Lord our God may be upon us. Establish thou the work of our hands; yea, the work of our hands, establish thou it. These blessings we ask for Christ's sake. Amen.

The delegates having been seated, Governor Morgan made the opening address, as follows:

GOVERNOR MORGAN'S ADDRESS.

Gentlemen of the Convention: The day and the hour have arrived at which the representatives of the Republican party were invited to assemble to nominate candidates for President and Vice-President of the United States; and, in obedience to the authority of the Republican National Committee, I now respectfully ask that you will maintain order.

In 1856, at Philadelphia, in 1860, at Chicago, and in 1864, at Baltimore, acting under the same general authority, it has been my privilege to call Republican conventions to order.

If I except the action of the convention of 1864, the duties which this intelligent body has to perform, in comparison with former ones, are the most important of all.

There is no special or parliamentary authority for any remarks from the chair. In the nature of things, there cannot be any. Custom, only, is my excuse (if excuse is needed) for even a few words.

In June, 1864, we were in the midst of the war for the preservation of the Union. We had great armies in the field, but they had achieved only partial successes, and when successful, always at very great cost of life. The bravest and best of our young men had fallen in battle by tens and hundreds of thousands, or were in prison at Andersonville and Libby. President Lincoln, seventeen months prior to this, had by proclamation, but only as a war measure, declared the slaves free, while their masters kept them within their lines, and held full dominion over them.

It was then modestly suggested by your chairman of the national committee, that the convention would not discharge its whole duty unless, among its resolves, it should declare for such an amendment of the national constitution as would, when adopted by the requisite number of states, forever prohibit African slavery on this continent. The suggestion was received with unexampled enthusiasm by the convention. The resolution to secure this national blessing was written in your party platform on that day: both houses of congress very soon after passed the required amendment: twenty-nine sovereign states ratified it: the noble Lincoln proclaimed the result to the people;—and from that hour to this "the sun has not risen upon a bondman nor set upon a slave" in all this fair land. Not to the North, not to the South, but to that Supreme Being alone who controls the destinies of nations as well as the affairs of individuals, let us give all the glory. But all this is past, and the past we conclude is secure.

Pardon me, gentlemen, if again, with like modesty, I make a suggestion or two bearing directly on the present. This convention should emphatically demand the prompt and efficient execution of those solemn promises of both houses of congress, and the president, to redeem in coin the legal-tender obligations of the government on the 1st of January, 1879, and signify its opposition to any modification or repeal of this law that does not guarantee a still earlier or better method of returning to specie payment. Let no doubtful word go out from this convention upon the subject of honest money. Prices are already at a specie point. Stand firmly by your numerous resolutions and platforms a little longer, and your currency basis will be transformed into a coin basis so easily and naturally that you will be yourselves surprised, regretting only, as you will, that it was not determined upon at an earlier day.

Resumption accomplished, then, in all human probability, will follow ten or fifteen years of prosperity equal to that of any former period, perhaps greater than the country has yet seen. If you will, in addition, put a plank in your platform declaring for such an amendment of the constitution as will extend the presidential office to six years, and make the incumbent ineligible for reëlection, you will deserve the gratitude of the American people.

As the mariner, when tossed for many days in thick weather, avails himself of the earliest glance of the sun to ascertain how far the elements have driven him from his true course, so in like manner, at the end of one hundred years from the foundation of our government, we too have come from the north, the south, the east, and the west, to take a political observation for the purpose of amending and improving our system of national government, so far as improvement is really necessary and possible. With this view we have come to this great and beautiful city of Cincinnati, on the banks of the grand but placid Ohio, containing nearly three hundred thousand souls, and where we now find every luxury that wealth, nature, or art can produce, but where not even a log cabin had been erected or a white man born when our government was organized.

The last three national conventions of our party have had indicated to them, in advance, the names of the candidates for the national ticket, so that they have been but little else than ratification meetings of decrees that had been made by the people, merely putting in form that which had already been decided upon. I allude to President Lincoln's second nomination, and to the nomination and renomination of the splendid soldier and patriot, General Grant. But such a state of things no longer exists. There appears to be at the present time no one to whom the unerring finger points as the only candidate. There seems to be no man rising so far above all others as to cause exultant voices to exclaim,—"Thou art the man!"

The consequence is, that many distinguished names among our party friends have been mentioned as candidates, and will be brought before the convention when the proper time arrives for making nominations. Therefore it is that I have expressed myself as seeing greater responsibilities resting upon the delegates to this Cincinnati convention than upon any or all that have preceded it.

The history of the Republican party furnishes abundant evidence of its desire that the government shall be administered with honesty and economy, and as a means to that end that the civil service should be elevated by the introduction of all needful and proper reforms. With such a history, and at a time like the present, it cannot be doubted that the choice of the convention will fall on some one, whomsoever he may be, clearly committed on this question—not only by his expressed opinions, but also by his public life and conduct.

I will not further anticipate the action of this honorable body, except to say that the firm support on the part of the nominees of all the recent amendments to the national constitution, and the support and maintenance of all other principles involved in the war for the preservation of the Union, must also be regarded as the pre-requisites for the high offices of President and Vice-President of the United States. With this accomplished, it will be the highest duty, and should be the greatest pleasure, for all in authority to extend the warm hand of fellowship to all good citizens of this Union, and as rapidly as possible to forgive and to forget the recent past, and to do every act to make us satisfied to be and remain in fact, as we are in name, one people, one country.

It is fit and proper, citizens of Cincinnati, that the Republican National Convention, in this centennial year, should be held in your city and under your auspices, as you, quite as fully as any other locality, represent in yourselves the industry, the enterprise, the sublimity, and the grandeur of our country's growth and greatness.

TEMPORARY CHAIRMAN.

Gov. MORGAN. I am further requested by the national committee to make a nomination of the temporary presiding officer of the convention, and therefore nominate the Hon. Theodore M. Pomeroy, of New York, for that office. [Applause.]

The question having been put, Governor Morgan declared Mr. Pomeroy chosen, and designated Governor Baldwin, of Michigan, and Governor Van Zandt, of Rhode Island, to conduct the temporary president to the chair.

On the arrival of the gentlemen on the stage with the temporary chairman, Governor Morgan said,—"I now present to you the Hon. Theodore M. Pomeroy, of New York." [Renewed applause.]

ADDRESS OF THE TEMPORARY CHAIRMAN.

Mr. Pomeroy spoke as follows:

Gentlemen of the Convention: I thank you most heartily for the compliment conferred by calling me to preside over the temporary organization of this convention.

I have been so long withdrawn from practical participation in political affairs, that it is in obedience to custom, rather than my own inclination, that I occupy even a few minutes of your time in the consideration of the political situation, and of the principles so long and so successfully entrusted to the keeping of the Republican party. Events have chased each other so rapidly, from the inauguration of President Lincoln to the closing year of the administration of General Grant, fraught with such fundamental changes in the whole theory and practice of government, that the consideration of them, in the briefest manner, is precluded upon an occasion such as this. Brief as may be considered the existence of the Republican party, none other in the history of the nation has for so long a consecutive period controlled its government without encountering popular defeat; and still, notwithstanding popular jealousy of political ascendency long continued by any party, it is in the power of this convention to designate the coming President of the United States. [Applause.] Our folly may concede what the wisdom of the opposition cannot achieve,—our defeat at the polls in November; but such defeat can come from no other source. We are met here, not as contending factions within the party to test under various leaderships our relative strength, but as representatives accepting a high responsibility to extract from the crucible of conflicting opinions that type of American statesmanship which shall be accepted as the worthy embodiment of the principles of the party. [Applause.] Men as well as measures are to be weighed in the balance during the coming canvass, and neither must be found wanting to secure success. [Applause.] The Republican party cannot continue to live by reason of its splendid achievements in the past, nor the Democratic party expect to be returned to power upon its glittering promises of reform in the future. [Applause.] The former party has but to present men representative of its principles; the latter must discover both its principles and its men. [Applause.] In former days, when party ties were firmer, when the immediate pressure of impending national calamity hedged us about and compelled party fidelity, the platform carried along the man, whomsoever he might be. Party ties are looser now, and no platform is buoyant enough to float an unworthy candidate. [Applause.]

The necessity for the continuance of the administrative policy of the Republican party, while not so apparent in immediate results, is as commanding respecting future consequences as at any time in its history. We are told that it has accomplished its mission, and, therefore, has no longer claim to live. Well, if it has, and the time for its dissolution has come, it can die triumphantly, like the apostle of old, exclaiming,—"I have fought a good fight; I have kept the faith." [Immense and continued applause.] It has fulfilled many missions. It fulfilled the mission of its birth in neutralizing the disastrous effects of the repeal of the Missouri Compromise, in saving freedom to the great territories of the North-west, and in bringing California into the sisterhood of states, undefiled by slavery, and adorned like a bride in the glitter of her golden promise. [Applause.] It fulfilled the mission of its youth in accepting the "irrepressible conflict," and it was a mission worth living for to have saved a nationality like ours; to have freed four million slaves and raised them to the dignity of American citizenship, and to have reconstructed the federal constitution so as to place the liberties of the citizen and the credit of the nation upon foundations strong enough to endure anything except the imbecility of a Democratic administration. [Loud applause.] The mission of the manhood of the Republican party, our mission of to-day, is, to establish on sure foundations and make secure for the coming ages the fruits of the war-debt, and taxation through which the present has been achieved. The benefits to be derived to the individual citizen from the fourteenth and fifteenth constitutional amendments are to be secured through such appropriate legislation as congress may devise. I ask the freedmen of the South, if they are ready to accept the Democratic party as the source of power [Voices—"No!" "No!" Speaker—I know it.] from which is to flow the appropriate legislation to give effect to those amendments. I ask a candid public, if the only anarchy that exists in the South to-day is not the anarchy caused by the opposition of the Democratic party, as such, to the principles adopted in the work of reconstruction, and now a fundamental part of the law of the land. The Democratic party claims to accept the situation respecting the sacredness of the national debt and the inviolability of the national credit, and yet $20,000,000 of taxation will not make good the annual loss to the American people, from the undefined and undefinable attitude and intentions of that party in regard to the payment of the principal of the public debt.

In the prosecution of the war to overthrow the rebellion, for the purpose of procuring the ready money to pay the army and the navy, and to provide the immense material of war, it became necessary to suspend specie payment, and to make a forced loan from the people, by declaring the greenback a legal tender in payment of public and private indebtedness; and yet, while claiming to be in favor of resumption of specie payment at some indefinite time, and by means of some indefinite process, although eleven years have elapsed since the close of the war, the Democratic party bitterly opposes the payment of the forced loan, or the taking of the first practical step toward assuming our position among the solvent nations of the civilized world. [Applause.]

No, gentlemen, the late war was not a mere prize-fight for national supremacy. It was the outgrowth of the conflict of irreconcilable moral, social, and political forces. Democracy had its lot with the moral, social, and political forces of the cause which was lost: the Republican party with those which triumphed and survived. The preservation of the results of that victory devolves upon us here and now. Democracy has no traditions of the past, no impulses of the present, no aspirations for the future fitting it for this task. The reaction of 1874 has already spent itself in a vain effort to realize the situation. It has simply demonstrated that no change in the machinery of the government can be had outside of the Republican party without drawing with it a practical nullification of the great work of reconstruction, financial chaos, and administrative revolution. The present house of representatives has succeeded in nothing except the development of its own incapacity. [Applause.] From the inception of the Republican party, in 1855, it has kept pace with the progress of the times, accepting each added responsibility of war, emancipation, taxation, and reconstruction, till the brightest pages of American history are but the life-story of the Republican party. [Applause.] Of the whole mass of its constitutional amendments and legislative enactments, it takes the responsibility without apology. It has often erred, but it has never failed to act, and through its action the nation has lived. There has been corruption;

but when it was discovered, the order went forth, "Let no guilty man escape." [Loud applause.] Gentlemen, that order has been executed. [Renewed applause.] There has been want of harmony; but a platform, unwavering in its declaration of principles, with candidates worthy of it, will weld together, as of old, into an unconquerable army, the great liberty-loving, law-abiding majority of the voters of the United States, and stamp with enduring success the results of the deliberations of this convention. [Great applause.] Again thanking you, gentlemen, I inquire, What is the pleasure of the convention?

Mr. David Atwood, of Wisconsin. I offer the following resolution:

Resolved, That Irving M. Bean, Esq., of Wisconsin, and Gen. H. H. Bingham, of Pennsylvania, serve as temporary secretaries of this convention.

The resolution was read and adopted, and the chair requested the secretaries to take their seats.

Mr. W. A. Howard, of Michigan. By request of the national committee, with the entire assent of the local committee, and by the earnest request of the Michigan delegation, I wish to present the name of Gen. E. W. Hinks, of Wisconsin, for sergeant-at-arms of this convention. He is a man covered all over with scars, and I hope that he will be elected by acclamation.

A vote was taken, and the chairman declared General Hinks elected.

Dr. Loring, of Massachusetts, offered the following resolution:

Resolved, That the roll of the states and territories be called, and the chairman of each delegation announce the names of the persons selected to serve on the following committees as each committee is named by the chair: 1. The Committee on Credentials. 2. The Committee on Permanent Organization. 3. The Committee on Rules and Order of Business. 4. The Committee on Resolutions.

The question being put, the resolution was declared adopted.

The Chair. Pursuant to the resolution, the secretary will call the roll of states.

Mr. S. B. Dutcher, of New York. I would inquire if that motion includes the territories.

The Chair. It does.

Mr. Dutcher. Then I move to reconsider the motion.

Mr. Albright, of Pennsylvania. I move to lay that motion on the table.

The Chair put this motion, and declared that Mr. Dutcher's motion to reconsider was laid on the table.

Mr. S. L. Woodford, of New York. I desire to ask if the roll of the states where there is a contest will be called.

The Chair. The convention has given no direction in respect to that. I presume as the states are called, when we come to states where there are contests, that question will be decided.

Mr. CUMBACK, of Indiana. Is it proposed to call the roll for each of these several committees?

The CHAIR. It was so ordered. They can be called in mass.

Mr. CUMBACK. I move that as the states are called they respectively announce their member for each of the committees.

The CHAIR. There is no objection, and the Chair considers that the motion is adopted. The gentlemen will therefore nominate the different committees at one time.

Mr. DUTCHER, of New York. I would move to add to the call, that the names of the gentlemen for vice-presidents and for members of the national committee be announced at the same time.

A DELEGATE from Pennsylvania. There is no propriety in that, because the Committee on Organization should select the vice-presidents.

Mr. DUTCHER. I withdraw the motion.

The roll-call was begun, Alabama being first called, and announcing as member of the Committee on Credentials, George Turner. Before the names of Alabama's members of the other committees had been announced,

Mr. WOODFORD, of New York, said,—It seems to me that there is a manifest impropriety in allowing those states or territories where there may be contests as to the proper delegation, to name members of the committee, and I think that either by unanimous consent or by some amendment of the resolution the usual parliamentary rule should be adopted,—that when a state is reached where there are contesting delegations, that state or territory should be passed on the roll-call. And I move you, sir, that in case of any state or territory where there is a contest as to the proper delegation, or where there are contesting delegations, such state or territory be passed upon the call of the roll.

Mr. CUMBACK. I move to add to the motion of the gentleman of New York, the district of Columbia.

Mr. WOODFORD. I accept the amendment of the gentleman from Indiana.

The question being put by the chair, the motion of Mr. Woodford, as thus amended, was agreed to.

The secretaries proceeded with the roll-call, passing Alabama under the above motion, and calling Arkansas. It being difficult to get the names correctly as they were announced by the chairmen of the delegations,

Mr. W. B. MANN, of Pennsylvania, remarked,—It is very evident this will consume a great deal of time, and there will be many inaccuracies in sounding names across the hall. I therefore move that the chairman of each delegation be requested to send the names in writing to the secretary on the platform.

No objection being made, it was so ordered.

A DELEGATE from Arkansas. I suggest that, to obviate confusion, the roll of states be called, and as each state is called the chairman of each delegation send the names in writing to the secretary.

Mr. CUMBACK. I think it would be better that, as the names are sent up, the secretary read them, so that the convention may hear who they are.

At the conclusion of the roll-call the secretary read the names of the various persons constituting the different committees, as follows:

COMMITTEE ON CREDENTIALS.

Arkansas,	O. P. Snyder.	Montana,	W. F. Sanders.
Arizona,	De Forest Porter.	Nebraska,	L. W. Osborn.
California,	Norman D. Rideout.	Nevada,	C. N. Harris.
Connecticut,	Joseph Selden.	New Hampshire,	Alonzo Nute.
Colorado,	J. B. Chaffee.	New Jersey,	Wm. J. Magie.
Dakota,	Alex. Hughes.	New York,	Thos. C. Platt.
Delaware,	James Scott.	North Carolina,	James Heaton.
Georgia,	James Atkins.	New Mexico,	Wm. Breeden.
Indiana,	Asbury Steele.	Ohio,	Wm. H. Upson.
Illinois,	G. S. Bangs.	Oregon,	J. V. David.
Iowa,	John T. Baldwin.	Pennsylvania,	Wm. S. Quay.
Idaho,	D. P. Thompson.	Rhode Island,	Wm. H. Howard.
Kansas,	A. H. Horton.	South Carolina,	Stephen A. Swails.
Kentucky,	J. W. Finnell.	Texas,	J. P. Newcome.
Louisiana,	Chas. E. Nash.	Tennessee,	A. G. Sharp.
Maine,	Seth L. Milliken.	Utah,	G. A. Black.
Maryland,	John T. Ensor.	Vermont,	Wheelock G. Veazey.
Massachusetts,	John E. Sanford.	Virginia,	J. F. Dezendorf.
Michigan,	Geo. Hannahs.	West Virginia,	Nathan Goff, Jr.
Minnesota,	W. G. Word.	Wisconsin,	Wm. David Atwood.
Mississippi,	R. C. Powers.	Washington,	G. T. Minor.
Missouri,	M. A. Rosenthal.	Wyoming,	Wm. Hunter.

RULES AND ORDER OF BUSINESS.

Arkansas,	R. A. Dawson.	Montana,	B. H. Tatem.
Arizona,	De Forest Porter.	Nebraska,	R. J. Brown.
California,	James M. Pierce.	Nevada,	R. S. Cloph.
Connecticut,	John T. Rockwell.	New Mexico,	W. P. Breeden.
Colorado,	Geo. W. Morgan.	New Hampshire,	Thomas C. Rand.
Dakota,	Alex. Hughes.	New Jersey,	John H. Kendrick.
Delaware,	J. H. Othcur.	New York,	Walter L. Sessions.
Georgia,	Jefferson S. Long.	North Carolina,	R. N. Worment.
Illinois,	E. S. Baker.	Ohio,	J. T. Updegraff.
Indiana,	Thos. M. Browne.	Oregon,	J. H. Foster.
Iowa,	S. M. Clarke.	Pennsylvania,	John Cessna.
Idaho,	Austin Savage.	Rhode Island,	J. S. Williams.
Kansas,	A. J. Banta.	South Carolina,	Robert Smalls.
Kentucky,	T. O. Shackelford.	Texas,	Richard Allen.
Louisiana,	George E. Hamlet.	Tennessee,	W. Y. Elliott.
Maine,	James M. Stone.	Utah,	J. B. McKean.
Maryland,	William Perkins.	Vermont,	Fred. E. Woodbridge.
Massachusetts,	William T. Davis.	Virginia,	J. F. Lewis.
Michigan,	Wm. H. Withington.	West Virginia,	J. E. Schley.
Minnesota,	John T. Ames.	Wisconsin,	S. R. D. Potter.
Mississippi,	J. J. Spellman.	Washington,	Elwood Evans.
Missouri,	H. E. Havens.	Wyoming,	J. M. Corey.

ON RESOLUTIONS.

Arkansas, . . .	C. C. Waters.	Montana, . .	W. F. Sanders.
Arizona, . .	R. C. McCormick.	New Mexico, . .	S. B. Axtell.
California, . .	Charles F. Reed.	Nebraska, . . .	A. R. Pinney.
Connecticut,	Joseph R. Hawley.	Nevada, ...	J. P. Jones.
Colorado, . .	James B. Belford.	New Hampshire,	Chas. H. Burns.
Dakota, . .	Andrew McHench.	New Jersey, . .	Fred. A. Potts.
Delaware, . . .	Eli R. Sharp.	New York, . .	Charles E. Smith.
Georgia, . .	Henry M. Turner.	North Carolina, .	P. C. Badger.
Illinois, ...	C. B. Farwell.	Ohio, . . .	Edward Cowans.
Indiana, . .	R. W. Thompson.	Oregon, . . .	H. K. Hines.
Iowa, ...	Hiram Price.	Pennsylvania,	Edward McPherson.
Idaho, ...	Austin Savage.	Rhode Island,	Charles Nourse.
Kansas, ...	J. D. Thacker.	So. Carolina,	D. W. Chamberlain.
Kentucky, . . .	James Speed.	Texas, ...	E. J. Davis.
Louisiana, . .	Henry Demoss.	Tennessee, .	A. A. Freeman.
Maine, . .	Nelson Dingley, Jr.	Utah, ...	J. B. McKean.
Maryland, . .	Dr. H. Steiner.	Vermont, . .	Geo. H. Bigelow.
Massachusetts,	Edward L. Pierce.	Virginia, ...	Wm. Miller.
Michigan, . . .	H. P. Baldwin.	West Virginia, .	J. W. Davis.
Minnesota, . .	J. E. Wakefield.	Wisconsin, .	James H. Howe.
Mississippi, . .	C. W. Clarke.	Washington, . .	Elwood Evans.
Missouri, . .	R. T. Van Horn.	Wyoming, . . .	Wm. Hinton.

ON PERMANENT ORGANIZATION.

Arkansas, . .	M. W. Benjamin.	New Mexico, . .	Wm. Breeden.
Arizona, . .	R. C. McCormick.	Nebraska, . . .	C. F. Bayha.
California, . .	Lucius H. Foote.	Nevada, ...	Frank Bell.
Connecticut,	Samuel Fessenden.	New Hampshire,	B. F. Whidden.
Colorado, . . .	John L. Routt.	New Jersey,	Garret A. Hobart.
Dakota, . . .	Andrew McHench.	New York, . .	Wm. Orton.
Delaware, . . .	J. R. Lockland.	Nebraska, . . .	Z. W. Osborne.
Georgia, . . .	Edwin Belcher.	North Carolina,	W. H. Wheeler.
Illinois, ...	G. B. Raum.	Ohio, . . .	R. P. Buckland.
Indiana, . .	K. G. Schryock.	Oregon, . . .	H. K. Hines.
Iowa, ...	W. G. Donnan.	Pennsylvania,	Charles Albright.
Idaho, . . .	D. P. Thompson.	Rhode Island,	Jas. M. Pendleton.
Kansas, ...	D. R. Lowe.	South Carolina,	H. S. Worthington.
Kentucky, . . .	J. J. Landrum.	Texas, ...	S. H. Russell.
Louisiana, . . .	S. B. Packard.	Tennessee, . .	Edward Shaw.
Maine, . . .	John L. Stevens.	Utah, ...	G. A. Black.
Maryland, . . .	Joseph Pugh.	Vermont, .	Warren C. French.
Massachusetts,	George B. Loring.	Virginia, . .	Ross Hamilton.
Michigan, ...	D. L. Filer.	West Virginia, .	T. H. Logan.
Minnesota, .	John L. Merriam.	Wisconsin, . .	Geo. C. Ginty.
Mississippi, . . .	J. T. Settle.	Washington, . .	T. T. Minor.
Missouri, . . .	George Bain.	Wyoming, ...	J. M. Corey.
Montana, . .	W. F. Sanders.		

A DELEGATE from Arkansas. I move that the chairman of each delegation hand to the chairman of the Committee on Permanent Organization the name of the vice-president from his delegation.

Agreed to.

Mr. EDWARD McPHERSON, of Pennsylvania. I offer the following resolution:

Resolved, That when this convention adjourns, it adjourn to meet at eleven o'clock to-morrow morning, and that immediately upon the meeting of the convention it shall proceed to nominate candidates for the office of President of the United States; that two speeches of presentation not exceeding ten minutes each, or one speech of twenty minutes, at the discretion of the friends of the respective candidates, be permitted, and that thereupon the convention will proceed to make the nomination."

General HAWLEY, of Connecticut. I move the reference of that resolution to the Committee on Rules and Order of Business.

Agreed to.

The chairman announced that a meeting of the Committee on Permanent Organization would be held immediately in a room adjoining the hall.

Judge DITTENHOFER, of New York. On behalf of the National German Republican Convention recently assembled in this city, over which I had the honor to preside, and in which twenty states were represented, I desire to present the following resolutions, which I will send up to the secretary. Without desiring to discuss them, I desire to call the attention of the convention to but three of them: first, the resolution in view of the recent decision of the supreme court of the United States, declaring state legislation on the subject of emigration unconstitutional, and that the national government should alone legislate on that subject; second, demanding the revision of the treaties between the foreign countries affecting naturalization and expatriation; and, third, demanding unsectarian schools [applause] and taxation of church property [renewed applause], as recommended by the President of the United States in his recent message. [Renewed applause.] I ask the permission of this convention that a committee of three, of which the Hon. Mr. Wolf, of Washington, is chairman, attend the Committee on Resolutions, and present them.

The resolutions, which were read from the stage, were as follows:

The German Republican delegates of the United States, in convention assembled, in the city of Cincinnati, June 12th and 13th, 1876, have adopted the following declaration of principles for the coming campaign, and present the same to the National Republican Convention for their favorable consideration:

1. We declare our unalterable allegiance to the principles of the Republican party, recognizing in their perpetuation the only safeguard of the republic.

2. Free, non-sectarian schools, compulsory education, taxation of church property, as expressed in the late message of the President of the United States.

3. No recognition of any system of worship by the state or Federal government. Sunday being recognized by the individual and not by the constitution of the United States, to enforce all legislation seeking to

abridge the personal rights of the citizens with respect to its "observings" is unconstitutional.

4. The protection of the immigrant by the Federal power is an indispensable necessity. Legislation fostering and protecting this important factor in the prosperity of the republic must be at once devised, in view of the recent decision of the supreme court declaring state legislation unconstitutional.

5. In a republic there can be but one class of citizens. The law must give the same protection abroad as at home. Any discrimination between those adopted and those native born is unjust, and such legislation savors of Know-Nothingism, and is unworthy of American statesmanship;—therefore we demand a revision of the existing treaties with foreign governments, especially that of Germany, affecting naturalization and expatriation.

6. The honor and integrity of the republic lie primarily in a regulated system of civil service, based on moral character and capacity, and not solely on political service.

7. Opposition to all inflation and repudiation heresies, and no step backward on the road to resumption.

8. The maintenance of every amendment to the constitution by the Federal power, and especially the rigid enforcement of every law affecting citizens South.

9. The nation is supreme, and not the state.

The resolutions were referred to the Committee on Resolutions.

The CHAIR. The following communication has been handed to the chair and will be read by the secretary.

The communication was read as follows:

To the Hon. the President of the National Republican Convention:

The courtesy of the reading-room and library of the Young Men's Mercantile Library of Cincinnati is cordially extended to the delegates of the convention. HERMAN GOEPPER, *President.*

Mr. DEZENDORF, of Virginia. It seems to me that there should be a meeting of the Committee on Credentials, as it will be impossible for us to transact any business until that committee reports, and we know who are delegates in this convention.

The CHAIR. The Chair will take the liberty of announcing that the several committees appointed will meet at the right of the Chair, in the committee rooms.

A DELEGATE from Missouri. I move that the convention now adjourn until four o'clock.

Gov. VAN ZANDT, of Rhode Island. I hope not until after the Committee on Permanent Organization shall have reported.

A DELEGATE from New York. I trust that the convention will not adjourn. We can hear the report of the Committee on Permanent Organization, and then adjourn until to-morrow morning.

At 1:25 P. M., while the several committees were retiring, the convention took an informal recess, and the band struck up.

At 2 P. M. the convention was again called to order by the Chair.

Mr. J. W. MASON, of New York. I offer the following preamble and resolution:

Whereas, We still remember with gratitude the services of the loyal women of the country during the late war, and their devotion in the hospitals of the North, and their fidelity to the nation in many of the disputed districts of the South; and,

Whereas, The Republican party has always advocated the extension of human freedom; therefore,

Resolved, That we favor the bestowal of equal civil and political rights on all loyal citizens of the United States, without regard to sex.

Mr. GEORGE WILLIAM CURTIS, of New York. Mr. Chairman, I hold in my hand an address of the Republican Reform Club of the city of New York, which I have been requested to lay before this convention, and to ask leave that it shall be read. I therefore move you, sir, that the address which I have the honor to submit be now read to the convention.

Objected to.

The CHAIR. The gentleman from New York states in his place that he has an address from the Republican Reform Club of the city of New York, which he desires to have read. Objection is made, and the question before the convention is, "Shall the address be read?"

The question being put, was decided in the affirmative.

Mr. Curtis, in response to repeated calls, ascended the platform and read the following

ADDRESS OF THE REFORM CLUB OF NEW YORK.

To the Republican National Convention of 1876:

The Republican Reform Club of the city of New York pray you to consider our respectful declaration of what we deem necessary to make the Republican party deserve and obtain success in this state, which is conceded to be the principal battle-ground of the canvass, and in which the apparent strength of the Democratic and Republican parties is nearly equal.

We believe that the people wish to keep the Republican party in power only upon condition that a new Federal administration shall fulfil the promises which were given by the Republican National Convention of 1872. Without pausing to argue whether they do demand something more, certainly they will insist upon nothing less. One of those promises committed the Republican party to a speedy resumption of specie payments, and another committed it to a thorough reform of the civil service. But the only measure that has been enacted toward fulfilling the first promise is a statute which pledges the honor of the nation to redeem its paper currency with specie on the 1st of January, 1879; and the second promise, after some beneficent experiments, has been openly, wilfully, and totally broken by congress and the President.

The long delay to resume specie payments keeps the business of the country depressed. Confidence is essential to prosperity. There cannot be confidence without a stable measure of value, and the only stable measure is gold. The neglect to reform the civil service exposes the people to a greater peril, for it encourages office-holders to conspire to keep their places without regard to their fitness for them. We leave the Republicans of other states, who are suffering from this grievance, to tell you their own story. Speaking for the state of New York, we testify to you of our own knowledge and experience, that Federal office-holders have here usurped the organization of the Republican party, and abuse it to exclude large classes of its members from any voice in its councils; that they treat the tenure of their offices as depending on the caprice of the Republican senator from this state, because he is the patron who dictated their appointment, and not on the will of the President or the people; and that they have banded themselves into an odious and intolerable oligarchy which menaces the very system of our government.

We believe that a great majority of the people deeply and justly distrust the motives which animate the Democratic party and the influences which guide it; that they are not reasonably hopeful of reform at its hands; and that they always will be reluctant to confide the Federal government to any party which is controlled by men who assailed the Union themselves, or sympathised with its assailants. Nor is this distrust inconsistent with fraternal feeling to our fellow-citizens who were recently in rebellion. But it is neither honest nor prudent to speculate upon imputations of disloyalty for a Republican success. If you neglect to prove by your resolutions and your nominations that the flagrant decay of official faith and integrity, which has occurred during the present Federal administration, is not the fault of the Republican party itself, but of unfaithful servants, whom you now, upon the first opportunity since 1872, are eager to depose, it is our solemn conviction that your proceedings will impel the people to put the Democratic party into power, for the sake, at least, of a change of the administrators of evil, since they cannot obtain from you a remedy of the evil itself.

Under this conviction, we earnestly attest to you our belief that a triumph of the Republican party in the approaching elections can be obtained only by your nomination of presidential candidates whose lives afford a more trustworthy pledge than the resolutions of any convention that they will spare no effort to fulfil the promises of the Republican party to resume specie payments speedily, and to emancipate the civil service from political control. We declare the desires of greater multitudes than our immediate constituency, when we demand all the assurances which you can give by your resolutions, and still more by your nominations.

1. That the sacred pledge of the honor of the United States to redeem and pay its legal-tender promises on the 1st of January, 1879, shall be followed by all the legislation needful to fulfil it, and never shall be repealed or modified without the substitution of an earlier and better method of specie resumption.

2. That all the powers of appointment to office, which are intrusted to the Executive by the constitution and the laws, shall be faithfully executed; that fixed methods shall be established for the selection of persons for appointment which shall protect merit against mere influence

and favoritism; that the legislature never shall encroach upon the executive in this department of authority, and especially that executive and executive powers shall not be confused by the delegation of the power of appointment by the President, or any other executive officer, to members of congress in order to conciliate their support or promote their ambition.

3. That the tenure of all the offices of the Federal government, whose faithful execution does not depend upon the political opinions of their holders, shall be independent of those opinions; and that honesty, capacity, and fidelity shall become the conditions of obtaining and retaining every Federal office.

Solemnly convinced that a Republican reform, and nothing but a Republican reform, can secure that Republican victory for which we pray, and to which we are anxious to give our heartiest aid, we beseech you to give us presidential candidates who can secure it, and to put no man in nomination who is responsible in any degree for the repudiation or evasion of the unfulfilled promises of the Republican National Convention of 1872, which it is the highest duty of the Republican party to renew and redeem.

A DELEGATE from New York. I move you that the document which has just been read be referred to the Committee on Resolutions.

A DELEGATE from Montana. I move you that the address be adopted as the sense of this convention.

The reference was ordered.

A DELEGATE from Maryland. Unless the Committee on Credentials are ready to report, I move that the convention take a recess until four o'clock.

Not agreed to.

Mr. E. L. PIERCE, of Massachusetts. I move that all addresses, memorials, and resolutions be referred to the Committee on Resolutions without reading and without debate.

Mr. J. B. SENER, of Virginia. I hope that the motion will be amended so as to except such communications as the chair shall judge should be laid before the convention. The wording of the gentleman's resolution is so broad that it will exclude all.

The CHAIR. The chair will take care of that.

Mr. Pierce's motion was put and agreed to.

At this point calls were made for various speakers, among whom was U. S. Senator John A. Logan, of Illinois. General Logan came forward, and was introduced by the chairman of the convention. He spoke as follows:

SPEECH OF GENERAL LOGAN.

Mr. President and Gentlemen of the National Republican Convention: I know not what I can say to you that will be of any benefit in directing your minds in that duty which you are now called upon to perform. You are the chosen representatives of the Republicans of the United States of America, assembled here for the purpose of nominating candidates for President and Vice-President upon a Republican platform, to be voted for at the next November election by the Republicans of the United States. To recite all that has been done by this party of ours, which has been of advantage to the whole people of this great country, and to enumerate the many things that have inured to the benefit of civilized man, would be a work I cannot now undertake. Our coming campaign, in my judgment, however, is to be one of no ordinary character. We have the evidence now before us in the demonstrations that are being made by the opponents of the Republican party sufficient to satisfy us that the time has again come for every lover of liberty and freedom in this land to buckle on his armor and be ready for the fray. That which has been achieved by our armies, that which has been made and perfected for the benefit of mankind by the intellect of our party, is before the country, for them to decide whether or not that which has been made so far a success shall be still continued as a success in this land, or whether all the fruits that have been gathered by the Republican party and by their exertions shall be destroyed. It is for you to say whether that which we have added to the constitution of the country shall be sustained and shall be carried out by the laws that shall be made by the legislative department of the government, and which can only be made with that department of the government in Republican hands, or whether you will turn it over to the hands of those who will legislate in opposition to the principles that have been embodied in that constitution by our amendments. To you, then, has this task been referred, so far as presenting to the country men that will stand upon this platform and carry out these principles. Let there be no uncertain sound in the platform that shall be adopted by the Republican party here to-day. It is not for me to indicate what your committee shall report, or what you shall adopt, except to say, as a Republican, Let there be no uncertain sound on any question that is at all a vital question before the American people.

This is a Republican convention, and it should be only captured by Republicans and only be sustained and supported by Republicans. I have learned, while being a Republican, that Republicanism in this land means liberty, freedom, the enjoyment of happiness, the protection under our laws alike to each and every citizen in the confines of this country, let him come from whence he may, whether born in a foreign land or upon our own soil. When you tell me that we have power to protect the American citizen on the high seas or in foreign lands, I say the government that has power to stretch forth its strong arm and protect the American citizen in foreign parts, has the power, and it is its bounden duty, to protect him at home. Sirs, the government that will not allow an insult to its flag from a foreign foe, but will allow its citizens to be trampled under foot, deprived of each and every right guaranteed to them by the constitution of the land in which they live, that will allow them to be plundered and robbed and murdered, is not a government of freedom and right, and the way to protect American citizens in their rights and in the enjoyment of that to which they are entitled under our constitution, is to enforce the laws, and to make such laws as will throw safeguards around each and every one of them, and to place in the presidential chair the man who will execute the laws for the benefit and protection of this people. The man that tells me that the four millions of unoffending people that have been made freemen in this land by the voice and the strong arm and will of the Republicans and Union men of the nation shall not have their rights protected the same as ours, but that they may become a prey at any day, or in any time or place, to the men who themselves will commit all kinds of depredations and fraud for the purpose of enforcing their victims either to acquiescence in wrong or into machinations against their friends, says that which is against the wishes of the great Republican party. It is our duty to say that this shall not be done.

Now, my countrymen, one word in reference to the signs of the times. What is it we see and hear all around and about us to-day, from those who oppose the success of the Republican party in this land? Do they sing the praises of the American nation? Do they sing the praises of quiet acquiescence of Americans in the laws of the country? Do they go forward to oppose the enemies of civilization, of Republicanism, of freedom, and say, "Here we stand with the banner of freedom in our hands, and we intend to wave it over this land and sustain all that it indicates for civilization"? Do we find that among the enemies of Republicanism? Most assuredly we do not!

We find this to-day. The men in this land who failed of success in overturning this government by force of arms, have undertaken, and they have had success to a certain extent, to destroy the government in a different manner. The destruction of this government is contemplated, not by arms, not by force, but by capturing the government, and then nullifying every law and every amendment to the constitution that gives that protection to our citizens that we ourselves said they should have when they were battling to preserve this nation. How do they do it? What is the commencement of this new revolution?—for revolution it means, and that is what it is. First, it is the assassination of the private character of every leading Republican in the land. The dagger of detraction is to be plunged into the very vitals of the men who stand firm against the storms that have been rolling against liberty and freedom in this country.

Sir, every man is to be stricken down who holds a prominent position in the Republican party. Every bold, earnest, and aggresssive man is to be destroyed; and when I say this, I have no reference to any individual. The commencement is this disintegration and destruction of the Republican party, by assailing and attacking every man that has been a prominent man within its ranks. With their destruction, the conquest is simple.

We need, then, a bold movement on this enemy, and another victory will be ours. Sir, I say the men that stand firm and boldly vindicate the rights of the people, the principles of Republicanism,—no matter who they are or where they live,—should be sustained by the Republican party, so far as they deserve being sustained. I do not mean this by way of saying that I have excuses to make for any one man or set of men, but I mean that the rights of the people should be guarded as well as they have been guaranteed.

Then, in conclusion, let me say this: Give us a Republican platform. Give us candidates for President and Vice-President that are men known to the land. Name them yourselves. I have naught to do with that. The man you name is my man. The man you name is the Republican standard-bearer, and he is the man that will be elected. I dislike to hear it said that we cannot elect this man or that man. The

Republican party, if it is true to itself, can elect whomsoever you shall nominate. You have collected together as wise men, as discreet men. In your hands is reposed the confidence of the Republicans of the United States. Whatever your wisdom shall decide, the Republicans of this country should be satisfied with and should acquiesce in; and, in my judgment, a Republican, after having called you together to make your nomination, who will fail to support that nomination, is not a true and genuine Republican. Now, gentlemen, I hope your deliberations will be calm and harmonious; that when we leave this place all asperity of feeling that may have arisen during this canvass will be wiped out, and that each and every one of us will take our departure to our homes satisfied that we have done the best we could for the country. Those who are disposed to be dissatisfied,—to them say only that it is the best we can do; that if they cannot be satisfied with that, we cannot help it, as we have done all we could do for the benefit of the country. Do that, my countrymen, without being deterred in any way, and you will satisfy the country, and the country will ratify your choice in November.

After Gen. Logan had concluded, there were loud calls for Ex-Gov. Joseph R. Hawley, of Connecticut, who, ascending the platform, was introduced by the chairman, and spoke as follows:

SPEECH OF GEN. HAWLEY.

Mr. President and Gentlemen: I am exceedingly sorry that I am not in a condition to address you. I wish, indeed, that I could talk with interest and power here upon the necessities of the hour, and the great duties of the Republican party. But I am not well; I have a severe headache; and I have much work before me in the meeting of the Committee on Resolutions this evening,—so I will say but a word, and leave you.

I wish I could believe, as our gallant and eloquent friend who has just addressed you has said, that the Republican party has but to nominate and go home and elect. I should be glad to believe this, expressed in as strong language as any sanguine temperament could devise; but I am not sure that it is precisely so. There has been growing up for some time in the country a wide-spread and serious dissatisfaction. It is simply common sense to recognize it. No wise officer goes into battle without understanding his ground and recognizing the power of his enemy. He is well on his way to victory when he has done that. Now, gentlemen, when you shall have nominated your candidates and laid down your platform, if that platform distinctly expresses and propounds sound Republican doctrine, and your candidate be an able, sound, and true Republican, I shall go to work with all my heart and all my strength to elect him. But now is the time: this afternoon, this night, and to-morrow are the precious hours given you to decide what you will do and how you will do it. I enter into no particulars, but you know, all of you,—there is not a man in this convention who does not know,—that you can so conduct yourselves in forty-eight hours that the three or four months between now and November will be unavailing.

I beg to point to one particular at least, in which it is the high duty of the Republican party to take clear, strong, honorable ground. I refer to the great questions of debt and of currency.

I heard an able and eloquent woman arguing once before a committee of congress in favor of female suffrage. She said that women might not always care to vote, because sometimes there might be pending merely financial questions. Merely financial questions! As if all questions involving that description did not carry with them tests of moral power, of the honesty and the integrity of the people. There is no higher test of our fitness for republican government than a financial test. A great country of forty millions can carry on a war. Everybody knows it. Summon them to the defence of the country against domestic or foreign foes, and we assume it is not difficult to call one or two millions into the field; but when the great and exciting contest is passed, and it becomes a question of how manufacturers shall carry on their work and pay the taxes necessary to raise the interest of the debt created by the war, then comes the test, and then come the insidious doctrines which have been promulgated by persons who think they see short ways to getting rid of the burden. Then we strike the moral vitals of the people. You can fight; but can you resolutely determine that you will pay every dollar of that debt according to the promise? that you will return to sound currency based upon economic laws? We hear much said about the great mysteries and the great and puzzling problems of financial science. These difficulties vanish very much when you apply to them the same very simple test. Tell the truth, and fulfil your promise. Do that, and you will solve half of the trouble. What do the bonds say? Read it, and do it. What does your enforced loan, your legal-tender note promise to do, and what did you promise to do when you issued them? Do it. There is no profound mystery in it, and no extraordinary difficulty in the performance of that duty.

I hold that perhaps the first of our many duties is to bring back our currency to a sound basis, to a resumption of specie payments. And this not alone as a question of honor and integrity for the nation, but as an indispensable pre-requisite to the restoration of business prosperity. Our business men are utterly unable to make any calculations with reference to the near future. They are waiting, in some measure, for the results of the campaign, that they may decide what to do. And I need not say that there is a profound anxiety throughout the whole Republican party, that we shall give new assurances to the country that all its affairs are to be administered with high honor and integrity; that the sacred trusts of office-holders are indeed sacred trusts, and not to be trifled with by bold and designing men.

I do not in any sense despair of the republic, or of the Republican party; but we find, however, in the great mass of our party, in the mind's eye, a very noble and very high ideal. We have been uplifted, under the providence of God during these fifteen years, to see a new glory in the constitution and a new glory in the flag; and when the young men of our country—sanguine and hopeful, honorable young men—see men in high office trifling with their duties and trading in office, winking at corruption, they become dissatisfied; and that general discontent, now prevailing throughout the country in the minds of many men, must not be disregarded by this convention, if you desire success.

After Gov. Hawley had concluded, there were calls for Ex-Gov. Edward F. Noyes, of Ohio, who spoke as follows:

SPEECH OF EX-GOVERNOR NOYES.

Mr. President and Gentlemen of the Convention: I am under very many obligations for the honor of being called upon to-day, but it seems to me it would be more modest for me to sit and listen rather than to speak in this presence. But as you have done me the honor to call upon me, I will say a single word, and a word only. It seems to me that a wonderful responsibility is resting upon this convention at this time. The people in this centennial year are demanding more of their representatives than has ever been asked of public servants before. This is a sentiment which we must recognize in all our action here. I have no sympathy with the vile slanderers who would destroy the reputation of our honest statesmen for political purposes. The reputation of our public men is too dear to us for us to afford that they should be unjustly destroyed. While we will defend them in everything where they are right, yet the spirit of criticism which seeks out wrong wherever it exists, and punishes the offender, is noble, and I trust will be evermore.

The Republican party, after its career of sixteen years, challenges honest criticism. We refer to our record, and what does it show? The shackles stricken off from the limbs of four or five millions of our fellow citizens; the ruinous heresy that a state of its own motion has a right to destroy our government, has been trampled out forever; we have settled that our foreign-born citizens here shall have the same rights among us as native-born citizens of the United States, and that they shall go up and down the earth protected by the entire power of the American government. We are going to settle the question that the American people will do as they have promised to do, and pay their honest debts as they have promised to pay them. We are going to settle the question, that in every part of our country, in the South as well as in the North, every man shall be protected in his rights of person or property, whether black or white, native or foreign-born.

The Republican party does not forget the millions of our colored fellow citizens of the South who stood by our flag, supported by only a few white men, and helped us fight the battles of the country. We remember that hundreds of these colored soldiers are sleeping to-day side by side with those of our heroic dead on fields of battle where they fell fighting for the government of the United States. Remembering these things, we propose, God helping us, so long as we exist as a party organization, to stand by them and their rights.

Whenever we discover thieves and rascals within the limits of our own party, we propose to hunt them out and punish them, and drive them out of the party and into the one where they belong.

As to the candidate of this convention, we, of Ohio, ask only this. We fight nobody. We assail no man's reputation. Whoever you nominate we will try to elect. But all we want, in the first place, is a man who is honest; in the second place, a man of comprehension enough to know what is right and what is wrong; and, in the third place, we want a man that is brave enough and strong enough to carry out his convictions. Give us a man of great purity of private life, and an unexceptional public record,and count on Ohio next November.

The Rev. Henry Highland Garnett, of New York, being called for, ascended the stage.

The CHAIRMAN. *Gentlemen:* I take pleasure in introducing to you a man well known before the abolition of slavery in these United States; a man who helped win the battle as well as his fellow citizens of this nation,—the Rev. Henry Highland Garnett, of New York.

SPEECH OF THE REV. HENRY HIGHLAND GARNETT.

Mr. President and Fellow Citizens: I regret extremely that your kindness has demanded my appearance upon this platform at this time. I would have been better satisfied to have listened to other gentlemen, whose names are well known, and to hear whom you have expressed your desires; and, to prove that I mean what I say, you will find that the remarks which I make shall be exceedingly brief. It has gratified me much to hear from gentlemen who have claimed your attention and gained your ear, that one particular desire that lies near the hearts of the delegates to this convention, is the purification of the government, and the election of men as President and Vice-President of the United States who shall not only have the sagacity of knowing what to do, but who shall surround themselves with men who know how to do, how to act, how to carry out the desires of the true Republicans of this country. There is another thing that I earnestly desire, but to which no allusion has been made. Gratified as I have been to hear it announced, by every speaker who has appeared upon this platform, that it is your purpose to give protection to the men who helped to secure the perpetuity of this Union, who helped you to lift up the old flag from the dust when it was smitten down by disloyal hands, let me beg of this convention to notice this: There were men from whose hands the fetters have been smitten, who got together their little earnings, and, by the advice and direction of their friends, laid it away for a rainy day, and, by the mismanagement of men who deceived you, they have been deprived of their little earnings; and to-day there are aching hearts all over the country, and especially in the South. If you can, Mr. President, try in your deliberations to put in a little plank that will give security to the freedmen of the South, that the suffering which they endure, in consequence of the rascality and villainy of the managers of the Freedmen's savings banks, shall be set right. Do n't forget that. If you do it you will have the gratitude, and love, and respect of that much injured people. Another thing, in conclusion: You may talk about your banks, your rag money, your silver and gold; you may talk about your civil service as much as you please,—but there is one thing that rises in importance above all these considerations. It is this: that in the South as well as in the North, every man,—not only the black Republicans, but the white Republicans,—shall be permitted to enjoy the highest privilege of citizenship at the polls, without being murdered by the pistol and the gun-shot. That is all I wish to say.

The CHAIR. The Committee on Resolutions is desired to meet at 260 Vine street, at seven o'clock this evening.

A DELEGATE from Michigan. I move that the convention do now adjourn till to-morrow morning at ten o'clock.

Loud calls being made for Hon. William A. Howard, of Michigan, the motion to adjourn was temporarily withdrawn, and Mr. Howard came upon the platform and said:

SPEECH OF MR. HOWARD.

Gentlemen of the Convention: You will excuse me for sitting while I speak. The success of the great Republican party must depend, in a great measure, upon enlisting the sympathies of all classes. To do that, we seek to give all classes representation here. Eloquent orators have already been heard,—leading men in the Republican party. Here our colored brother has been heard. Two classes have been represented; and I suppose, sir, that I am indebted for this honor to the fact that I am a cripple. Gentlemen, I stand before you [rising to his feet] representing the great body of the cripples in the Republican party. It is the only claim I have to be heard. But there was a time when I was not a cripple. There was a time when I was the only nominee for congress under the Republican party under that name, and, for a wonder, I was elected. Since that time the Republican party has been instrumental in making more history than any party that has ever existed under the heavens, and better history. To-day it represents certain great principles, certain ideas.

Liberty has always been the leading characteristic of the party. The Democratic party, our opponents,—they also, as an organization, are champions of liberty. They claim the liberty to murder negroes and assassinate white men's reputations. We claim that there should be in this broad land one manner of citizens, so far as rights are concerned. We claim that there should be one manner of laws, and that the laws should be enforced in every place in the land. We claim that if the Federal government has the right to fight pirates on the seas in defence of American citizens, they have the right to fight Ku-Klux in our own land.

Now, fellow citizens, I come from a state where the Republican banner has never trailed. A wise general, going into battle, will strengthen the weakest parts of the line. I come here to say that Michigan can, and will, carry any candidate triumphantly you may nominate, be he whom he may. We ask for no reinforcements; we will hold our fort: and yet, looking to the future of the Republican party, we ask that you will not fail to meet the demands, the just demands, of the people. The great body of the Republican party demand to-day that no guilty man shall escape, and that no innocent man shall have his reputation assassinated. For these two things,—for the protection of every citizen in every part of the land,—we are ready, not only to vote, but to fight; and, cripple as I am, I would rather die in the ditch than see the Republican party take one step backward. I have said that it was a principle of the Republican party that we must have one kind of citizen only, so far as rights are concerned. No matter about the color; no matter about wealth or poverty: if he be a citizen, he is entitled to equal protection. The broad principle of our constitution is simply this: no man in the land is entitled to any privileges over any other man. This is the principle that underlies our whole creed. Do not go back on it. Never fear your enemies. A bold fight is the best: we should advance, and not retrograde. But, sir, I ought not to have consented to come up here to-day. I did not want to. There is a black Douglass in this hall, and while he is not much blacker than I am, he is a great deal smarter; so I hope you will let me off and call for him.

A DELEGATE from Michigan. I now renew my motion to adjourn to 10 o'clock to-morrow morning.

The motion, being put, was lost.

Mr. Fred. Douglass being loudly called for, stepped forward upon the platform.

The CHAIR. *Gentlemen of the Convention:* Frederick Douglass needs no introduction anywhere in the United States.

SPEECH OF MR. DOUGLASS.

Mr. President and Gentlemen of the National Republican Convention: Allow me to express my deep, my heartfelt gratitude to you for the warm, the cordial invitation you have extended to me to make my appearance on this platform at this time. The work to which you have called me is somewhat new. It is the first time in my life that I have ever had the pleasure of looking the Republican party squarely in the face. And I must say,—and I hope you will acquit me of everything like a disposition to flatter,—that you are a pretty good looking *man.* But I will not detain you here by any attempt at a speech. You have had speeches,—eloquent speeches, glorious speeches, wise speeches, patriotic speeches; speeches in respect to the importance of managing correctly your currency; speeches in defence of purity of administration; and speeches in respect to the great principles for which you struggled, and for which the race to which I belong struggled on the battlefield, and poured out their blood.

The thing, however, in which I feel the deepest interest, and the thing in which I believe this country feels the deepest interest, is, that the principles involved in the contest which carried your sons and brothers to the battlefield; which draped our Northern churches with the weeds of mourning, and filled our towns and our cities with mere stumps of men,—armless, legless, maimed, and mutilated; those for which you poured out your blood, and piled a debt for after-coming generations higher than a mountain of gold, to weigh down the necks of your children and your children's children,—I say that those principles, those interests involved in that tremendous contest, ought to be dearer to the American people, in the great political struggle now upon them, than any other principles we have.

You say you have emancipated us. You have; and I thank you for it. You say you have enfranchised us. You have; and I thank you for it. But what is your emancipation?—what is your enfranchisement? What does it all amount to, if the black man, after having been made free by the letter of your law, is unable to exercise that freedom, and, after having been freed from the slaveholder's lash, he is to be subject to the slaveholder's shot-gun? Oh! you freed us! You emancipated us! I thank you for it. But under what circumstances did you emancipate us? Under what circumstances have we obtained our freedom? Sir, ours is the most extraordinary case of any people ever emancipated on the globe. I sometimes wonder that we still exist as a people in this country; that we have not all been swept out of existence, with nothing left to show that we ever existed. Look at it. When the Israelites were emancipated, they were told to go and borrow of their neighbors,—borrow their coin, borrow their jewels, load themselves down with the means of subsistence: after, they should go free in the land which the Lord God gave them. When the Russian serfs had their chains broken and were given their liberty, the government of Russia—aye, the despotic government of Russia—gave to those poor emancipated serfs a few acres of land on which they could live and earn their bread. But when you turned us loose, you gave us no acres: you turned us loose to the sky, to the storm, to the whirlwind, and, worst of all, you turned us loose to the wrath of our infuriated masters.

The question now is, Do you mean to make good to us the promises in your constitution? Talk not to me of finance. Talk not of mere reform in your administration. I believe there is honesty in the American people; honesty in the men whom you will elect; wisdom in the men to manage those affairs,—but tell me, if your heart be as my heart, that the liberty which you have asserted for the black man in this country shall be maintained? You say, some of you, that you can get along without the vote of the black man of the South. Yes, that may be, possibly; but I doubt it. At any rate, in order to insure our protection hereafter, we feel the need, in the candidate whom you will place before the country, of the assurance that, if it be necessary, the black man shall walk to the ballot-box in safety, even if we have to bring a bayonet behind us. And I have this this feeling, that, if we bring forth either of the gentlemen named here, the government of the United States and the moral feeling of the country will surround the black voter as by a wall of fire; and, instead of electing your President without the black vote, you may count in the number of your victorous Republican states five or six, at least, of the old master states of the South. But I have no voice to address you longer; and you may now move, down there, for an adjournment.

PERMANENT ORGANIZATION.

Mr. Geo. B. Loring, of Massachusetts, then came forward and read the following report of the Committee on Organization:

PRESIDENT.

Edward McPherson, of Pennsylvania.

VICE-PRESIDENTS.

State	Name	State	Name
Alabama,	——— ———	New Jersey,	William A. Newell.
Arkansas,	M. W. Gibbs.	New York,	Marshall O. Roberts.
California,	George S. Evans.	North Carolina,	James H. Harris.
Colorado,	Henry McAllister.	Ohio,	Benjamin F. Wade.
Connecticut,	Martin J. Sheldon.	Oregon,	J. H. Foster.
Delaware,	David W. Moore.	Pennsylvania,	J. Smith Futhey.
Florida,	——— ———	Rhode Island,	Henry Howard.
Georgia,	R. L. Mott.	South Carolina,	R. H. Gleaves.
Illinois,	John T. Rinaker.	Tennessee,	Horace H. Harrison.
Indiana,	James S. Fraser.	Texas,	A. B. Norton.
Iowa,	W. T. Shaw.	Vermont,	George Howe.
Kansas,	William Martindale.	Virginia,	R. H. Carter.
Kentucky,	E. R. Weir.	West Virginia,	W. E. Stevenson.
Louisiana,	George Y. Kelso.	Wisconsin,	James Bintliff.
Maine,	J. B. Brown.	Arizona,	D. Forest Porter.
Maryland,	James A. Gary.	Dakota,	Alexander Hughes.
Massachusetts,	P. A. Chadbourne.	District of Columbia,	——— ———
Michigan,	Henry P. Baldwin.	Idaho,	Austin Savage.
Minnesota,	L. Bogen.	Montana,	Benjamin H. Tatem.
Mississippi,	M. Shannessee.	New Mexico,	Samuel B. Axtell.
Missouri,	G. A. Finkelnburg.	Utah,	James B. McKean.
Nebraska,	H. S. Kaley.	Washington,	Ellwood Evans.
Nevada,	Thomas Wren.	Wyoming,	William Hinton.
New Hampshire,	E. A. Straw.		

SECRETARY.

Irving M. Bean, of Wisconsin.

ASSISTANT SECRETARIES.

State	Name	State	Name
Alabama,	——— ———	New Hampshire,	Geo. W. Marston.
Arkansas,	H. M. Cooper.	New Jersey,	James L. M. Stratton.
California,	Isaac Hecht.	New York,	James W. Husted.
Colorado,	James B. Osborn.	North Carolina,	T. M. Owen.
Connecticut,	John A. Tibbitts.	Ohio,	L. J. Critchfield.
Delaware,	John H. Hoffecker.	Oregon,	J. B. David.
Florida,	——— ———	Pennsylvania,	Henry H. Bingham.
Georgia,	J. T. Collins.	Rhode Island,	Edward L. Freeman.
Illinois,	Thos. A. Boyd.	South Carolina,	Wm. J. McKinley.
Indiana,	L. Noble.	Tennessee,	J. T. Wilder.
Iowa,	J. D. Hunter.	Texas,	Adolph Zadek.
Kansas,	A. L. Redden.	Vermont,	Mason S. Colburn.
Kentucky,	T. E. Burns.	Virginia,	W. N. Stevens.
Louisiana,	W. G. Brown.	West Virginia,	J. D. Ramsdell.
Maine,	C. A. Boutelle.	Arizona,	——— ———
Maryland,	F. M. Darby.	Dakota,	Andrew McHench.
Massachusetts,	Smith R. Phillips.	District of Columbia,	——— ———
Michigan,	B. D. Pritchard.	Idaho,	D. P. Thompson.
Minnesota,	R. B. Langdon.	Montana,	W. F. Landers.
Mississippi,	J. A. Haskins.	New Mexico,	William Breeden.
Missouri,	Daniel S. Twitchell.	Utah,	George A. Black.
Nebraska,	R. G. Brown.	Washington,	T. T. Minor.
Nevada,	C. N. Harris.	Wyoming,	J. M. Carey.

And the chairman has been requested to say to the convention, that when the questions of contesting delegations from Alabama and Florida and the District of Columbia are settled, the vice-presidents and secretaries from those states will be reported to the convention.

A DELEGATE from Pennsylvania. I move to adopt the report of the committee.

Mr. MCCLURE, of Arkansas. I think the adoption of this report at this time is a little premature. There is no gentleman in this convention who knows that these gentlemen are delegates to the convention. I hope the report will not be adopted until the adoption of the report of the Committee on Credentials. Until that time I hope the report will not be acted upon. I therefore move that action upon said report be deferred until the reception of the report of the Committee on Credentials.

Mr. LORING. This question was before the committee, and, upon turning to the report of the convention at Philadelphia, in 1872, it was found that the Committee on Permanent Organization reported before the Committee on Credentials, and it was on that account that this report has been made, feeling that the convention has a perfect right to accept it or not, as they please, and that provision has been made for the contesting delegations by the report of the committee.

Mr. MASON, of New York. I move that the report be adopted, so far as relates to those states where there is no question of contest, and that the remainder—

The CHAIR. That motion is not in order.

A DELEGATE from Maryland. I move to lay upon the table the motion of the gentleman from Arkansas to postpone.

Agreed to.

Mr. MCCLURE. I submit this point of order,—that the motion to lay upon the table carried with it the subject-matter of the original motion.

The CHAIR. The convention has adopted no rules, and therefore must make its own rules as it goes along. The Chair therefore decides that the motion to lay upon the table only carried with it the motion of the gentleman from Arkansas to lay upon the table. The question therefore recurs upon the motion of the gentleman from Pennsylvania, to adopt the report of the Committee.

The question being put, the report of the committee was adopted, and the officers named declared duly elected.

THE PERMANENT CHAIRMAN.

The CHAIR. The first business now in order, and the only business, is to surrender the chair to the permanent chairman named by the Committee on Organization. The chair therefore names Messrs. Orton of New York, Donnan of Iowa, and McCormick of Arizona, as a committee to conduct the permanent chairman to the platform.

Mr. McPherson came forward, accompanied by the escort, and was greeted with cheers.

The retiring CHAIRMAN said: I take pleasure in introducing as your permanent president the Hon. Edward McPherson, of Pennsylvania.

SPEECH OF MR. M'PHERSON.

Gentlemen of the Convention: None of you know better than myself how entirely unworthy I am of this high distinction. It has come to me not only unsought, but with a feeling of absolute and uncontrollable surprise. But I have been reared in a school of duty; and in the politics of Pennsylvania it is a fundamental doctrine, that every Republican shall do his whole duty; and, therefore, I am here to accept the honor tendered by your committee and ratified by yourselves, as an honor tendered to the great commonwealth which has sent me as one of its delegates to this convention, which, since 1856, in no one of the great contests has ever faltered, and which, in this centennial of the nation, determined, inflexible, defiant, turning its face to the enemy striped all over with treason and malignity and hate at everything that is national, has determined to roll up for the nominees of this convention such a vote as will entitle her to continue to be what she has been —and I say it with all respect—foremost in the Republican column. The chair is ready for business.

Mr. CARTER, of Virginia. I move that the rules of the House of Representatives be adopted for the government of this convention.

A DELEGATE from Pennsylvania. That belongs to the Committee on Rules.

Mr. JOHN CESSNA, of Pennsylvania. I desire to announce that the Committee on Rules and Order of Business, not being able to find a place of meeting, will meet this afternoon, at four o'clock, in the parlor of the Gibson house.

The PRESIDENT. I would suggest the appointment of a member of the Committee on Resolutions to take my place, vacated by my election to this position.

Mr. CUMBACK. I move that the convention do now adjourn till ten o'clock to-morrow morning.

Which was agreed to, and the President declared the convention so adjourned.

SECOND DAY—THURSDAY, JUNE 15, 1876.

It having been generally understood that the convention had adjourned to meet at eleven o'clock this morning, the President waited until that hour before calling the body to order. He announced that prayer would be offered by the Rev. George B. Beecher, of the First Presbyterian church of Cincinnati.

OPENING PRAYER.

Almighty and ever-living God! Our father's God and our God! We look to thee for strength and guidance. Thine is the dominion and the power and the wisdom. Thou hast been the God of our fathers; and when, in other times of trouble they called on thee, thou heardst and helpst them. Thou hast been our God, and, in our days of trial, thou didst defend and shield us. We acknowledge that the power is thine; that it is not of us or of our fathers that is the greatness of this land, but due is it all to thy goodness: and now we thank thee for it: and as thou hast ruled in our midst in the years that are past, rule thou still over us. Be thou our God and our wisdom; and grant, we pray thee, our Father in heaven, that all we do this day may be to thy honor and glory. We pray thee that thou wilt be here this day, giving to those who are gathered here for this great and responsible work thy Spirit and thy guidance. Grant, we pray thee, that as thou hast for thy people of old, and as thou hast for us in other days, raised up great leaders to go out and in before thy people, so to-day wilt thou raise up a great leader, that shall go out and in before this nation, and lead them in the paths of righteousness and truth. We pray thee to this end that thou wilt choose for us: and grant, we beseech thee, that thy Spirit may be here in the hearts of thy servants, so that they shall be kept from every wrong decision; that they shall be guided into every right decision. We pray thee that thou wilt drive away all low and all earth-born passions, if such there be, all selfishness, all prejudice, all pride, and all hatred and strife; and grant, we pray thee, that an unselfish devotion to public good, a love for country, for humanity, and for God, may fill every breast, and produce harmony and peace and unity. And grant, we pray thee, that divine wisdom may characterize the proceedings of this hour and the principles that shall go forth from this assembly, so that purity and righteousness and peace may prevail throughout the length and breadth of our land.

Bless, we pray thee, the officers of this meeting. Give them strength for the duties devolving upon them. Bless our nation. Bless, we pray thee, all those that are in authority: our chief magistrate, and all his counsellors and advisers. Bless the nations of the earth: and grant that thy kingdom, which is righteousness, and peace, and joy, may fill the whole earth. And as all the strength and wisdom comes from thee, so unto thee be all the honor and glory, forever and ever. Amen.

WOMAN SUFFRAGE.

Mr. GEORGE F. HOAR, of Massachusetts. *Mr. Chairman:* I am requested to present to this convention the memorial of a large class of our citizens, who are excluded from any representation here, or from any share in the government of the country. I desire to present the memorial of the National Woman Suffrage Association. Under the order adopted yesterday, this memorial goes to the Committee on Resolutions at once; but I desire to move that Mrs. Sarah J. Spencer, who has been deputed by the association for that purpose, be heard by the convention for ten minutes.

The motion was agreed to.

The PRESIDENT. I have the pleasure of presenting to the convention Mrs. Sarah J. Spencer.

REMARKS OF MRS. SPENCER.

Citizens of the United States—Members of the National Republican

Convention: The request would not have been made to this convention that any woman's voice should be heard in a convention of men called by men for men, if yesterday, when the grand opportunities were presented, your noble speakers had remembered that there were women citizens in the United States who had no voice in this honorable body. The first plank in your platform of 1872 declares that "the Republican party has emancipated four millions of slaves, and has established universal suffrage." Where were the ten million women,—citizens of the United States? When will you make this high-sounding declaration true? The second plank in your platform declares that you have established "justice, perfect liberty, and perfect equality for all." Where are the wives and mothers and daughters of this republic? In plank 14, it begins to dawn upon the Republican party that there are women in the United States; and plank 14 reads,—

"The Republican party is mindful of its obligations to the loyal women of America, for their noble devotion to the cause of freedom. Their admission to wider fields of usefulness is viewed with satisfaction; and the honest demands of any class of citizens for additional rights should be treated with respectful consideration."

Yesterday, when Gen. Logan, who voted for us in the United States senate, forgot to mention us, I reminded him of it. He said,—"I forgot the women." I said,—"Beware, lest ten millions of women in the United States, with the ballot in their hands, forget you." When Frederick Douglass, yesterday, also forgot the women, I reminded him that to a woman—to Harriet Beecher Stowe—he owed more than to all the men of the United States.

Frederick Douglass once said that the proposition had been established for men, that a man's head is his head, his body is his body, his feet are his feet, and if he chooses to run away with them it is nobody's business. Now we want the proposition established for women, that a woman's head is her head, her body is her body, her feet are her feet, her hands are her hands, and that she should hold in them the ballot for self-protection.

The Republican party promised to give our claims respectful attention in 1872. It cannot afford to recede in four years. It cannot afford to stand still, for to be still is to die. Nothing is still that lives. It must move forward. In this bright new century, let me ask you to win to your side the women of the United States—the wives, daughters, and sisters of this republic.

The following is the memorial presented, but not read:

To the President and Members of the Republican National Convention:

Gentlemen: The National Woman Suffrage Association asks you to place in your platform the following plank:

"*Resolved,* That the right to the use of the ballot inheres in the citizens of the United States."

We ask the insertion of this plank. We propose no change of fundamental principles. Our question is as old as the nation. Our government was framed on the political basis of the consent of the governed. From July 4, 1776, until the present year, 1876, the nation has constantly advanced toward a fuller practice of our fundamental theory that the governed are the source of all powers. Your nominating convention occurs in the centennial year of the republic, and is a most opportune moment for the reäffirmation and complete recognition of these principles. Our government has not yet answered the end for which it was formed, while one half the people of the United States are deprived of the right of self-government. Before the Revolution, Great Britain claimed the right to legislate for the colonies in all cases whatsoever. The men of the nation now as unjustly claim the right to legislate for women in all cases whatsoever. The call for your nominating convention invited the coöperation of all voters who desire to inaugurate and enforce the rights of every citizen, including the full and free exercise of the right of suffrage. Women are citizens, declared to be so by the highest legislative and judicial authorities, but they are citizens deprived of a full and free exercise of the right of suffrage. Your platform of 1872 declared,—"The Republican party, mindful of its obligations to the loyal women of the nation for their noble devotion to the cause of freedom." Devotion to freedom is no new thing for the women of this nation. From the earliest history of our country, woman has shown herself as devoted as man to the cause of freedom. At every vital period in the nation's life, from the Revolution to the present hour, woman has stood by the side of father, husband, son, and brother, in defence of liberty. The heroic and self-sacrificing deeds of the women of the Revolution must not be forgotten. Men and women then fought together for liberty. Together, men and women have made the country what it is; and to-day, in this hundredth year of our existence, the women of the country, as members of the nation, as citizens of the United States, ask national recognition of their right of suffrage. The Declaration of Independence struck a blow at every existent form of government by declaring the individual the source of all power. Upon this, one newly proclaimed truth over native error arose; but if states may deny suffrage to any classes, according to the *Minor* v. *Hoppersott* decision of the supreme court, a decision rendered under the auspices of the Republican party against suffrage as a constituent element of United States citizenship, we have nothing truly national in the character of this government. National supremacy does not chiefly mean the power to levy war, conclude peace, contract alliances, and establish commerce. It means national protection and security in the exercise of the right of self-government, which comes alone by and through the use of the ballot. Even granting the premise of the supreme court decision,—"that the constitution of the United States does not confer suffrage on any one,"—our national life does not date from that instrument. The constitution is not the original declaration of rights. It was not framed until eleven years after our existence as a nation, nor fully ratified until nearly fourteen years after the commencement of our national life. This centennial celebration of our nation's birth does not date from the constitution, but from the declaration of independence. The declared purpose of our civil war was the settlement of the question of supremacy between the states and the United States. The documents sent out by the Republican party in this present campaign warn the people that the Democrats intend another battle for state sovereignty, to be fought this year at the ballot-box. The National Woman's Suffrage Association calls your attention to the fact that the Republican party itself has reopened the battle, and now holds the anomalous position of having settled the question of state sovereignty in the case of black men, and again opened it through the Minor-Hoppersott decision, not only in the case of women citizens, but also in the case of men citizens, for all other causes save those specified in the fifteenth amendment. You have yet another opportunity to retrieve your party from this false position. The political power of this country has always shown itself superior to judicial powers, the latter ever shaping and basing its decisions on the policy of the Democratic party. A pledge, therefore, by your convention to secure national protection, enfranchisement, perfect equality of rights, civil and political, to all citizens, will so define the policy of the Republican party as to open a way to a full and final adjustment of this question. Aside from these higher motives of justice, we would suggest your adoption of this principle of equal rights to women as a means of securing your own future existence. The party that ceases to respect the vital principles of truth and justice is the party that dies. If you would have the party of the future be the Republican party, you must now take the broad, noble ground of citizens' suffrage. By this step you will pay the most honor to your ancestors; by this act you will do most to promote the general welfare, and secure the blessings of liberty to yourselves and your posterity; by this act you will reduce to practice the theory of a hundred years, and establish a genuine republic that shall know no class, caste, race, or sex, where all the people are citizens, and all the citizens are equal before the law.

On behalf of the National Woman's Suffrage Association.

SUSAN B. ANTHONY.

REPORT ON RULES AND ORDER OF BUSINESS.

The PRESIDENT. The first business in order is the report of the Committee on Rules and Order of Business.

Mr. CESSNA, of Pennsylvania. *Mr. Chairman:* On behalf of the Committee on Rules and Order of Business, I beg leave to submit the following report:

To the Honorable the President and Members of the Republican National Convention:

Your committee, to whom was referred the matter of rules and order of business, beg leave to submit the following rules, including the order of business, for the government of this convention, as follows, to wit:

Rule 1. Upon all subjects before the convention the states shall be called in alphabetical order, and next the territories and the District of Columbia.

Rule 2. Each state shall be entitled to double the number of its senators and representatives in congress, according to the late apportionment, and each territory and the District of Columbia shall be entitled to two votes. The votes of each delegation shall be reported by its chairman.

Rule 3. The report of the Committee on Credentials shall be disposed of before the report of the Committee on Platform and Resolutions is acted upon; and the report of the Committee on Platform and Resolutions shall be disposed of before the convention proceeds to the nomination of candidates for President and Vice-President.

Rule 4. In making the nominations for President and Vice-President, in no case shall the calling of the roll be dispensed with when it shall appear that any candidate has received the majority of the votes cast. The president of the convention shall announce the question to be, "Shall the nomination of the candidate be made unanimous?" but, if no candidate shall have received a majority of the votes, the chair shall direct the vote to be again taken, which shall be repeated until some candidate shall have received a majority of the votes cast; and when any state has announced its vote, it shall so stand until the ballot is announced, unless in case of numerical error.

Rule 5. When a majority of the delegates of any two states shall demand that a vote be recorded, the same shall be taken by states, territories, and the District of Columbia—the secretary calling the roll of the states and territories in the order heretofore stated, and the District of Columbia.

Rule 6. In the record of the votes by states, the vote of each state, territory, and the District of Columbia shall be announced by the chairman; and, in case the votes of any state, territory, or the District of Columbia shall be divided, the chairman shall announce the number of votes cast for any candidate, or for or against any proposition.

Rule 7. When the previous question shall be demanded by the majority of the delegates from any state, and the demand seconded by two or more states, and the call sustained by a majority of the convention, the question shall then be proceeded with and disposed of according to the rules of the House of Representatives in similar cases.

Rule 8. No member shall speak more than once upon the same question, nor longer than five minutes, unless by leave of the convention, except that delegates, presenting the name of a candidate, shall be allowed ten minutes in presenting the name of such candidate.

Rule 9. The rules of the House of Representatives shall be the rules of this convention, so far as they are applicable and not inconsistent with the foregoing rules.

Rule 10. A Republican National Committee shall be appointed, to consist of one member from each state, territory, and district represented in this convention. The roll shall be called, and the delegation from each state, territory, and district shall name, through their chairman, a person to act as a member of such committee.

JOHN. CESSNA, *Chairman.*

R. A. DAWSON, *Secretary.*

DEBATE ON THE REPORT.

Mr. EUGENE HALE, of Maine. I move to strike from Rule 3 that part of it which postpones the nomination of candidates until after the adoption of the platform.

Mr. CESSNA. I rise to a point of order. I make a motion to recommit, my object being to secure the division of the report, as it appears that the convention desire to discuss it. I ask that the report be divided into two divisions,—the first division to embrace the whole of it except Rule 3, and the second to embrace Rule 3.

Mr. HALE. That will be perfectly satisfactory. I had no indication of the object of the gentleman. I oppose the rule, because I do not believe it is usual in bodies of this kind to adopt the platform before the nominations are made.

Mr. CESSNA. If there be no other objection, I ask that this report be divided as indicated.

Mr. SILLIMAN, of New York, said he desired, before the question should be put upon the adoption of the report, to suggest an amendment, as follows:

Resolved, That after each ballot, and until some candidate shall receive a majority of the votes cast, this convention will take a recess for the space of half an hour.

Mr. SILLIMAN. I will state, in another word, that this will enable the delegates from each state to meet, confer, consult, and decide upon their next ballot, and also to consult with other delegations.

Mr. CESSNA. I desire to suggest to the convention, that, in my judgment, the desirability, if not the necessity, of having some rules, will very soon appear; and I now say to my friend from New York, that, if he will let the vote be taken on the first division, I will not object to his offering that as a new rule to come in at the end of the report.

Mr. Silliman withdrew his amendment temporarily.

The PRESIDENT. The proposition, of which notice was given by the gentleman from New York, of the proposed amendment to the report of the committee, will be read. Although it has been temporarily withdrawn, it may be renewed after the division of the report itself. It will now be re-read for information only.

The secretary read the amendment for the information of the convention.

The PRESIDENT. The previous question has been called upon the adoption of the report,—the report being divided into two parts, the first to embrace the whole of it except Rule 3. The secretary will read Rule 3 for information.

The secretary read the rule, as follows:

"The report of the Committee on Credentials shall be disposed of before the report of the Committee on Platform and Resolutions is acted on; and the report of the Committee on Platform and Resolutions shall be disposed of before the convention proceeds to the nomination of candidates for President and Vice-President."

The PRESIDENT. The question on the adoption of that rule is reserved; and the pending question is on the adoption of the remaining rules.

The remaining rules were then adopted by a unanimous vote.

Mr. CESSNA. I move to reconsider and lay upon the table.

The PRESIDENT. That is unanimously agreed to, no objection being made.

The question then recurred upon the adoption of Rule 3.

Mr. HALE. I move to strike out that portion of the rule that postpones the balloting for candidates until after the platform is settled. I do not object, and cannot conceive of any one objecting, to the first part of the rule, that the report of the Committee on Credentials shall be first settled, and therefore do not desire to antagonize the whole rule. I move to strike out the last part of it, which the secretary will please read.

The secretary read as follows:

"And the report of the Committee on Platform and Resolutions shall be disposed of before the convention proceeds to the nomination of candidates for President and Vice-President."

The PRESIDENT. The proposition is to strike from the rule the words read, so that the rule will stand as follows:

"The report of the Committee on Credentials shall be disposed of before the report of the Committee on Platform and Resolutions is acted on."

Mr. CESSNA. Before the vote is taken, I desire to know if my friend from Maine wishes to discuss the amendment.

Mr. HALE. The whole point presented by my motion, Mr. President, must be so clear that I do not desire before this body of men to take up their time. I will only say that so far as my knowledge goes, neither in local or state conventions or national conventions, where I have attended before, has the platform or the resolutions of the party been presented before the nomination and selection of candidates. I believe, sir, that gentlemen present will see, that unless this motion of mine be carried, this convention may remain here for hours, uneasy and impatient, with nothing essential to do, while the Committee on Resolutions may be waiting, debating upon their report.

Mr. S. W. KELLOGG, of Connecticut. Was that not the case in 1860, when President Lincoln was first nominated?

Mr. HALE. I am informed by gentlemen about me that it was not. The gentleman has had more experience than I, and was perhaps present at that convention.

Mr. KELLOGG. I was not. I understand the Committee on Platform will be ready to report in five minutes. Therefore I do not see any necessity for changing the rule.

Mr. HALE. That only places the result of the deliberations of the committee before the convention, and leaves us engaged upon resolutions to be first considered, when I believe that the feeling of the gentlemen I see before me now is that when the organization of this convention is completed we should proceed at once to the nomination of its candidates.

Mr. G. W. HOTCHKISS, of New York. *Mr. Chairman:* In 1860 we made a platform before we placed our candidates upon it. Practically it may make no difference to-day, but theoretically it would be an absurdity to place a man on horseback before you get your horse. If there ever was a time in the history of the Republican party when we needed deliberation in our proceedings, it is to-day. In behalf of New York, I ask this convention that they make no forced march, but first let us know what our platform demands of the candidates. You may make a platform that will lessen the number of candidates materially. In 1860 the Republican party was composed of elements that had not come together and congealed, and they had to know what the principles of the party were in order to get a fit candidate. More new questions exist to-day in the Republican party than existed in 1860. We had then an overshadowing question. Now we are circumstanced differently, and every speaker upon that stand has told us that we were to meet new issues and new questions. Let us know what new questions we are to agree upon; then we can put forward a candidate reflecting our views, and he must be a candidate who is known and assured to be a fit exponent of those views, an earnest one, and not one who has to make up his mind after the platform is made.

Mr. NOYES, of Ohio. The gentleman from Maine is decidedly mistaken in his history of 1860. As the gentleman has just stated, the platform was reported before the candidate was nominated eight years ago. I am informed by Lieutenant-Governor Lee, of the New York delegation, who was then one of the Committee on Resolutions, that the convention waited a long time for the Committee on Resolutions to report. As the gentleman says, it is absurd to nominate a candidate until you know what he is to stand upon. It may make all the difference in the world when a platform is reported. It might turn out that one candidate was fitted to it, and another was not.

Mr. CESSNA. *Mr. Chairman:* I have no feeling whatever on this subject. I consider it, however, but proper and fair that, on behalf of my committee, I should stand by what was its unanimous action as to the report to this convention. The resolution which is now pending for adoption before this body has neither an "i" dotted nor a "t" crossed from the resolution and the rule, and its number is the same adopted by the last national convention, held in 1872. I beg to say to my friend from Maine, and any other gentlemen who entertain different views, that this rule is not introduced, and it is not now advocated, by the present speaker at least, in the interest of any candidate, nor in a spirit of opposition to any other candidate. I believe a platform should be made, and I believe, as my friend has said, that if ever there was a time when deliberation was necessary at the hands of a national convention, that hour is now. I have been in conventions in former times, and I know and I feel to-day, that if we go to work and nominate our ticket before we make our platform, one half of the delegates will be on their way home before we get to the platform, and there will be no deliberation or discussion of it.

Mr. HALE. Let me ask the gentleman a question.

Mr. CESSNA. Certainly.

Mr. HALE. My main point in making the motion was to have something for the convention to do. I wish to ask if the chair has authoritative information that the Committee on Resolutions is ready to report.

The PRESIDENT. The chair has not; but the chairman of the committee is present.

Mr CESSNA. This is a matter of very immaterial difference, because, under the rules, I would state to my friend from Maine, that the report of the Committee on Credentials must be considered before the report of the Committee on Resolutions, and before any nominations; and, from what I have heard in relation to that report, I think my friend from Maine will find that we have enough to do when that report comes in.

Mr. HALE. I only asked the question to get from my friend from Rhode Island the information whether the committee was ready to report.

A DELEGATE from Rhode Island. I am so informed by my colleague on that committee.

Mr. HALE. Then, Mr. President, I withdraw the motion.

Mr. CESSNA. I demand the previous question.

The previous question was ordered, and the motion agreed to; and Rule 3 was adopted as reported by the committee.

THE QUESTION OF A RECESS AFTER EACH BALLOT.

The PRESIDENT. The next business in order is the motion of Mr. Silliman, from New York, for the addition of a new rule. The secretary will read the proposition made by the gentleman from New York, which is now pending as an addition.

The secretary read as follows;

Resolved, That after each ballot, and until some candidate shall receive a majority of the votes cast, this convention will take a recess for the space of half an hour.

Cries of "No!" "No!"

The PRESIDENT. Is the convention ready for the vote?

Mr. SILLIMAN. Perhaps the necessity of the resolution will appear, when I state that after each ballot is taken each delegation may wish to have time to consult and confer with other delegations.

Mr. VAN ZANDT, of Rhode Island. I trust, before the motion is put, it may be amended; and I offer as an amendment, that, before the thirty minutes recess be taken, each delegation, or the chairman of each delegation, shall be suitably labelled for what they ask, and whether they take "cash" or "country produce."

A DELEGATE from Virginia. I move to lay on the table.

The president put the vote on laying on the table the motion of the gentleman from New York, which provides that after each ballot there shall be a recess of thirty minutes; and the motion to lay on the table was adopted.

The PRESIDENT. The next business in order is the report of the Committee on Credentials. Mr. John T. Ensor, of Maryland, chairman of the Committee on Credentials, will now read the report.

Mr. Ensor read the following report:

REPORT OF COMMITTEE ON CREDENTIALS.

The Committee on Credentials have attended to the duties assigned them, and respectfully report that full delegations are present from all the states and territories, with the following exceptions:

The states of North Carolina and Nevada each have one absent delegate, and the committee recommend that in each of these cases the delegates present be authorized to cast the full vote of their respective states.

No seats are contested, except from the states of Alabama, Florida, and the District of Columbia, and the committee recommend that the following delegates and alternates be admitted from Alabama, viz.:

Delegates.	AT LARGE.	*Alternates.*
Jeremiah Haralson.		James Q. Smith.
Willard Warner.		Charles W. Buckley.
Samuel F. Rice.		George M. Duskin.
Wm. H. Smith.		George F. Sommerville.

DISTRICTS.

Delegates	Alternates
1—Morris D. Wickersham.	
Frank H. Threatt.	
2—Robert A. Knox.	Patrick Robinson.
Hershal D. Cashin.	George W. Sewell.
3—M. S. Patterson.	James R. Treadwell.
Robert T. Smith.	J. A. C. Parker.
4—James V. McDuffie.	
Green S. W. Lewis.	
5—Charles H. Miller.	
William H. Nichols.	
6—J. A. Cowdery.	
William Miller.	
7—Joseph W. Burke.	
Robert A. Mosely.	
8—J. R. Coffrey.	
Thomas Masterson.	

Your committee also recommend that the following delegates and alternates be admitted to seats from Florida, viz.:

Delegates.	AT LARGE.	*Alternates.*
S. B. Conover.		Reuben S. Smith.
W. J. Purman.		Wm. J. Stewart.
John G. Long.		Geo. W. Witherspoon.
John R. Scott.		Joseph E. Lee.

DISTRICTS.

Delegates	Alternates
1—Manuel Gorin.	James D. Thompson.
Peter W. Bryant.	John W. Wyatt.
2—Harrison Reed.	G. J. Arnold.
J. W. Menard.	Thos. W. Long.

Your committee also recommend that the following delegates and alternates be admitted to seats from the District of Columbia, viz.:

Delegates.	*Alternates.*
S. J. Bowen.	Andrew Gleason.
A. M. Green.	C. Crusor.

The state of Arkansas has elected twenty-four delegates, who are all present, and the committee recommend that they all be admitted to seats in the convention, with the right to cast the twelve votes to which their state is entitled.

JOHN T. ENSOR, *Chairman.*

DAVID ATWOOD, *Secretary.*

Mr. HEATON, of North Carolina. I desire to correct an error in the report. At the time the committee first met, the North Carolina delegation was not full, but now, I am pleased to say, it is full, Mr. Russell, delegate from the first district, having arrived.

Mr. CHARLES N. HARRIS, of Nevada, read the following minority report of the Committee on Credentials:

MINORITY REPORT.

The undersigned, members of the Committee on Credentials, feel constrained to differ from the report of the majority of the committee, in so far as the same relates to the seating of the delegates from Alabama. From the limited opportunities afforded the committee to investigate this case, the minority are led to the conclusion that the delegation from Alabama, headed by Hon. Geo. E. Spencer, is the only legitimate and truly representative delegation applying for admission to this convention from that state. We base our opinion on the following facts and considerations:

In August of 1874, a Republican state convention was held at the city of Montgomery, Alabama, for the nomination of state officers, to be voted for in that state for that year. There was at this time no faction in the party in the state. All Republicans were represented in the convention, and were satisfied with its action. This convention appointed a state executive committee, consisting of twelve members, to conduct the succeeding campaign, and to act for and in behalf of the party in the state in all things until the convention to be called in 1876, two years thereafter. The committee met and elected as chairman Charles E. Mayer. The campaign was conducted under the auspices of this committee, and its actions were acquiesced in by all except the Democrats, so far as the minority of your committee are informed. These facts are undisputed. A quorum of this committee met in Montgomery on February 2, 1876, under the call of its chairman, and put forth a call for the convention of May 24, 1876, which assembled and sent to this convention the delegation headed by Mr. Spencer. If there be any virtue in legitimacy and regularity, the convention held on May 24, last past, was the regular Republican state convention of Alabama, and the delegation sent by that convention to represent the Republican voters of Alabama, in our body, are the delegates that should be admitted.

The delegation, headed by S. F. Rice, while admitting, as we understand, the facts as above set forth, claim that on December the 29th the committee created by the last state convention was reorganized by the committee itself, in obedience to the demands of a mass meeting held at Montgomery on said day. The claim, briefly stated, is as follows: That when the original committee was created in 1874, there were but six congressional districts in the state, and the committee was formed by appointing two members of the committee from each of said congressional districts; but that at the session of the legislature for 1874–5 the congressional districts of the state were reorganized, by reason of the increased representation allowed Alabama in the lower house of congress by the new apportionment, and eight districts were created, thus creating two new congressional districts in the state, and changing the boundaries of the old districts. The claim is, that this rendered a reorganization of the state executive committee necessary, in order that each district might be represented thereon, and that the committee, in compliance with the demands of the mass meeting before referred to, met and added twelve new members to itself for this purpose. The committee, as thus constituted, would be one of twenty-four members, and not twelve. The minority of your committee, from the best information they have been able to gain, find it to be true that a mass meeting was held in the city of Montgomery on the 29th day of December, 1875; but its representative character is denied, the organization, headed by Mr. Spencer, claiming that it was local in its character, and that it represented only the county of Montgomery, with trifling exceptions. We find it to be true, further, that some members of the committee did, at the dictation of this mass meeting, consent to elect twelve new members to be added to the twelve already constituting the committee; but we find that this action was not taken by the committee itself, after having been duly called by its recognized chairman. Members of the committee, being in the city at the time, voluntarily assembled and took the action as stated. Such action, had under such circumstances, is diametrically opposed to every idea entertained by us of order or regularity in a political body, or of legality in a legislative body.

This convention, yesterday, adjourned until this morning at ten o'clock. If, at ten o'clock last night, four hundred of its members had assembled in this hall and pretended to nominate candidates for President and Vice-President, without notification to or the acquiescence of the other three hundred and odd members, it would be a precisely parallel case. The committee afterwards, under the regular call of its chairman, assembled, and refused to recognize or acquiesce in the action of its members at the former unauthorized meeting. This fact shows that the committee have never acquiesced in the action first taken; and subsequent events show that the Republican party has never acquiesced therein. But we do not recognize the right of a committee, even if regularly called and fully attended, to increase or diminish its number, or to change its constitution in any form. Any attempt to do so is but an attempt at revolution, and can never have validity, except when universally acquiesced in by the party, wherein sovereignty in such matters rests. The convention that created the committee did not confer on it the power of making a new committee. It clothed the committee with the power and responsibility of conducting the affairs of the party, and not for the purpose of having it divide that power and responsibility with others unknown to and unrecognized by the convention.

These considerations derive additional force, when the pretext upon which the pretended reorganization was based is fully considered. That pretext is, that the reorganization of the congressional districts rendered a reorganization of the state executive committee necessary. But, in our view, such was not the case. It is presumed that the congressional districts were taken as the basis of representation on the committee, because they were fair geographical divisions of the state; and it was the desire of the state convention to give each section of the state representation on the committee. The addition of new districts, then, or the abolition of old ones, could not change those geographical divisions. They still existed, and each section of the state was as well represented on the committee after as before the change in the districts. Further: we understand it to be a fact, that the law creating the new districts does not go into effect until November, 1876. According to party usage, a state convention would have to be held before the August election of the present year. Why, then, resort to disorganization and disintegration to re-form the committee, to conform to the law going into force eight months thereafter, when, by waiting only three months, if there was any justice in the claim, the committee could be reorganized by a regular state convention chosen by the people for that purpose?

No evidence was adduced before the committee to show the relative strength of the different organizations before the Republicans of Alabama. In the discussions, however, and in published statements submitted to the committee, mention was made of a proposition of compromise made by Hon. Simon Cameron, chairman of the Union Republican Congressional Committee, and by Hon. Wm. E. Chandler, secretary of the Republican National Committee. Said proposition is as follows:

WASHINGTON, D. C., March 21, 1876.

Dear Sir: The following plan of compromise, by which to unite the Republican party in Alabama, is presented, after mature deliberation, as being fair and equitable in its terms, and in full confidence that it will be accepted by all parties:

1. The chairman of the two executive committees shall withdraw the calls already made, and unite in calling a convention to be held on the 23d day of May next.

2. Mr. Chas. E. Mayer, the chairman of one committee, shall call the convention to order, and name Hon. William H. Smith, chairman of the other committee, as temporary chairman of the convention.

3. The temporary chairman shall appoint two committees and no more, viz., the committees on credentials and on permanent organization, and no other business shall be transacted, or additional committees appointed, until the convention shall have been permanently organized.

4. The committees on credentials and on permanent organization shall be selected in the following manner: Mr. Mayer and Governor Smith shall each name two members of each committee, and the four thus selected shall select a fifth. All five members of each committee shall be selected before the meeting of the convention.

A letter identical in its terms with this has been sent to Hon. William H. Smith.

You will please call your committee together without delay, and at your earliest convenience notify Hon. J. M. Edmunds, of Washington, D. C., of the acceptance or rejection of these terms of compromise.

Very respectfully, your obedient servant,

SIMON CAMERON,
Chairman Republican Congressional Committee.
W. E. CHANDLER,
Secretary of the Rep. Nat'l Committee,
appointed by the Philadelphia Convention.

This proposition was promptly and unconditionally accepted by the organization that called the convention of May 24th, and that sent the delegates to this convention headed by Mr. Spencer,—thus showing a commendable willingness to test their strength and rest their cause in the hands of the Republican voters of their state.

The proposition of Mr. Cameron and Mr. Chandler was undoubtedly as promptly and unconditionally declined by the other organization. Right here let it be observed, that the point of the Cameron-Chandler proposition was to bring both parties together on one day and in one convention, under such safeguards that it could not but give a fair expression to the views and feelings of the Republicans of the state.

Mr. Cameron and Mr. Chandler, with a commendable zeal for party unity and harmony, did not stop here, but made the following reply to the declination of their proposition.

WASHINGTON, April 28, 1876.

SIR: We have to acknowledge receipt of yours of April 13, in answer to our letter of March 23.

In making our former communication, we did not desire to express an opinion or to invite a discussion of the actual merits of the controversy going on between two rival organizations of the Republican party in Alabama.

Whatever the merits of that controversy may be, we desire to end it all by securing a state convention fairly representing the Republicans of the state.

Neither do we desire to enter into the merits of your complaints of Senator Spencer and Mr. Chas. E. Mayer, or their associates.

It is sufficient to say, that, while you make assertions against them, they generally and specifically deny that they are correct or just; and our object is to remit them to one convention fairly and impartially constituted, instead of having them result in an injurious division of the party.

To the plan proposed by us you take no specific exception; and certainly upon its face it indicates perfect fairness toward both sides, and gives neither side an advantage over the other. It does not seem to us that either side can refuse to accept it, unconditionally, without admitting its belief that it will be in a minority of a Republican convention fairly constituted, and legitimately entitled to represent the Republicans of Alabama.

We therefore repeat our request that you will accept our suggestions, and we trust upon reflection you and your committee will conclude to do so.

The propositions suggested are repeated at the foot of this letter.

Very respectfully yours,
SIMON CAMERON,
Chairman Republican Congressional Committee.
WM. E. CHANDLER,
Secretary Republican National Committee.

Hon. W. H. SMITH, Wedowee, Ala.

Is it not apparent that the strictures of Messrs. Cameron and Chandler were just? The proposition submitted by them provided for a perfectly fair organization of the convention. It proposed to place the question in the hands of the people for their decision, and the only reason we can see for either side declining the proposition was a conscious weakness of their cause with the people, for the organization that had the most voters would control the convention.

Therefore, the conclusion is most convincing that the side refusing to accept it could only be actuated in their refusal by one of two motives, namely,—by a desire to divide and disrupt the party, or by the fear and knowledge that the people were not with them, and would not send a majority of their delegates to the convention.

The foregoing considerations induce us to dissent from the majority, and to recommend that the following gentlemen be admitted to this convention.

DELEGATES AT LARGE.

George E. Spencer,.............Decatur, Morgan county.
Charles Hays,..................Hayesville, Greene county.
Alexander White,...............Salem, Dallas county.
Alex. A. Curtis,...............Marion, Perry county.

DISTRICTS.

1—George Turner,.................Mobile, Mobile county.
Constantine Perez,.............Mobile, Mobile county.
2—Paul Strobach,.................Montgomery, Montgomery co.
Allen Alexander,...............Montrose, Baldwin county.
3—Isaac Heyman,..................Opelika, Lee county.
Alex. E. Williams,.............Eufaula, Barbour county.
4—Prelate D. Barker,.............Selma, Dallas county.
Thomas Walker,.................Selma, Dallas county.
5—Daniel B. Booth,...............Prattville, Autauga county.
Harry C. Bryan,................Wetumpka, Elmore county.
6—Charles C. Sheats,.............Houston, Winston county.
John G. Stokes,................Pikeville, Marion county.
7—Arthur Bingham,................Talladega, Talladega county.
Robert S. Heflin,..............Medoma, Randolph county.
8—Jerome J. Hinds,...............Decatur, Morgan county.
P. J. Kaufman,.................Huntsville, Madison county.

All of which is respectfully submitted.

C. N. HARRIS, Nevada.
JAMES ATKINS, Georgia.
STEPHEN A. SWAILS, South Carolina.
A. STEELE, Indiana.
A. G. SHARP, Tennessee.
M. A. ROSENBLATT, Missouri.
C. E. NASH, Louisiana.
JAMES HEATON, North Carolina.
M. S. QUAY, Pennsylvania.
T. C. PLATT, New York.
JAMES P. NEWCOMB, Texas.

A DELEGATE from Maryland. I move that the subject-matter referring to this particular delegation be recommitted.

Mr. CESSNA. I ask that the report be divided, and that the first part be the adoption of the whole of it, except the part relating to Alabama.

The president stated the motion for a division.

Mr. CESSNA. I presume I have a right to demand that division, without putting it to a vote. I have learned,—and I beg not to be considered offensive toward the committee,—partly from the committee and partly on my own responsibility, that, in the case of the District of Columbia, neither of the delegations comes with that regularity and form that would entitle them to seats in this convention. I feel that the states of New York, Pennsylvania, Ohio, and other states, have been very generous and liberal in giving the territories places upon all these committees, giving them five or six places on the most important committees, to make a platform on which candidates for President and Vice-President are to stand. After so learning, in the interest of peace and harmony, I move to amend that portion of the report, by striking out the name of Sayles J. Bowen, and inserting the name of Frederick Douglass, so that each delegation from the District of Columbia may be represented here.

The PRESIDENT. The report of the committee has been divided. The pending proposition is to adopt the whole of the report except that relating to Alabama. The gentleman from Pennsylvania moves to amend that part relating to the District of Columbia by striking out the name of Mr. Bowen, and inserting the name of Mr. Douglass.

Mr. KELLOGG, of Connecticut. I wish to ask by what authority any delegates are recognized as entitled to seats in this convention from the District of Columbia? Formerly, for a few years under the laws, it was entitled to a delegate in congress the same as the territories, and, I presume, was under the same custom allowed delegates in national conventions.

The PRESIDENT. Such is the custom.

A DELEGATE from West Virginia. I would ask if the call for this convention did not ask for the election of delegates from the city of Washington?

The PRESIDENT. It so appears from the call.

Mr. JAMES N. TYNER, of Indiana. Before the vote shall be taken upon the motion of the gentleman from Pennsylvania, I desire to call his attention to the fact that he has stated, in general terms, that the action of the Republicans in the District of Columbia was somewhat irregular in sending the two delegates here, whose admission has been recommended by the majority report. Now, will the gentlemen tell us in what respect those proceedings were irregular?

Mr. CESSNA. I answer the gentleman from Indiana that all the information I have got is from the Republican organs in the city of Washington, and that kind of Republicans who come here headed by Frederick Douglass, who needs no indorsement anywhere in this country.

Mr. TYNER. Then, Mr. President, I treat the gentleman with entire respectfulness when I say that he has no information on the subject. Therefore, it is fair to assume that the gentleman makes his proposition because Frederick Douglass happens to represent an interest here in which he fully concurs and other delegates do not.

Mr. ENSOR. I wish to make but a single remark on this part of the report. While there were differences of opinion in regard to other subjects before the committee, the committee will bear me out that if we were not entirely, we were almost unanimously, in favor of the admission of the delegates we have reported as entitled to seats in the convention for the District of Columbia. In regard to the regularity of the credentials, it cannot be denied that the credentials of Mr. Bowen and Mr. Green were regular upon their face, and were proper credentials; and permit me to say, when the gentleman who represents the other side was called upon for his credentials, he admitted that he did not have them. He had no credentials to present to the consideration of that committee. It is true, he claimed that he had the credentials, and had handed them in to the secretary of the National Executive Committee; but he brought no credentials to us. We, therefore, strictly speaking, could take no notice of his case, but, aside from that, it was clearly demonstrated to the committee that the credentials of Mr. Bowen and Mr. Green were regular in every respect.

Mr. CESSNA. *Mr. Chairman—*

Mr. REDDEN, of Kansas. This convention has adopted a rule that no gentleman shall speak twice upon the same subject, and the gentleman from Pennsylvania has already spoken twice upon the subject.

Mr. CESSNA. I desire before the chair rules on that point of order to make this statement.

Cries of "Order!" "Order!"

The PRESIDENT. The chair states that he will rule upon the question of order raised by the gentleman from Kansas upon ascertaining the precise facts. The discussion was so desultory that he cannot recollect the fact whether the gentleman from Pennsylvania has spoken more than once upon the proposition. I am not aware that the gentleman has made any remarks upon this proposition.

Mr. CESSNA. I do not desire to make any now. What I desire, is—

Cries of "Order!" "Order!"

The PRESIDENT. The gentleman from Pennsylvania has withdrawn his proposition.

Mr. CESSNA. That is all I want to do.

The PRESIDENT. The question then recurs upon the adoption of the report of the Committee on Credentials, except that portion relating to Alabama.

This question, on being put, was agreed to, and the report, with that exception, adopted, and the delegates reported declared entitled to seats in the convention.

Mr. ENSOR. I move that the portion relating to Alabama be recommitted. I shall not occupy more than five minutes in replying to the long written argument of my friend who has introduced the minority report. I wish simply to call attention to facts—plain, simple facts. The state central committee of Alabama was constituted in 1874. There were then six congressional districts in the state; and the committee was composed of twelve members—two from each congressional district. That committee met. It considered itself not large enough, and it called in Mr. Charles E. Mayer, and elected him chairman of that committee. Mr. Mayer was not appointed a member of that committee by the state convention. He was called in by the members of the committee, without authority, and, after having been called in, he was made chairman of that committee. This seemed to be regular, as the party accepted it; and they went on for a year or two, until many Republicans considered they ought to have more members on the committee. Inasmuch as Mayer had been called in irregularly, without authority, members of the party said,—"We wish others called in: we wish the committee increased from twelve or thirteen to twenty-four."

The Republicans of the state called a meeting. The members of that committee were invited to it. They went to it, most of them. It was there determined that this committee should be increased, in just the same manner as the chairman had been added to it. This was acquiesced in by the people. It was acquiesced in by most of the old committee. The committee was then made up of twenty-four members. In February last, when they wished to call a convention to elect delegates to this convention, the committee met, six of the old members of the committee meeting with the twelve new members, making eighteen. These eighteen members of the state central committee called a convention that elected the delegates to this convention. The other six not being satisfied, and not, by the way, being a quorum, went off and called another convention, and sent delegates, who are contesting the seats of those whom the committee have reported in favor of seating. If there was any irregularity in this committee, it was inaugurated in the beginning by calling in a man who was not a member of it, who had not been appointed by the state convention. But that was acquiesced in, and when the committee of twenty-four was appointed it was acquiesced in at the time by at least a portion of the old committee, and by the great body of the people of Alabama, who wanted success for the Republican party in the state of Alabama. The committee being thus constituted, twelve of that committee called the convention which has sent its delegates here. Six of the others, looking to disorganization, have sent the other delegates.

Mr. CUMBACK, of Indiana. I do not wish, sir, to take up much time in discussing this report,—

Mr. ENSOR. I should have stated that this matter was fully discussed in the committee. The vote was taken by calling the roll; and it appeared that there were twenty-six in favor of the one delegation, and thirteen in favor of the other.

Mr. CUMBACK. I propose to reply to that proposition at once. The gentlemen knew when they came before this convention with this majority report that the minority report would be made, setting forth the facts of the minority; and yet the gentlemen of the majority come without a single fact to sustain their report. I think, therefore, it is conclusive that this majority of the committee have no facts from which they could draw the conclusion they have presented; and they propose to seat this delegation without any facts. Now, the minority of this committee have come before this convention with such an array of facts, undisputed by the report of the majority, as should leave no doubt in the mind of every fair-minded Republican that the minority report should be adopted. Another thing that is conclusive to me, irrespective of the acts of the committee, is this: The National Committees fairly and squarely presented a compromise to these gentlemen, and asked them to leave it to the Republicans of Alabama. The delegation represented by the majority of the committee declined any such proposition. I therefore conclude two facts: First, that the majority of this committee had not sufficient facts to sustain their report; and that the delegation had not sufficient facts to justify their action so that they could dare to submit it to the Republicans of Alabama.

Mr. TYNER. *Mr. President:* After listening carefully to the argument of the gentleman in charge of the majority report, I come to the conclusion that he made only one single point in behalf of his report. That point was this: That, after the regular executive committee had been appointed by the state convention in Alabama, in 1874, they went outside of their list and chose a chairman of that committee. Now, can the gentleman tell me that that committee did not have the authority of that convention to do so?

Mr. ENSOR. It was not claimed on the part of the Spencer delegation that the convention delegated any such authority.

Mr. TYNER. It is claimed upon the part of the Spencer delegation that they had the authority, in accordance with the usage of the party from its organization down to this day.

Mr. ENSOR. That is an affirmative proposition; and if that convention ever had such authority, by resolution, it is in your power to produce it, and I ask for it here.

Mr. TYNER. Then, Mr. President, the gentleman has presented authoritative conclusions for the admission of certain gentlemen from Alabama. I return upon him, by asking him for the proof that these gentlemen are entitled to admission on this floor.

Mr. ENSOR. Allow me to interrupt you. Is it customary that a committee on credentials shall read all its proof—read all its evidence? If so, we can produce it.

Mr. TYNER. Then, Mr. President, my response to that is, that the gentleman should not question my statement on this floor until he is prepared to substantiate his own. Again, sir: I want to say, that after looking this matter over as carefully as I can, I come to the conclusion that the only authority for the convention of May 16 was authority which emanated from a mass convention called without authority of the state central committee; and, if I am right, then it follows that the duly organized and regular delegation here from the state of Alabama is that headed by George E. Spencer. One word more, sir, and I have done. There are many gentlemen about me who have been associated with me in legislative life for more than six years. They will bear me testimony that my history and my record will indicate that I never took an unfair advantage of any man. I say, then, gentlemen, presuming upon my own spirit of fairness in this matter,—I say, that the gentleman who stands here as the friend and supporter of any candidate who is to be benefited by the admission or rejection of either of these delegations, cannot afford to ask this convention to do an unfair thing. Whoever shall be the nominee of this convention must win the prize fairly.

Mr. DEZENDORF, of Virginia. I wish to speak in behalf of the majority report. In presenting this case to the convention, I shall endeavor to confine myself to the facts as they appeared before that committee—the Committee on Credentials. It appears, sir, that in 1874, at the state convention, there was a committee appointed consisting of twelve members. That committee, as has been here stated, proceeded to elect a chairman outside of its own number. That, I claim, they had a right to do, if they saw fit so to do. It is the case in a great many states that such a proceeding has been taken. Time passed; and, from the statements made to the Committee on Credentials, it appears that the party in Alabama became very much demoralized. It got into a very bad shape indeed; and a large number of Republicans of that state published a call calling upon the state central committee to call a meeting of conference, to be composed of delegates or members from all portions of the state of Alabama. That conference was held. It was participated in by a large number of this old convention or committee. In the process of their considerations and deliberations, they came to the conclusion that it was necessary to enlarge the state central committee, and make it composed of twenty-four instead of twelve delegates, in order that all the districts in the state of Alabama might be properly represented. That was assented to by at least a majority of the old state committee. In consequence of the absence of the chairman of the state central committee, Mr. Mayer, who, I believe, was a clerk of a committee in the city of Washington, and absent from the state a large portion of the time, they decided to elect a temporary chairman, which they did. That committee of twenty-four—a majority of it, consisting of eighteen members—called a convention, which convention elected the delegation to this house headed by Jere Haralson, as he is commonly called. Six of the committee dissented from the views of the majority, and called another convention, which elected the Spencer delegation. The question, then, gentlemen, it seems to me, resolves itself down to whether or not the majority of the committee shall rule, or the minority. Gentlemen have alluded to the fact that the offer of compromise was not accepted. The people recognized no two committees. There was but one committee.

Mr. JAMES ATKINS, of Georgia. *Mr. President and Gentlemen of the Convention:* I desire to present a few facts and considerations that justify me, as a member of the minority of this committee, in recommending the seating of the Spencer delegation; and, to my mind, these facts and reasons are entirely unanswerable. A state central committee, or, as they called it, an executive committee of Alabama, was appointed in 1874. There is no dispute about this one great fact. This committee, in accordance with the custom prevailing in the party in Alabama, appointed a chairman outside of their own number. We may say that this is irregular; that it is not the best way; that it is not the right way;—but the Republicans of Alabama have always acted under that system. It will not do for us to come now and dictate to them, especially in regard to transactions that have already taken place. The party followed this committee, worked with this committee, responded to the call of this committee, in all the campaigns that took place from the time of its appointment until this difficulty arose. There is no difficulty, no doubt, no question of fact, for a moment, about the regularity of this committee. The question arises right here, Had any power but a convention, regularly called, composed of delegates from the Republican party from the state of Alabama, any right to appoint another committee? Had they any right to increase the old committee, or diminish it, in any way whatsoever? In a political sense, is there any sovereignty in the state of Alabama, so far as the Republican party is concerned, except the people, the Republicans of Alabama? I think not, and I think you will all agree with me. If so, then this committee being appointed, it would remain and continue as it was, except as it might be changed by acts of Providence. A set of gentlemen conceived the idea of taking possession of the Republican party of Alabama, and they are represented by the delegation that opposes the Spencer delegation here. They attempted it by a *coup d'état*—by revolution; it is nothing else but revolution. If it succeeded, and was ratified by the Republicans of Alabama, it was a success. But did they succeed? Let us see. Did their revolution succeed? What was the first step? Was a convention called? Not at all. There was a mass meeting in Montgomery, attended by the local Republicans and Democrats around Montgomery. There is no pretence that it was a representative body at all. Was their attempted revolution successful? Was it acquiesced in? No call of the central committee was made at the time of this mass meeting in Alabama; but a number of the members of this committee were present in the city of Montgomery, and they, overawed by this mass meeting, consented, so far as they were concerned, and added these twelve men to the old twelve of the committee.

Mr. MILLIKEN, of Maine. I wish, Mr. President, to say but a single word upon this subject. It seems to me that gentlemen have so treated the matter as to give us an entire misconception of it. The gentleman who preceded me wished this convention to understand that somebody was ousted there; that there was a *coup d'état;* that there was a revolution. Now, the facts are these: When the people of Alabama found it was necessary to vitalize that state committee, found that the Republican party was languishing for the want of activity, members of the state committee being out of the state, they called a mass meeting to consider this question. At that mass meeting the old committee was present. They recommended that new additions should be made. Those additions were made by the committee with the consent of every one, nobody objecting. The new committee and the old, acting harmoniously together, nobody objecting, called a convention. Then Mr. Mayer, who was elected chairman of the old committee from the outside, and who held a place, as I understand it, in Washington, found it necessary for some purpose, I know not what, to come down and make trouble. I understand that this new committee was acting in entire harmony; that the people were satisfied until this Mr. Mayer,—never elected by the executive committee, but only chosen by the state committee,—I say, this Mr. Mayer called a convention, but he was not sustained by a quorum of the old committee of twelve. It is a significant fact, gentlemen, that this committee which elected the Haralson delegates, as they are called, was called by eighteen delegates. It must have included six of the old committee at least. This new convention, which the gentleman calls legitimate, was called simply by Mr. Mayer, not sustained by a quorum, as I said before, of the old committee. One gentleman who spoke before me said that he acted in fairness towards the prevalent sentiment of the state. I say, it appeared to the committee that they who lived there, who voted there, they who fought the Republican battles, and not those who held fat places away out of the state,—I say, it appeared to the committee, by overwhelming testimony, that the people of Alabama, who stayed there, were unanimously in favor of the Haralson delegation. It was hardly denied at all.

Mr. POMEROY, of New York. *Gentlemen of the Convention:* I would not take a moment of your time upon this question, so far as it has any political bearing; but it goes further than that, and we are sitting here as jurors, upon our honor, to pass upon a question of fact and law involving the rights of the state of Alabama, and perhaps deciding the fate of this convention. Now, when it comes to a question like that, where I am sitting upon my honor as a juror to pass upon the rights of others, then I say I will act upon it without fear, favor, affection, reward, or the hope thereof, and so, no doubt, the members of this convention feel. Now, what are the facts of this case? We came here yesterday: we understood there were contestants from the state of

Alabama, and the matter of the contest was referred to the Committee on Credentials. They come in this morning, and a majority of that committee present to us—what? The facts? Not one. They present a simple conclusion of law not based upon a single fact. As a juror sitting to pass upon this case, I find that there is nothing before me. Now, I say that any court, upon the presentation of such a report as this, would set it aside without argument. They would not allow it to be discussed. There is nothing there. Now, if that was all there was of this thing, I should before this have moved that the subject be again referred to the Committee on Credentials, to give us something to act upon; but there is no necessity of that. A minority report has been presented here which does embrace the facts, and it does arrive at a different conclusion of law. Not one vital fact in that report is controverted. There is no necessity, then, to send this back to the committee for a further report. We have the facts, all of them. Not one of them essential to our finding is disputed, and the only question is, Shall Alabama be turned out of this convention? There is not a man of the majority of those who presented that report that dare stand here and say that, upon that majority report, Alabama should be represented at all. The mass meeting they bring in here to purify the state of Alabama is a mass meeting whose functions ended with the state lines of Alabama. We are not dealing here with mass meetings. We are dealing with regular organizations; and except we show credentials from regular organizations, none of us could have any status here. Now, the undisputed fact, as it appears from the report of the minority, which is the only report before the convention, is, that George E. Spencer and his associates represent a convention emanating from the committee appointed two years ago, and which is the only committee holding any power from any source in the state of Alabama entitled to recognition here. The question therefore is, simply, Shall George E. Spencer and his associates be admitted, or, shall Alabama be denied representation in this convention?

Mr. HEATON, of North Carolina. *Mr. President and Gentlemen of the Convention:* I am a citizen of the tar-heel state. I know what the people throughout this Southern Union desire; and I stand here to-day, although a native-born Ohioan, to say that while I love that state, this beautiful land of the middle section, I still love the state of my adoption more, the state of North Carolina. Now, then, the question presents itself to you in this wise: Who are the proper men to be seated here as delegates from Alabama? According to the evidence that was adduced before the Committee on Credentials last night, I have no hesitation in saying, in every point of view, in every fact that is material to the issue, that Mr. Spencer, with his followers, backed up by the regularly organized element of the Republican executive committee of that state, is the man, and they are the delegates entitled to seats upon this floor.

Now, then, gentlemen, there is something behind the curtain that I wish to speak of here. When that committee was in open session, in the hall of the Grand Hotel, down here, last night, there was a strenuous effort—an effort that was somewhat successful—before that committee, by the illustrious chairman of it, to suppress debate in favor of Mr. Spencer and his delegation. I say it with all due deference to him,—but I tell him, that if he takes up the battle-cry of the Horace Greeley disorganizing, disintegrating element of the South, and fights it out in his contest as he did last year, you may bid farewell to Republican success. I have nothing to say against Greeley,—for, when God puts his hand on a man, I always take mine off;—but I do say this,—that if we had been thoroughly heard before that committee, and had had proper time to represent the facts and issues, that report would have been different entirely. But we were suppressed. We were denied that opportunity, and the gentleman here knows it.

A DELEGATE from Wisconsin. I think there is altogether too much eloquence wasted upon this question. We are of opinion that the only sensible way to settle it is, to adopt the majority report. Therefore, Mr. Chairman, I move the previous question.

Mr. R. C. POWERS, of Mississippi. I move, sir, that when that vote is taken, it be taken by the call of states.

Mr. VAN ZANDT, of Rhode Island. The previous question is seconded by Rhode Island.

The PRESIDENT. The chair begs to state to the convention, that he was not aware that the gentleman from Wisconsin demanded the previous question. Under the rules of the house, it is required that a majority of the delegation of any one state shall demand the previous question. The demand must be made on behalf of a majority of the delegation. Does the gentleman represent a majority of the delegation?

A DELEGATE from Wisconsin. The demand is made on behalf of every living soul in Wisconsin.

The PRESIDENT. The chair now understands that the rule has been complied with. The previous question has been demanded and seconded, and the question now is, Shall the main question be now put? It appears to be agreed to. It is agreed to, and the question arises upon the adoption of the substitute proposed by the minority of the committee.

A DELEGATE from Connecticut. I now move that the roll of states be called on that motion, and that the chairman of each delegation rise in his place to respond.

The PRESIDENT. Under the rule, it is required that a majority of the delegates of two states shall concur in ordering the yeas and nays.

A DELEGATE. The call is seconded by Kansas.

Another DELEGATE. And Indiana.

The PRESIDENT. The clerk will call the roll of the states, and the question is on the adoption of the substitute offered by the minority of the committee. The majority of the committee made a report in favor of seating the delegation headed by Jeremiah Haralson. The minority of the committee made a report in favor of seating the delegation headed by George E. Spencer. The pending question is the motion to substitute the resolution of the minority committee for the resolution of the majority, and, under the rules, as each state is called, the chairman of the delegation will announce the vote of his delegation. The clerk will call the roll.

The roll was accordingly called, the states voting as follows:

States.	*Ay.*	*No.*	*States.*	*Ay.*	*No.*
Alabama	—	—	Delaware	—	6
Arkansas	11	1	Florida,	7	1
California	5	7	Georgia	11	11
Colorado	—	6	Illinois	10	32
Connecticut	8	4	Indiana	30	—

States.	*Ay.*	*No.*	*States.*	*Ay.*	*No.*
Iowa	7	15	Rhode Island	8	—
Kansas	—	10	South Carolina	11	3
Kentucky	—	24	Tennessee	13	11
Louisiana	9	7	Texas	11	4
Maine	—	14	Vermont	—	10
Maryland	3	13	Virginia	9	13
Massachusetts	—	26	West Virginia	2	8
Michigan	—	22	Wisconsin	2	18
Minnesota	—	10	Arizona	2	—
Mississippi	11	5	Dakota	—	2
Missouri	21	9	District of Columbia	—	2
Nebraska	—	6	Idaho	—	2
Nevada	6	—	Montana	—	2
New Hampshire	4	6	New Mexico	—	2
New Jersey	3	15	Utah	—	2
New York	59	9	Washington	—	2
North Carolina	18	2	Wyoming	—	2
Ohio	15	25			
Oregon	6	—	Totals	354	375
Pennsylvania	58	—			

When the vote had proceeded as far as California, Mr. Van Zandt, of Rhode Island, arose and asked the chair to put the question more definitely, as there appeared to be some misunderstanding among the delegates.

The PRESIDENT. In order to get a clear comprehension of the question, the chair has been requested to state what it is. Those gentlemen who vote Aye, vote in favor of seating the Spencer delegation, and those who vote No upon this question, vote in favor of seating the Haralson delegation.

Before the result was announced, Mr. Thomas, of Maryland, asked to change the vote of that delegation.

Mr. Cumback raised the point that it was not competent for the chairman of the Maryland delegation to change the record.

The PRESIDENT. The gentleman from Maryland rises to make a correction of the report he made in the vote. He reported four affirmative and twelve negative votes, and he wants to make it stand three affirmative and thirteen negative votes. The gentleman from Indiana raises the point of order, that it is not competent for the chairman of the delegation to change the record.

Mr. Thomas explained that the vote was reported under a misapprehension.

Mr. CUMBACK. Well, if it was a misapprehension, I will withdraw my objection.

Mr. PHELPS, of New York. I understand that Colorado is reported as having cast six votes. I find they are only entitled to two.

The PRESIDENT. Under the call of the National Committee, as I understand it, the state of Colorado was conceded six votes. At all events, that question can hardly arise now, as the convention has settled it.

Mr. E. R. HOAR, of Massachusetts. I would like the vote of Massachusetts to stand twenty-six noes instead of twenty-four noes. Two gentlemen who were thought absent were present, and wished to vote in the negative.

The PRESIDENT. Were these delegates within the bar of the convention before the last name on the roll was called?

Mr. Hoar replied in the affirmative.

The chair then ordered the change made.

Mr. WOODFORD, of New York. I wish to correct the vote of New York. One delegate counted in the affirmative we found was absent when the vote was taken.

The change was made.

A DELEGATE from New York. I demand that the vote be announced in detail.

The secretary accordingly read the vote in detail.

The PRESIDENT. Upon the proposition to substitute the minority for the majority report, the affirmative has 354 votes, and the negative 375 votes. So the substitute is disagreed to. The question recurs upon the adoption of the majority report.

A DELEGATE from Maryland. I move the adoption of the majority report.

Mr. CUMBACK. I demand the vote upon the adoption of the report by states.

At the suggestion of delegates, Mr. Cumback withdrew his demand.

A vote was then taken *viva voce* on the majority report, and it was declared adopted.

REPORT OF COMMITTEE ON RESOLUTIONS.

The PRESIDENT. The next thing in order is the report of the Committee on Resolutions.

General J. R. HAWLEY. You must be aware that your Committee on Resolutions, upon assembling, found themselves constituted of men of somewhat different sentiments and widely separated localities, mostly strangers to each other. We have in general agreed upon the statement we are about to present to you, and respectfully submit it to you for your consideration, and for your amendment, if you please.

General Hawley then read the report, as follows:

PLATFORM.

When, in the economy of providence, this land was to be purged of human slavery, and when the strength of government of the people by the people for the people was to be demonstrated, the Republican party came into power. Its deeds have passed into history, and we look back to them with pride. Incited by their memories, and with high aims for the good of our country and mankind, and looking to the future with unfaltering courage, hope, and purpose, we, the representatives of the party, in national convention assembled, make the following declaration of principles:

1. The United States of America is a nation, not a league. By the combined workings of the national and state governments, under their respective constitutions, the rights of every citizen are secured at home and protected abroad, and the common welfare promoted.

2. The Republican party has preserved these governments to the hundredth anniversary of the nation's birth, and they are now embodiments of the great truths spoken at its cradle, that all men are created equal; that they are endowed by their Creator with certain inalienable rights, among which are life, liberty, and the pursuit of happiness; that for the attainment of these ends governments have been instituted among men, deriving their just powers from the consent of the governed. Until these truths are cheerfully obeyed, and, if need be, vigorously enforced, the work of the Republican party is unfinished.

3. The permanent pacification of the Southern section of the Union, and the complete protection of all its citizens in the free enjoyment of all their rights, are duties to which the Republican party is sacredly pledged. The power to provide for the enforcement of the principles embodied in the recent constitutional amendments is vested by those amendments in the congress of the United States; and we declare it to be the solemn obligation of the legislative and executive departments of the government to put into immediate and vigorous exercise all their constitutional powers for removing any just causes of discontent on the part of any class, and securing to every American citizen complete liberty and exact equality in the exercise of all civil, political, and public rights. To this end we imperatively demand a congress and chief executive whose courage and fidelity to these duties shall not falter until these results are placed beyond dispute or recall.

4. In the first act of congress, signed by President Grant, the national government assumed to remove any doubt of its purpose to discharge all just obligations to public creditors, and solemnly pledged its faith "to make provision at the earliest practicable period for the redemption of the United States notes in coin." Commercial prosperity, public morals, and the national credit demand that this promise be fulfilled by a continuous and steady progress to specie payment.

5. Under the constitution, the President and heads of departments are to make nominations for office, the senate is to advise and consent to appointments, and the house of representatives is to accuse and prosecute faithless officers. The best interest of the public service demands that these distinctions be respected; that senators and representatives who may be judges and accusers should not dictate appointments to office. The invariable rule for appointments should have reference to the honesty, fidelity, and capacity of appointees, giving to the party in power those places where harmony and vigor of administration require its policy to be represented, but permitting all others to be filled by persons selected with sole reference to the efficiency of the public service and the right of citizens to share in the honor of rendering faithful service to their country.

6. We rejoice in the quickened conscience of the people concerning political affairs. We will hold all public officers to a rigid responsi-

bility, and engage that the prosecution and punishment of all who betray official trusts shall be speedy, thorough, and unsparing.

7. The public school system of the several states is the bulwark of the American republic; and, with a view to its security and permanence, we recommend an amendment to the constitution of the United States, forbidding the application of any public funds or property for the benefit of any school or institution under sectarian control.

8. The revenue necessary for current expenditures and the obligations of the public debt must be largely derived from duties upon importations, which, so far as possible, should be so adjusted as to promote the interests of American labor and advance the prosperity of the whole country.

9. We reäffirm our opposition to further grants of the public lands to corporations and monopolies, and demand that the national domain be devoted to free homes for the people.

10. It is the imperative duty of the government so to modify existing treaties with European governments, that the same protection shall be afforded to adopted American citizens that is given to native born, and all necessary laws be passed to protect emigrants, in the absence of power in the states for that purpose.

11. It is the immediate duty of congress fully to investigate the effect of the immigration and importation of Mongolians on the moral and material interests of the country.

12. The Republican party recognizes with approval the substantial advances recently made toward the establishment of equal rights for women, by the many important amendments effected by Republican legislatures in the laws which concern the personal and property relations of wives, mothers, and widows, and by the appointment and election of women to the superintendence of education, charities, and other public trusts. The honest demands of this class of citizens for additional rights, privileges, and immunities should be treated with respectful consideration.

13. The constitution confers upon congress sovereign power over the territories of the United States for their government. And in the exercise of this power it is the right and duty of congress to prohibit and extirpate in the territories that relic of barbarism, polygamy; and we demand such legislation as will secure this end, and the supremacy of American institutions in all the territories.

14. The pledges which our nation has given to our soldiers and sailors must be fulfilled. The grateful people will always hold those who perilled their lives for the country's preservation in the kindest remembrance.

15. We sincerely deprecate all sectional feeling and tendencies. We therefore note with deep solicitude that the Democratic party counts, as its chief hope of success, upon the electoral vote of a united South, secured through the efforts of those who were recently arrayed against the nation; and we invoke the earnest attention of the country to the grave truth, that a success thus achieved would reopen sectional strife, and imperil national honor and human rights.

16. We charge the Democratic party with being the same in character and spirit as when it sympathized with treason; with making its control of the house of representatives the triumph and opportunity of the nation's recent foes; with reässerting and applauding in the national capitol the sentiments of unrepentant rebellion; with sending

Union soldiers to the rear, and promoting Confederate soldiers to the front; with deliberately proposing to repudiate the plighted faith of the government; with being equally false and imbecile upon the overshadowing financial questions; with thwarting the ends of justice, by its partisan mismanagement and obstruction of investigation; with proving itself, through the period of its ascendency in the lower house of congress, utterly incompetent to administer the government;—and we warn the country against trusting a party thus alike unworthy, recreant, and incapable.

17. The national administration merits commendation for its honorable work in the management of domestic and foreign affairs; and President Grant deserves the continued hearty gratitude of the American people, for his patriotism and his eminent services in war and in peace.

Respectfully submitted, on behalf of the committee.

JOSEPH R. HAWLEY, *Chairman.*

CHAS. E. SMITH, *Secretary.*

THE MONGOLIAN QUESTION.

General Hawley having concluded the reading of his report, Mr. Edward L. Pierce, of Massachusetts, addressed the convention as follows:

Mr. President and Gentlemen of the Convention: I desire to move an amendment to the platform which has been offered, and to make a few remarks in support of that amendment. I move to amend by striking out what appears upon the eleventh page in relation to the Mongolian immigration. The Republican party this year, this centennial year, is twenty years old, and meets to-day for the sixth time in national convention, and this is the first time in all that long period that any attempt has ever been made to put in its platform a discrimination of race. In 1858, on the prairies of Illinois, Abraham Lincoln met his great antagonist on this ground,—that nowhere in the Declaration of Independence had its doctrine of equality been confined to the Caucasian or Aryan, to the exclusion of African, Mongolian, or Semitic races. Standing on that ground, he won the victory, and ascended to the highest office in this world. I denounce, therefore, that resolution as a departure from the life and memory of Abraham Lincoln. I denounce it as a departure from every Republican platform adopted by every Republican national convention. I denounce it as a violation of the principles of the Declaration of Independence. I denounce it as contrary to that great law of Christian love which proclaims that there is no difference between men, no matter of what race they may be, whether Greeks or Jews, Barbarians or Scythians. I therefore move this amendment. I will not accept this resolution. It is not the doctrine of New England. There was but a single member of the committee from New England who voted for it, and the only African on the committee recorded his vote against it.

Mr. S. B. AXTELL, of New Mexico. In relation to the proposed amendment, I desire the patience of the convention but for one or two words. The Republicans of the Pacific states, in fact, all persons, irrespective of party, desire that congress should investigate the question of Mongolian or Chinese immigration. There is no other action called for by the resolution but simply to investigate that question. It is claimed by those best informed upon this subject, that this immigration is not in good faith; that it is, in fact, an importation of coolies and slaves; that it is an importation of labor hired in China, at the prices paid there, we will suppose four dollars a month, with contracts running three or four years under the coolie system. It is claimed that they come under the pretence of immigration to this country, and, by their presence, by their custom, by their pagan and filthy habits, degrade American labor; and we ask that congress shall investigate the subject. We ask that the great Republican party, that has always been opposed to servile labor, that has always been opposed to the slave trade, should investigate this subject. We believe that the time has come for this step to be taken, and we trust that this simple request of our brethren on the Pacific slope will be acceded to, simply and only for the purpose of having an investigation.

Mr. JOHN P. JONES, of Nevada. *Mr. President and Gentlemen of the Convention:* I do not propose, after so long and tedious a session as you have had to-day, and in view of the vast amount of business you have yet to perform, to occupy the attention of this convention more than a very few minutes on this question. The question is one of the greatest importance, not only to our own citizens, to our own laborers with regard to the reward that they shall get for their labor, but in regard to the morals of the community. The people on the Pacific coast have suffered an invasion there worse than the grasshopper plague, worse than the plague of the locusts. They have found a people who bring with them no respect for our government, no knowledge of our language; a brutalized people; a people that recognize neither honesty among their men, nor virtue among their women; and they have planted themselves like a leprous sore in our midst; and I believe there is scarcely any difference of opinion on the Pacific coast with regard to the action that should be taken by this convention on the resolution submitted by the Committee on Resolutions. Many of us there are in favor, a majority of the law-abiding people on that coast are in favor, of protecting the Chinese; but we find that public opinion is so strong against them there, that it is almost impossible to do so. The very language of the Chinaman has degenerated into a libidinous slang. They do nothing to support the schools of the country. They do nothing to support organized society in the country. One of these Chinamen can work for ten cents a day, and, perhaps, successfully compete with the American laborer, who supports schools and raises a family, and, when the country is in danger, places himself in the foremost ranks of defence. In the resolutions already offered here, and to which no opposition has been made, I find one in relation to the tariff, providing that the duties on imports shall be so levied that the rights of the American laborer shall be protected; that he shall receive as high wages as it is possible for him to receive. I have no doubt that the gentleman who addressed you, opposing the present resolution submitted by the committee, is in favor of these imposts of tariffs for the protection of the American laborer; that is to say, he is in favor of imposing a tariff upon the introduction of goods or manufactures from abroad under the pretence that the American laborer will be protected; but he shows himself to be in favor of an unlimited free importation of the coolie semi-servile laborers to compete with the honest American laborers of the Pacific coast. This resolution asks for nothing but this,—that this convention shall call upon congress to appoint a committee to inform itself, so that it shall know as much about this question as those who live on that side of the country, and have been subject to all its horrors. All it asks is, that congress shall investigate, and if nothing shall be necessary, then of course nothing will be done; and I hope that there will be no serious opposition to the passage of the resolution as offered by the committee.

Mr. S. B. DUTCHER, of New York, called for the reading of the resolution under debate.

The secretary read as follows:

"It is the immediate duty of congress fully to investigate the effect of the immigration and importation of Mongolians on the moral and material interests of the country."

The PRESIDENT. Mr. Pierce of Massachusetts moves to strike out that resolution. Is the convention ready for the question?

Mr. DUTCHER. I desire to say a word upon this question. Mr. President and gentlemen of the convention, I will occupy your time but for a moment. I listened with pleasure, as I have listened before, to the eloquent representative from Massachusetts. I always listen with pleasure to these earnest, strong phrases in behalf of liberty, by whomsoever they may be uttered; but, standing as we do upon the threshold of the second century of the republic, we must give careful consideration to all questions that come before this convention. We cannot afford to be unjust. We cannot afford to be unfair. We will not be unjust, we will not be unfair, to any one; and while we recognize the right of all men, whatever their color, whatever their creed, or whatever their condition, to come to our shores, and we promise them a hearty welcome, yet our own American-born freemen, and the freemen who come from other sections of the earth, have rights which we should guarantee and protect; they have rights which we should protect against importations under contract of labor, as stated to us to-day to be the case regarding this Mongolian race. We cannot be unjust to them; and I hope that no haste and no hurry, no desire to return to our homes, to our wives and our children, will prevent us from giving careful consideration to every question that comes before this convention.

Mr. THORNBERG, of Tennessee. In behalf of the Tennessee delegation, I call for the previous question.

General HAWLEY. In behalf of the committee, and I think for all of them, I suggest that an opportunity should be given for brief talks upon a great subject.

Mr. THORNBERG. I withdraw my motion.

Mr. GEORGE WILLIAM CURTIS, of New York. *Mr. President and Gentlemen of the Convention:* One hundred years ago the colonies of America declared themselves free and independent in a document which laid down fundamental principles of human rights. Under that sign they conquered. With the Declaration of Independence in front, they carried their independence, they secured your independence, and the freedom of all who come after you. For nearly one century the Declaration of Independence, in a part connected with a very essential portion of the representation in this convention, was trampled under the feet of the American people. And you Republicans, you are sprung from the Declaration of Independence, you are the children of the Declaration of Independence; and our first, great, revered, martyred leader, Abraham Lincoln, was the first man plainly to declare that the platform of the Republican party was the Declaration of Independence.

Now, then, as we begin a new century, as my friend and associate from New York says, is it for us,—is it for the Republicans of America who are resolving, as I believe that they will, to purify and elevate their government,—to declare that the principles of the Declaration of Independence shall now be virtually revoked? For what is this platform? It is simply a declaration of faith of this party. It is not a means of asking that this or that shall be done. It is a declaration of our purpose. It is a declaration of the things that we, as a party, mean shall be accomplished; and, Mr. President and gentlemen, if you mean to draw a cordon along the coasts of this country,—if you mean to say that any man of any race shall be excluded,—then you have revoked the original principle of your party; then, gentlemen, you have accused your own statesmanship, for, under the Declaration of Independence, we have freed the colored men of the South; we have made them voters: and to-day the country is strong, and the government is surer than ever. I beg you, therefore, gentlemen, to understand, that if you are to make this declaration of principle at this time, and at the beginning of this year, you, in my judgment, declare that the fundamental principle, not only of the Republican party, but of the American republic, demands revision at your hands.

The PRESIDENT. The question pending is the adoption of the motion of the gentleman from Massachusetts, to strike out the eleventh resolution.

Mr. R. H. DANA, of Massachusetts. The delegation from Massachusetts has instructed me to call for a vote by states.

Mr. J. B. BELFORD, of Colorado. In common with the senator from Nevada, I come here to represent the interests of the people of the Pacific slope. I have always been a devoted and consistent and persistent friend of human freedom; and, because I have occupied that relation to all parties who have been oppressed, I am in favor of the adoption of the resolution reported to the convention by this committee. I hold, Mr. President, that the chief object of this convention is to bring our national honor up to par; and, in bringing our national honor up to par, it is equally our duty to protect the honor, and purity, and virtue, and integrity of the pioneers of this country, who have swelled the mere path of the pioneer into the magnificent highway of the nation, and have built an empire beyond the Rocky Mountains. I say, that in the state of California exists a people where the men are thieves and the women are prostitutes, and they are brought from China and Asia. I say that it is impossible for the laboring man, whether he be of American, German, Irish, or any other nationality, or in any degree connected with the Caucasian race, to compete with those people in the prices of labor. The gentleman from Massachusetts has stated that we should adhere to the principles of the Declaration of American Independence. I state to him, that here is a class of people who refuse to assimilate with our civilization. Here is a class of people who ignore our school system, ignore our church system, and in no manner contribute to support the government; who decline to become citizens of the republic by virtue of the naturalization laws enforced there, and who dislike our institutions so much that they leave word for their friends and brethren, after they are dead, to ship them back to China for burial.

Mr. THORNBERG, of Tennessee. Tennessee demands the previous question upon the adoption of the platform, reserving the resolution referring to the financial question, upon which a gentleman from Texas has a minority report.

A DELEGATE from Montana. I object.

The PRESIDENT. Are there two other delegations seconding the demand of the delegation from Tennessee for the previous question?

Mr. WM. J. SEWELL, of New Jersey. New Jersey seconds the call for the previous question.

Delegates from Rhode Island, Connecticut, and Mississippi announced that those states seconded the demand.

The PRESIDENT. The question is, Shall the main question be now put, reserving the financial plank?

The question being put, was agreed to.

The PRESIDENT. The question recurs upon the motion of the gentleman from Massachusetts, upon which a vote by states is demanded by the delegation from Massachusetts and the delegation from Rhode Island. The proposition is to strike out the eleventh section, which will now be read, after which the roll of states will be called.

The secretary read as follows:

"It is the immediate duty of congress fully to investigate the effect of the immigration and importation of Mongolians on the moral and material interests of the country."

A DELEGATE from Montana. I ask unanimous consent to protest, in the name of my territory.

Objected to.

The PRESIDENT. The vote will now be taken upon the proposition to strike out this section which has been read in your hearing. The clerk will call the roll.

Mr. J. M. HARLAN, of Kentucky. I beg leave to say, Mr. President, that, in my judgment, the convention has been too hasty in adopting the previous question, and would inquire whether it would be in order to move a recess for twenty minutes, in order that we may confer further in reference to the question.

The PRESIDENT. The motion would not be in order.

Mr. HARLAN. I move to reconsider that vote, in order that we may have further consideration on the subject. The whole state joins me in the motion, and California and Indiana seconds it.

Mr. CESSNA, of Pennsylvania. Will it be in order now to demand a division of the question? If so, I ask a division of the question into three parts,—the first to embrace the Coolie question; the second, all the resolutions except the finance plank; and the third, the finance plank. It is especially to get at the Coolie question and the financial plank.

The PRESIDENT. We are now operating under the previous question. The difficulty is, that there can be no further discussion on the Coolie question.

A DELEGATE from Virginia. I move to lay upon the table the motion to reconsider the vote.

The president put the question, and decided that the motion to reconsider was laid upon the table, and that the question then recurred on the motion of the gentleman from Massachusetts, to strike out the eleventh section.

Mr. CUMBACK, of Indiana. After this vote shall be taken, if the resolution to strike out prevails, will it then be in order, under the operation of the previous question, to offer a substitute for the resolution to strike out?

The PRESIDENT. I think not.

The president then put the question; and, the roll being called, the states voted as follows:

States.	*Ay.*	*No.*	*States.*	*Ay.*	*No.*
Alabama	10	10	New York	30	35
Arkansas	8	4	North Carolina	3	17
California	—	12	Ohio	19	25
Colorado	—	6	Oregon	—	6
Connecticut	5	7	Pennsylvania	—	58
Delaware	2	4	Rhode Island	5	3
Florida	—	8	South Carolina	14	—
Georgia	7	15	Tennessee	2	22
Illinois	2	40	Texas	—	16
Indiana	10	20	Vermont	4	6
Iowa	12	10	Virginia	—	22
Kansas	—	10	West Virginia	3	7
Kentucky	14	10	Wisconsin	—	20
Louisiana	5	8	Arizona	—	2
Maine	6	8	Dakota	—	2
Maryland	15	1	District of Columbia	—	2
Massachusetts	20	6	Idaho	—	2
Michigan	6	16	Montana	2	—
Minnesota	—	10	New Mexico	—	2
Mississippi	11	5	Utah	—	2
Missouri	12	17	Washington	—	2
Nebraska	—	6	Wyoming	—	2
Nevada	—	6			
New Hampshire	2	8	Totals	215	532
New Jersey	—	18			

The PRESIDENT. On the motion of the gentleman from Massachusetts to strike out the eleventh section, the ayes have 215 votes and the noes have 532 votes, and the convention refuse to strike out.

The eleventh resolution was then agreed to; and the president said, the question now recurs upon the adoption of the financial resolution, for which Mr. Davis, of Texas, offers a substitute.

Mr. E. J. DAVIS, of Texas. *Mr. President:* I desire to offer the following minority report:

To the President of the Republican National Convention: The undersigned, one of the Committee on Resolutions, dissents from the majority, in regard to the fourth resolution—that bearing on the question of resumption of specie payments. He considers said resolution improper in this, among other respects, that it is uncertain and vague in its promises, leaving the time of resumption unsettled, and being thereby calculated further to disturb public confidence. The undersigned therefore submits the following, and recommends that it be adopted as a substitute for said resolution:

"*Resolved*, That it is the duty of congress to provide for carrying out the act known as the Resumption Act of congress, to the end that the resumption of specie payments may not be longer delayed."

Mr. President: I do not propose to make a speech, but, as a test, I move that this report be substituted in the place of the fourth resolution,—the financial resolution as reported by the majority of the committee. In that resolution reference is made to the declaration made by the Republican congress some eight years ago, that they would go on, without any unnecessary delay, and redeem our promises by resuming specie payments. We have gone on year after year, congress after congress, convention after convention, and have repeated these promises, until finally, in the early part of last year, our Republican friends in congress, having there a majority of two thirds of both houses, finally nerved themselves to the passage of an act providing for resumption, not to-day, or to-morrow, as they should have done, but three years hence, in January, 1879. I think, gentlemen, when you scrutinize the resolution as adopted by the majority of the committee and reported here this morning, you will find that it is nothing more than a step backward, and a return to promises again. I, for one, and I hope a majority of the convention will sustain me, am opposed to making any step backward.

At the request of the delegates the fourth section of the platform was re-read; also the substitute offered by the gentleman from Texas.

Mr. J. R. HAWLEY. *Mr. President and Gentlemen:* I will detain you but a short time. I think it quite fair that the minority of the committee, a very respectable and honorable gentleman, who has moved a substitute, should be allowed to say a word or two in behalf of his motion. It is best, in my opinion, always, in dealing with principles for the guidance of a party during a year, or four long years, to confine ourselves to an emphatic declaration of sound principles, and not tie ourselves to details in measures. That was the general rule which governed us in drafting that resolution. In drafting it, we recited that first great act of Grant's administration,—that act which is an honor to him and to the Republican congress, which removed all possible doubt as to the purpose of the government to fulfil in letter and in spirit the obligations of this nation to redeem in coin every dollar of the debt, save where there was an express provision to the contrary in the bill. That great act, framed in clear, strong language, asserted it the high moral duty of the nation to fulfil all these obligations. We knew not how to express ourselves more emphatically than by referring to that representative act of legislation, and adding to it, "The commercial prosperity, public morals, and national credit demand that the promise be fulfilled by a steady and continuous progress to specie payment." The gentleman wants to confine the whole declaration of duty to passing laws to carry the resumption act into effect. The act provides for resumption two years from next January. You cannot propose any law with any chance of its going through congress until a year from next January or two or three months after that, even provided you have the next congress Republican, and then only ten or eleven months elapse before the taking effect of that act. Whether it is best to bring about specie payments in that way, I do not know; but I am not desirous of being tied to the advocacy of that bill. I regard it as a very imperfect bill. I voted against it. I should not care to spend an hour on the stump in defending it. I do not care for the details of resumption. I plant myself, not only upon a high political, but upon a high moral, duty to resume specie payment—to do so at the very earliest practicable moment; and when I say that, I mean it. It is necessary for us to bring paper to par with gold, for that is essential to commercial prosperity, public morals, and national credit.

The question was then put upon the substitution of the minority report, and the President announced that it was disagreed to. The report on the fourth section of the platform was then agreed to.

The platform as a whole was then unanimously adopted.

NOMINATION OF CANDIDATES.

At 2:50 P. M. (Cincinnati time) the President announced that the nomination of candidates for the office of President of the United States was in order.

A DELEGATE from Pennsylvania. I move that the convention adjourn until ten o'clock to-morrow morning.

Not agreed to.

Mr. HALE, of Maine. I move that this convention now proceed to put in nomination and select a candidate for President of the United States.

The PRESIDENT. That is the next business in order without a motion. That is our duty. For if we are not here to nominate a President of the United States, what are we here for? The Chair is ready to receive any nomination—if there be any candidate!

A DELEGATE from Montana. I move that we adjourn till to-morrow at ten o'clock.

Several Delegates. That has just been ruled out of order.

Mr. EDICK, of New York. I move that the secretary call the roll of the states in their alphabetical order, and that each state, if it has a candidate, present his name to the convention.

MARSHALL JEWELL.

The call of the states was then begun by the secretary, and when he had reached the state of Connecticut, Mr. Stephen W. Kellogg, of that state, arose in his seat to present the name of a candidate. The Chair invited the gentleman to the stage, whence he spoke as follows:

SPEECH OF MR. KELLOGG.

Mr. President and Gentlemen of this Convention: I am instructed by a majority of the delegates from Connecticut to present for your suffrages the name of the Honorable Marshall Jewell, of Connecticut, now Postmaster-General of the United States; and, in a single word, I call your attention to the fact that while Connecticut is often called a Democratic state (and when we talk to you about our shares in the Republican victories you call us a Democratic state), bear in mind, that from the hour of the organization of the Republican party,—in 1856, and through five successive presidential elections,—we never failed you in a single instance. Overpowered as we are on other elections, yet, by dint of unwearying exertion and determined energy in presidential contests, we have carried our state in line with the ranks of the Republican party from the first hour of its organization. We present to you the name of Marshall Jewell, as our governor who redeemed the state from the rule of the Democracy in 1869. We elected him three years. He was then absent as minister to Russia. During the last two years, or a portion of them, he has been your Postmaster-General, and you, men of the broad West, know that you never had a man in that position that has inaugurated reform, that has done so much to bring speedy intelligence to your doors every day and hour, as he who now holds that office. We present his name to you, not desiring to detain you longer,—but we believe he has all the qualifications of an executive officer that will make him fit to adorn that seat, as he has adorned all other positions he has ever filled.

OLIVER P. MORTON.

When the state of Indiana was called, Mr. R. W. Thompson ascended the stage and said:

SPEECH OF MR. THOMPSON.

Mr. President and Gentlemen of this Convention: I am instructed by the entire Republican party of Indiana to put before this convention the name of Oliver P. Morton as a suitable nominee for President of the United States. We present his name to you because we not only believe but know him to be worthy,—to be a faithful, honest, and untiring representative of the great fundamental principles upon which the Republican party has always stood, and must always stand. These principles may be preserved,—they may be carried out by other means than his election. But you must allow us to say that we do not believe that they can be more surely preserved or better carried out than under the presidential administration of our old war governor. We have conferred this title upon him, not merely by way of empty compliment, but because he has won it in the field of duty well discharged in the hour of his country's peril, when men's hearts were tried, and tried in that fiery ordeal which alone tested not only the courage but the virtue of the patriot. He was equal to every crisis during the darkest hours of our rebellion, and he has been equal to every crisis since that darkness was dispelled, and he stands to-day in the senate of the United States the peer of the best and ablest statesmen of the land. And whenever there is an assault made upon the rights of humanity, upon the rights of the Southern colored men, upon the rights of the nation, of the Union, and of the honor of the flag, who is before Oliver P. Morton in their defence? or who defends them with more ability and more manliness? None! Then we do not arrogate to ourselves any superiority over our sisters when we say that while our war governor is no better than anybody else, he is equal to the best of them. We have never had a president from Indiana. It may be assumption in us to say that we feel old enough to have one. And we do not regard ourselves as any the less worthy than our neighbors and our friends; and we simply say to you now, that if you nominate in this convention our candidate for the presidency, we assure you that in the October elections of this year there shall go up from the prairies of Indiana such a shout of victory as will do good to the heart of every Republican in the land.

I have heard it said since I came to this city, more than ever before, that Governor Morton was physically unfit for the duties of this position. I affirm to-day, in the presence of this large and respectable audience, with a perfect knowledge of what I say, and with the full sense of the responsibility of its utterance, that there are not out of any hundred men in this convention ten persons of it who can perform more physical labor to-day than he. True, he has been afflicted in his legs, but it does not require legs to make a statesman! If he had been in the condition of Jeff. Davis, his legs would have been of service to him. His head is clear. His heart is sound. His will is unconquerable. His devotion to the union is unabated, and he is ready now, to-morrow, or the next day, to give his life for the honor of the old flag. Therefore, sir, we say—and I desire only to repeat this, for I will not weary you—if the rights of all the people without regard to color, if the rights of all sections are to be preserved, if the constitution is to be preserved in its integrity, if the Union is to stand, if the great principles of the Republican party are to be preserved, we insist, sir, that no man in this nation is better calculated to secure these results than our nominee for the presidency.

Mr. P. B. S. PINCHBACK, of Louisiana, rose to second the nomination. The time allotted by the convention for presenting the name of each candidate—ten minutes—having expired, the chair asked the convention if leave would be granted to Mr. Pinchback to second the nomination. Leave was granted, and Mr. Pinchback spoke as follows:

SPEECH OF MR. PINCHBACK.

Mr. President and Gentlemen of the Convention: In the name and in behalf of the truly loyal people of Louisiana, whom I in part have the honor to represent in this convention, I rise to second the nomination of the Hon. Oliver P. Morton. A man of spotless integrity, matchless courage, broad and catholic views, his nomination will secure the combined and united patriotism of the party. Mr. President, when president Grant made that utterance, "Let no guilty man escape," he struck the chord of the national heart. In whatever audiences those utterances have been repeated, they have been greeted with thunderous applause. Sir, the elevation of Hon. Oliver P. Morton of Indiana will not only secure the arrest and the prosecution of the defrauders of the national revenue, but it will do more than that; it will strike terror to the hearts of those monsters in the South who are driving away capital from that section, destroying its commerce, persecuting and murdering white and black Republicans in that section. More than this, Mr. President, it will be the consummation of all of the past and the aspirations of lovers of liberty everywhere. It will be a combined and a complete and final settlement of all the great questions arising out of the late unfortunate war. Then, sir, with Oliver P. Morton as our standard-bearer, with the rights of all citizens guaranteed by the amendments of the constitution secured, and the protection of every man in his civil rights as an incentive, victory must and shall perch on our banners.

BENJAMIN H. BRISTOW.

Mr. John M. Harlan, on the call of the state of Kentucky, spoke as follows:

SPEECH OF MR. HARLAN.

Mr. President and Gentlemen of the Convention: The name which has been given me, by the unanimous Republican party of the state of Kentucky, for presentation to this convention as a fit nominee for President of the United States, is that of Benjamin H. Bristow, of the state of Kentucky. I speak whereof I know, when I declare to those Republicans, both from the North and from the South, that from the earliest days of his manhood he has been true to those great principles which are dear to the Republican party of the United States. Since his name has been prominently mentioned in connection with the presidency, his record has been carefully scrutinized in every part of our common country. I need only say to-day, that he was reared in that school of politics which taught me and you that these United States do not constitute a league, but a nation. In 1861, when Abraham Lincoln called upon the freemen of this country to rally to its defence against an attack coming from a causeless and wicked rebellion, Benjamin H. Bristow promptly announced to his fellow citizens of Kentucky, that, let come what would, and cost what it would, he intended to stand by the flag of our fathers. His devotion to his country was not shown by mere words: it was followed by acts. He entered the Federal army as the lieutenant-colonel of a Kentucky infantry regiment. He was subsequently colonel of the Eighth Kentucky Cavalry. While serving his country in the field, he was called upon by his senatorial district to serve that people in the legislature; and there he was the acknowledged head of the Republicans of that period. In 1865, when the question was presented to Kentucky, in official form, whether she would ratify the thirteenth amendment to the Federal constitution abolishing slavery throughout this land, he, with a small band of Republicans in the senate, voted in favor of its ratification. He voted in favor of and approved the fourteenth amendment, which gave every man in this country the rights of citizenship, without regard to color. He approved and endorsed the fifteenth amendment. In 1866, as United States attorney for the district of Kentucky, he performed signal service in the prosecution of men charged with violations of the Ku-Klux and Civil Rights bills. In 1871, standing upon the soil of his native state, addressing his fellow citizens of that state, when asked what he had to say with reference to the amendments to the constitution, he used this language: "Neither those constitutional provisions, nor any statute passed in relation to them, oppresses or harms a single human being. The Civil Rights and Ku-Klux acts aim solely at the lawless people who have no respect for law; and that government that cannot protect its humblest citizens from outrage and injury is unworthy the name, and ought not to command the support of the people." When asked, upon the same occasion, what he had to say in relation to the education of the people, he responded,— "In the name of our high and sacred duty to see that the commonwealth suffers no injury, and that the best interests of society are cared for, let us make free schools *for all.* If I am asked how it is proposed to raise money to defray the expenses of such schools, I answer, by taxing all the property of the state. I would tax the rich man's property to educate his poor neighbor's child. I would tax the white man's property to educate the black man's child, and *vice versa.* In a word, I would tax *all* the property of the state to educate *all* the children of the state." On the same occasion, and in the same connection, he was asked what he had to say with reference to the law which then excluded the colored men of Kentucky from the right of testifying. He replied,— "The statute of Kentucky, which denies to 225,000 colored people of the state the right to testify in any case, civil or criminal, affecting a white person, has its origin in the supposed necessities of slavery, and is indefensible in a land of freedom. This denial is a monstrous and a grievous wrong to both races. It is a practical denial of freedom to the colored race. Yes, it is even worse than that: it is a license, if not an invitation, to base miscreants and cowardly ku-klux to gratify their brutal passions and satiate their murderous propensities on this unoffending and defenceless race."

But, my countrymen, I am to be followed by gentlemen as seconds to this nomination who will tell you more about General Bristow, and in better language than I can do, and I will not detain you longer than I intended to do. I have, however, pride in referring to the record which Mr. Bristow has recently made as secretary of the treasury of the United States. He had not been at the head of that department thirty days before every employé in that department, from one end of this land to the other, felt that there was at last a man at the head. It is his proud record, and we of Kentucky are proud of it, that no man has been able to say that Colonel Bristow, in the administration of the duties of that office, has favored his own party. He has shown no favoritism of any sort. His mode has been to execute the law; and, if the Republican party contained offenders who betrayed their trust, or who were thieves, he let them be punished as well as anybody else.

Now, I have said enough. My time is out. I would beg leave to make one single suggestion. I do not quite share the ardent hopes that some have in reference to the future of the Republican party of this country. We of the South feel that our destiny is in your hands. We of the South feel that it is in your power to avert from this country that direst of all political calamities, the return of the national Democratic party to power. We believe that the man whom we present to you can combine with enthusiasm all elements of opposition in this country to the Democratic party, and thereby secure not only honest government, but the perpetuation of Republican principles; and therefore we express the earnest hope that this convention will not adjourn its deliberations till they have made him our leader in this contest in the war for Republican principles against corruption and fraud.

At the conclusion of Mr. Harlan's speech, the rule was extended in order to allow Mr. Luke P. Poland, of Vermont, to second the nomination of Mr. Bristow. Mr. Poland spoke as follows:

SPEECH OF MR. POLAND.

Mr. President and Gentlemen of the Convention: I come here as a delegate from one of the smallest states, both in territory and population, but in that state a larger proportion of its people belong to the Republican party than in almost any other state in the Union. No portion of the Republican party in this country believes more firmly in its principles, or believes more firmly that the success and dominion of that party in the government of this country is essential to its welfare and perpetuity. We have no candidate of our own to present. We have no special interest to be served by the nomination of any particular man. Our only desire is the general good of the cause, the good of the party, and the good of the country. The Republicans of Vermont look upon the forthcoming presidential election as involving great peril to this great country. For long years the Democratic party of this country was kept in power by a close alliance with the power of slavery in the South. By and by, when the Republicans overcame this joint alliance and got into power, the South rebelled, and aid and comfort were given to that rebellion by the Democracy in the North. Now that the war is over and slavery is ended, and these states are again in the Union, the old alliance is renewed. The boast of the Democratic party is, that they go into the election with the entire South in their favor. If that be so, and it will probably be nearly so, only a small fraction of the North is required in order to enable them to obtain power, and the result would be that the power of this government would practically go out of our hands and into the hands of those who for years sought to destroy and break up the government. We have the warnings of last year. If the Democratic party in this presidential election can carry as large a proportion of the country as they carried in the elections of last year, with what they will get in the South they will carry the presidential election. Now, it is perfectly well known that the victories they obtained last year were not on account of any change of political opinion: they grew out of doubt, distrust, and dissatisfaction in our own party. It is the part of wisdom to avoid this. The presidential candidates that have been named, some of them, are our neighbors and friends. All personal considerations would induce us to vote for them. But it seems that the cause is everything, and that we should go forth united, and that the gentleman who has been named can better combine all the united strength of the Republican party than any other. Mr. President, Vermont and Kentucky came into this Union together. For many years, in the days of Harry Clay, they stood side by side. I trust that now and henceforth Vermont and

Kentucky, upon a higher and purer platform, are again to stand shoulder to shoulder. I second the nomination of Benjamin H. Bristow.

At the conclusion of Mr. Poland's speech, Mr. George William Curtis, of New York, spoke as follows:

SPEECH OF MR. CURTIS.

Gentlemen of the Convention: On behalf of that vast body of Republicans of New York who have seen, as the country and the world have seen, that reform is possible within the Republican party,—because they have seen the heavy arm of the government descend upon the thieves of the treasury,—I rise to second the nomination of Benjamin H. Bristow, of Kentucky. We know, gentlemen, as you know, that the real question which is submitted to us in the contest of this year is the continued ascendency of the Republican party. Not more truly was slavery the mortal peril of this country twenty years ago, than political corruption and demoralization in every form are its perils now; and as the conscience and intelligence of the patriotism of this country, organized as the Republican party, saved the government then, so must those same qualities, still organized as that party, save the character of the government now. There is one man, in my judgment, of all the great names that have been presented,—there is one man who more truly than the others represents the true issues of this campaign. You heard, yesterday, our friend General Logan, from Illinois; you heard our friend of many years' standing, Frederick Douglass, of the District of Columbia: and what did they tell you? They told you that the Republican party must remain in power, in order that the rights of all the white and black men at the South should be absolutely respected. I believe, with them, that that is indispensable. I believe, with them, that the only condition of peace in that part of the country is a continued ascendency of the Republican party. But you must believe with me, that the condition of the continued ascendency of that party is, that it shall stand to-day as it stood yesterday, and that it shall meet the issues of this hour in the same spirit of concord and enthusiasm and resolution that it met the issues of the past. Now, in my judgment, the real issues of the campaign are two. But one is, in my mind, supreme, because it is the only guaranty and security of the other. Now, then, fellow citizens, this gentleman—Benjamin H. Bristow—is a citizen of Kentucky. But we in New York have learned afar off what those men, our neighbors in New England, also knew at a safe distance. When it was easy for me,—when it was easy for you, my own associates,—to be Republicans, Benjamin H. Bristow took his life in his hand, and marched forth a Republican. And I say, more especially to my fellow delegates from the Southern states, that the one man in this country who, since the end of the war and during the great storms and contests of reconstruction, during which hundreds and thousands fell by the wayside, was the man who, armed with the power of the government of the United States as district-attorney of Kentucky, hunted and hunted and hunted the Ku-Klux until the Ku-Klux disappeared. The life, the liberty of every man at the North,—the liberty, the life of every man at the South,—is safe in the hands of this man from Kentucky, who has known, as you of the South have bitterly learned, as we of the North have distantly seen, the mortal perils of the struggle.

And still further, Republicans, if Governor Morgan, who presided at the first convention of the Republican party, did not look yesterday on the last convention of a successful Republican party, it will be because we go into this contest with these three cries: First, absolute protection of all rights, North and South, with the utmost power of the government; second, the hardest kind of hard money, and the earliest return to it possible; and third, and more important, I say, because itself the security and the guaranty of all this, will be our cry of victory,—"No rings, no cliques, no combinations of personal interest against the interest of all the people; no personal government; nothing but the clear will of the people, clearly and directly expressed." Therefore, not what we have said in this platform, but that which we are about to do, will speak to this country for our purpose. Beyond us, gentlemen, stands the country watching. We have been tried long; and, Republicans, you know we have not always commanded the confidence of the Republicans. You know that we have not altogether satisfied the scrutiny that has been fixed upon us. Let us now show the country that we understand ourselves. Let us now prove that we know what this country wants to-day; and we may be sure that the country will not insist upon doing it without our leadership, if it can have it with that. And one word more, and only one. The opportunity is sublime. Napoleon before Austerlitz, Washington before Yorktown, could not know the future, but they knew the present. They had the opportunity offered. Each improved it in his own way. Napoleon became emperor of France. Washington became the saint of American liberty. To us at this moment the opportunity is offered. Let us use it as Washington used it. Let us understand that this government must be purified if the party is to be saved, and that Benjamin H. Bristow is the one man who stands before the country as the embodiment of the spirit of governmental purification, and I know, gentlemen, what the verdict of the country must be.

Mr. Richard H. Dana, of Massachusetts, then spoke as follows:

SPEECH OF MR. DANA.

Mr. President and Gentlemen of the Convention: I am deeply grateful for my state and the delegation here that we have been permitted and invited on the part of Massachusetts to second the nomination of Benjamin H. Bristow. When that proposition was submitted to us, I asked the advice of my brethren of the Massachusetts delegation, and by a vote not quite unanimous, but representing a very large majority of the delegation, I was authorized and requested to second the nomination of General Bristow; and when this large majority of the Massachusetts delegation spoke those words to me, they spoke the voice of the old commonwealth of Massachusetts. I tell you, gentlemen of the convention, I know no other name which is sure to carry the old commonwealth of Massachusetts next November. Mark what I said: I did not say no other man would, but no other man am I sure would do it. Gentlemen may make such oral demonstrations as are in accordance with their habits and their nature. But Massachusetts has done something in the past for the Republican party, has she not? Well, I claim no credit. It was easy to be loyal and to be Republican. We rested on seventy thousand majority in our loyal state, but by one cause or another, by mismanagement, by the settling down of a great cloud over the Administration, we almost lost the state of Massachusetts. But now, gentlemen, now, Mr. President, our hope returns. Let me say to you,—and I wish to speak seriously and earnestly to this convention, not for applause, but in order to present the views I am instructed to present,—let me say, therefore, first, it is the belief of Massachusetts that the body politic is laboring under a severe and dangerous disease. It is our belief that it requires the administration of strong and severe and unwelcome remedies. It is our belief that the disease must be cured by the work of a strong hand; a strong hand and a strong will of a man of mighty courage; a man who, when he is president, will devote himself to the duty of being the president of the United States.

Gentlemen, Massachusetts is satisfied with the loyalty of Benjamin H. Bristow. Every man is satisfied with the loyalty of Benjamin H. Bristow. We know that he is from the other side of the line; but we know that his loyalty has been all the more tried for that cause. It has been tried in the furnace; and, therefore, gentlemen, thanking you—I was about to say, thanking you for the attention you have all given me—and knowing the respect in which you hold the commonwealth that I partially represent, and in behalf of the large part of the delegation which has honored me by placing me at its head, I second the nomination, with all my heart, of Benjamin H. Bristow.

JAMES G. BLAINE.

After the conclusion of Mr. Dana's speech, the call of the states proceeded until Illinois was reached, when Mr. Robert G. Ingersoll of that state was introduced by the president, and said:

SPEECH OF MR. INGERSOLL.

Massachusetts may be satisfied with the loyalty of Benjamin H. Bristow. So am I. But if any man nominated by this convention cannot carry the state of Massachusetts, I am not satisfied with the loyalty of Massachusetts. If the nominee of this convention cannot carry the grand old commonwealth by seventy-five thousand majority, I would advise them to sell out Faneuil Hall as a Democratic head-quarters. I would advise them to take from Bunker Hill their old monument of glory. The Republicans of the United States demand as their leader in the great contest of 1876 a man of intellect, a man of integrity, a man of well-known and approved political opinions. They demand a statesman. They demand a reformer after as well as before the election. They demand a politician in the highest, the broadest, and the best sense of that word. They demand a man acquainted with public affairs, with the wants of the people, with the requirements of the hour not only, but with the demands of the future. They demand a man broad enough to comprehend the relation of this government to the other nations of the earth. They demand a man well versed in the powers, duties, and prerogatives of each and every department of this government. They demand a man who will sacredly preserve the financial honor of the United States; one who knows enough to know that the national debt must be paid through the prosperity of this people;

one who knows enough to know that all the financial theories in the world cannot redeem a single dollar; one who knows enough to know that all the money must be made, not by law, but by labor; one who knows enough to know that the people of the United States have the industry to make the money, and the honor to pay it over, just as soon as they can. The Republicans of the United States demand a man who knows that prosperity and resumption, when they come, must come together; when they come they will come hand in hand through the golden harvest fields; hand in hand by the whirling spindles and the turning wheels; hand in hand past the open furnace doors; hand in hand by the flaming forges; hand in hand by the chimneys filled with eager fire, raked and grasped by the hands of the countless sons of toil. This money must be dug out of the earth. You cannot make it by passing resolutions in a political convention. The Republicans of the United States want a man who knows that this government should protect every citizen at home or abroad; who knows that any government that will not defend its defenders, and will not protect its protectors, is a disgrace to the map of the world. They demand a man who believes in the eternal separation and divorcement of church and school. They demand a man whose political reputation is spotless as a star; but they do not demand that their candidate shall have a certificate of moral character signed by the Confederate congress. The man who has, in full, complete, and rounded measure, all of these splendid qualifications is the present grand and gallant leader of the Republican party, James G. Blaine.

Our country, crowned by the vast and marvellous achievements of its first century, asks for a man worthy of her past and prophetic of her future; asks for a man who has the audacity of genius; asks for a man who has the grandest combination of heart, conscience, and brain the world ever saw. That man is James G. Blaine. For the Republican hosts, led by this intrepid man, there can be no such thing as defeat. This is a grand year,—a year filled with the recollections of the Revolution; filled with proud and tender memories of the sacred past; filled with legends of liberty;—a year in which the sons of freedom will drink from the fountain of enthusiasm; a year in which the people call for the man who has preserved in congress what their soldiers won upon the field; a year in which they call for the man who has torn from the throat of treason the tongue of slander; the man who has snatched the mask of Democracy from the hideous face of the rebellion; the man who, like the intellectual athlete, hath stood in the arena of debate challenging all comers, and who up to the present moment is a total stranger to defeat. Like an armed warrior, like a plumed knight, James G. Blaine marched down the halls of the American congress and threw his shining lance full and fair against the brazen forehead of every traitor to his country and every maligner of his fair reputation. For the Republican party to desert that gallant man now is as though an army should desert their general upon the field of battle. James G. Blaine is now and has been for years the bearer of the sacred standard of the Republican party. I call it sacred, because no human being can stand beneath its folds without becoming and without remaining free.

Gentlemen of the Convention: In the name of the great republic, the only republic that ever existed upon the face of the earth; in the name of all her defenders and of all her supporters; in the name of all her soldiers living; in the name of all her soldiers that died upon the field of battle; and in the name of those that perished in the skeleton clutch of famine at Andersonville and Libby, whose sufferings he so vividly remembers,—Illinois—Illinois nominates for the next president of this country that prince of parliamentarians, that leader of leaders, James G. Blaine.

The next speaker was Mr. Henry M. Turner, one of the colored delegates from Georgia, who spoke as follows:

SPEECH OF MR. TURNER.

Mr. President and Gentlemen of the Convention: [A voice, louder!] I will be loud enough directly. When I left my home in Georgia I went eastward, and determined, in passing through several of the states, to ascertain the will of the people. I knew it would almost be impossible to give Georgia's electoral vote to any Republican, notwithstanding the dead have been raised. Everywhere I went, everywhere I mingled with the people, the name of Blaine seemed to be talismanic. It extorted a cheer, and the people seemed to be alive at the very announcement of it. I rise to-day to second the nomination of James G. Blaine, of Maine. And in doing this, Mr. President and gentlemen of the convention, I want it understood that some of the names that have been mentioned I revere with a reverence that my tongue cannot express. The name of Morton, the champion of Gov. Pinchback, the defender of the outraged people of Louisiana! I would borrow a Raphael's pen, and dip it in the sunlight of heaven, and write on Morton's brow,—"Honor, eternal honor." But, Mr. President, I believe that we have before us now a name that will arouse the people of this great country in a remarkable manner that the name of Morton cannot. I have nothing to say against Mr. Bristow. I listened to the eloquence of the great poet(!) of New York, as he defended the name of Bristow; and I paid equal deference to that learned son of Massachusetts, our minister to England(!). But, Mr. President, in the person of James G. Blaine we have a Republican about whom there is no question. He commenced with the party, and for twenty-five years he has been in its front, and to-day he stands the champion of Republican principles, I believe, in the United States of America. He gave his own state,—so says an aged and learned doctor of divinity of Maine—to that party, and forever, I expect, buried Democracy on that sacred soil. It will never lift its head there again, I trust. He originated the spirit of the fourteenth amendment. He stood by the immortal Lincoln during the great struggle this country was passing through for freedom and justice and equality to all mankind, and to chase out of this nation a set of insurgents who lifted impious hands against that flag that still floats over us, thank God. Mr. President, there is one thing I like about Mr. Blaine: he is a representative of Young America. He is no dead fossil. He is not tied on to any old constitutional barriers that shut out a parcel, a class, of God's humanity, and tie him to a set of principles that are antiquated. One thing more I wish to say of Mr. Blaine, and—I have a dozen points to make, but will make but one now—it is this: But for Mr. Blaine you would have no Republican party to-day. Wait, and I will show it. When the Democrats carried this country, at the last election, the Republican party of those days all over this land was thunderstruck, paralyzed, dead, and bleeding. It was Blaine, standing on the floor of congress, who shook aloft the banner of the Republican party, united the party, and defied the Democracy of this nation, and breathed again the spirit of activity and hope into this prostrate Republican party. Who can deny it?

SPEECH OF MR. WM. P. FRYE, OF MAINE.

Mr. Frye said:

Gentlemen of the Convention: The impatience of the convention is a warning to me which I take heed of as I start, and I would not trespass one word upon your patience or time did I not feel bound, as a citizen of Maine, as a Republican of Maine, to stand here before this great convention, and declare her confidence in her favorite, her idol son, James G. Blaine. She is a daughter of the old commonwealth of Massachusetts. But, sir, I say here, and I say now, that whoever is nominated in this convention as the candidate of the Republican party shall carry the state of Maine by 20,000 majority. And why? It is a contest for life; it is a contest between right and wrong, between liberty and slavery, between barbarism and civilization; and in God's name, is this republic to go down now at the commencement of the second century forever and ever? Are we to take this beloved republic, baptized again and again in the blood of our sons, sanctified and purified by the prayers and tears of our mothers and our wives, and pass it over into the hands of the men who, bloody-handed, within a score of years endeavored to destroy its life forever? My friends, that is the question which is to be settled here and now; and when we have nominated our candidate, we know he will sweep all the loyal Union men of the whole country as a tornado sweeps the prairies of the great West. For twenty-five years, we of Maine have known James G. Blaine as we know our own households. He is honest; he is pure; he is spotless; he is sagacious; he is wise; he is brave; he is a power with us; he is a power in the congress of the United States. He will be a power to salvation as the candidate of the Republican party.

ROSCOE CONKLING.

When New York was called, Mr. Stewart L. Woodford said:

SPEECH OF MR. WOODFORD.

Mr. President and Gentlemen of the Convention: In obedience to the injunction of our state convention, with the thoughtful and absolute endorsement of our deliberate reflection and conviction, and with the earnest enthusiasm that his fidelity in friendship, his private worth and his public services demand, New York presents for the presidency of the republic the honored name of Roscoe Conkling. Broad in culture, eloquent in debate, wise in council, fearless in leadership, and as true to the old Republican party as the needle to the pole,—Roscoe Conkling needs no defence nor eulogy. He is a positive quantity in our politics. He, through the dark and trying hours, when slander and misrepresentation hissed at the silent and brave man whom we have twice placed in the presidential chair, was the faithful and true friend of Ulysses S.

Grant. In presenting his name, New York fully recognizes and cordially honors all the names that have been presented upon this platform to-day. When Connecticut suggested the candidacy of Marshall Jewell, we recalled the energy, economy, and executive ability that have marked and adorned his admirable administration of postal affairs. When Indiana presented the name of her great war governor, our hearts went back to that dark hour when organized rebellion seized on the legislature of Indiana, and when Oliver P. Morton strangled the treason, and won as great a victory in the council as our best and bravest soldiers in the field. When Kentucky,—birthplace of Abraham Lincoln—Kentucky,—where sleep the ashes of Harry Clay—when Kentucky named the great secretary, she sought to name one to whom New York gives her heartiest love and highest honor. You and I remember how all the animosities of partisanship died, when we learned that the great commoner of Maine was stricken, and the awful silence which fell upon us as we feared approaching death had settled over him. From every heart there rose most earnest prayers,—from opponent as well as supporter, when faithful friends and loving wife were waiting by his side,—that the God of all life would spare James G. Blaine; and to-day, with the most loving of his friends, New York congratulates him that his strength is renewed, and his health so fully restored.

But, gentlemen, let us not nominate with our hearts, but with our heads. Four years ago we gave to Grant, and that grand old patriot, John A. Dix, 50,000 majority in the state of New York. Two years ago and that same state gave 53,000 majority to Samuel J. Tilden. Only this last spring the state of Connecticut, right on the eve of the presidential battle, gave 5,000 Democratic majority. Only the other day, as we were gathering for this convention, the wires whispered across the continent that Oregon had gone Democratic. To-day, Indiana has a Democratic governor; to-day, New Jersey has a Democratic governor; to-day, Connecticut has a Democratic governor; to-day, New York has a Democratic governor;—and unless you can secure the votes of Indiana, Ohio, Connecticut, and New York, or, failing one, the votes of all the rest, in spite of all our enthusiasm, in spite of all our zeal, we may follow the banner of our party to defeat. I do not claim that Roscoe Conkling is the only Republican who can carry the state of New York. I believe that he can. If I did not so believe I would cut that hand off before I would stand in a Republican convention and plead for his nomination. Mark this, and it is in all soberness of judgment, there is in New York a vote that is neither Republican, nor yet Democratic; a vote that went for Dix in 1872; a vote that went for Tilden in 1874.

Gentlemen of the convention: I pray you this hour let all personal ambition, let all pride, be put aside. Remember what Democratic victory means. It means destruction of the national credit. It means madness in all legislation touching finances and the tariff. It means that all through the South-land white Republicans must put padlocks on their lips, while the black Republicans will be hunted like the wolves before the hounds.

Gentlemen of the convention: Not for Roscoe Conkling, not for New York, but for the ideas of the Republican party; for the cause,—for the cause that we followed, some of us, through fields of battle; in the name of those who have died, in the name of the loyal men to whom we would give protection through all the land, in the name of all the interests of humanity that in this centennial time are committed to the Republican party, I plead that you to-day give us a candidate with whom and under whom we can achieve, not personal ambition, but a victory that means honesty in finance, loyalty in government, and absolute protection to the lowliest and humblest under the flag of our fathers.

RUTHERFORD B. HAYES.

Ohio being called, Mr. Edward F. Noyes, of that state, addressed the convention.

SPEECH OF MR. NOYES.

Mr. President and Gentlemen of the Convention: On behalf of the forty-four delegates from Ohio, representing the entire Republican party of Ohio, I have the honor to present to this convention the name of a gentleman well known and favorably known throughout the country; one held in high respect and much beloved by the people of Ohio; a man who, during the dark and stormy days of the rebellion, when those who are invincible in peace and invisible in battle were uttering brave words to cheer their neighbors on, himself in the fore-front of battle, followed his leaders and his flag until the authority of our government was reëstablished from the lakes to the gulf, and from the river around to the sea; a man who has had the rare good fortune since the war was over to be twice elected to congress from the district where he resided, and subsequently the rarer fortune of beating successively, for the highest office in the gift of the people of Ohio, Allen G. Thurman, George H. Pendleton, and William Allen. He is a gentleman who has somehow fallen into the habit of defeating Democratic aspirants for the presidency; and we in Ohio all have a notion, that, from long experience, he will be able to do it again. In presenting the name of Governor Hayes, permit me to say we wage no war upon the distinguished gentlemen whose names have been mentioned here to-day. They have rendered great service to their country, which entitles them to our respect and to our gratitude. I have no word to utter against them. I only wish to say that Governor Hayes is the peer of these gentlemen in integrity, in character, in ability. They appear as equals in all the great qualities which fit men for the highest positions which the American people can give them. Governor Hayes is honest; he is brave; he is unpretending; he is wise, sagacious,—a scholar and a gentleman. Enjoying an independent fortune, the simplicity of his private life, his modesty of bearing, are a standing rebuke to the extravagance, the reckless extravagance, which leads to corruption in public and in private places.

Remember now, delegates to the convention, that a responsible duty rests upon you. You can be governed by no wild impulse. You can run no fearful risks in this campaign. You must, if you would succeed, nominate a candidate here who will not only carry the old, strong Republican states, but who will carry Indiana, Ohio, and New York, as well as other doubtful states. We care not whom the man shall be, other than our own candidate. Whoever you nominate, men of the convention, shall receive our heartiest and most earnest efforts for his success. But we beg to submit that in Governor Hayes you have those qualities which are calculated best to compromise all difficulties, and to soften all antagonisms. He has no personal enmities. His private life is so pure that no man has ever dared to assail it. His public acts throughout all these years have been above suspicion even. I ask you, then, if, in the lack of all these antagonisms, and with all these good qualities,—living in a state which holds its election in October, the result of which will be decisive, it may be, of the presidential campaign,—if it is not worth while to see to it that a candidate is nominated against whom nothing can be said, and who is sure to succeed in the campaign?

In conclusion, permit to say, that if the wisdom of this convention shall decide at last that Governor Hayes's nomination is safest and is best, that decision will meet with such responsive enthusiasm here in Ohio as will insure Republican success at home, and which will be so far-reaching and wide-spreading as to make success almost certain from the Atlantic to the Pacific.

SPEECH OF MR. BENJAMIN F. WADE.

Mr. Wade, of Ohio, said:

After what has been said by my colleague, there remains but very little for me to say. In fact, Gen. Hayes needs no second to name him as a nominee for president. He is well known in Ohio. He is well known by all the Republicans of Ohio, and respected by all the Democracy of Ohio. He is a gentlemen about whom nothing can be said to his discredit; a man who will run without opposition; a man who will enter the field without the fear of any opposition whatever. We of Ohio know him well. He is not unknown in official life. He has occupied high and responsible official positions, not only in the state but in the nation; and in the whole period of his official life he has acquitted himself to the entire satisfaction of those who placed him there. And two years ago, when the Republican flag seemed to be trailing, when the Republicans stood in fear that their cause might temporarily be lost, he was the man that we put up to bear the standard of this state in the face of the nation, when the eyes of the whole people were upon us, looking at us with the most intense anxiety. I need not tell you, in whatever portion of the United States you may reside, that the result of his canvass cheered the hearts of Republicans in every part of this Union, and turned the tide of victory against Democracy. Gen. Hayes has ever been a sound Republican, never deviating from his course when others have fallen, and always abetting the cause of Republicanism, spending his fortune and his power and strength to promote its interest; an undeviating Republican, in whom there was never any mistrust. He stood by the Republican party in the blackest hour of our peril. He stood by it in council and in peace, and he stood by our guns in war; and we intend to stand by him as he stood by us.

SPEECH OF MR. ST. GEM, OF MISSOURI.

Mr. President and Gentlemen of the Convention: I claim the right to raise a voice from the state of Missouri in support of the nomination of Governor Rutherford B. Hayes, of Ohio. Without reflecting upon the great and illustrious names that have been presented, yet I must say, that, in the present state and condition of the country, it is the duty of the Republican party and of this convention to reflect upon the selection of a standard-bearer that will win in the contest of November.

I will say, that on the nomination of Rutherford B. Hayes, of Ohio, a response will be heard, not only from the great valley of the Ohio, but from the still greater valley of the Mississippi, that has not been heard in many contests since the great Republican party was organized. The man who has been known as the citizen-soldier, and afterwards to have been so honored by the great state of Ohio as to have thrice defeated the leaders of the Democratic party, and last, but not least, when the state of Ohio rested under the cloud of defeat, was the only man who, like Cincinnatus of old, forsook the plow, saved Ohio, and defeated William Allen,—that man was Governor Rutherford B. Hayes; and, gentlemen of the convention, there will be a response of all the elements of the Republican party, and a concentration of disaffected elements that, I believe, no other man could concentrate upon the ticket. You would hear no more of Liberal Republicans, or of Reformers. It would be a general arousing of the Republican party for the ticket: it would be the most triumphant victory since the days of the illustrious and immortal Lincoln. Give us Rutherford B. Hayes as the champion of honest money and popular education, and a shout will be raised through the land that no other candidate can raise. Give us Rutherford B. Hayes as the candidate of the Republican party, and there will be no such thing as defeat.

SPEECH OF MR. J. W. DAVIS, OF WEST VIRGINIA.

Mr. President: In behalf of myself and of my colleagues, I heartily second the nomination of the gentleman who has preceded me. The character of Governor Hayes is irreproachable and unreproached. As a soldier, he inspired enthusiasm among his followers and respect among his foes. He has filled the highest offices of the state, civil and military, legislative and executive, state and national, and on every occasion he has been found equal to the situation which he filled. His devotion to the principles of civil liberty is such that his election would be a guaranty of the freedom of every citizen of the United States. His hand would hold firmly the reins of government. Nominate him here to-day, and he will surely be elected. Elect him, and you have a president that every American citizen, at home or abroad, will be proud to call his president. Without saying anything against anybody else, I feel sure that the nomination of Hayes is an assured fact. His election is just as certain as that the sun is to rise to-morrow morning. Nominate him, and he will be the president of the United States when the next presidential election shall occur.

JOHN F. HARTRANFT.

Mr. Linn Bartholomew, as the representative of Pennsylvania, took the platform and said:

SPEECH OF MR. BARTHOLOMEW.

Mr. President and Gentlemen of the Convention: The manifest anxiety that pervades this assembly to depart, shall hasten me to a conclusion. I know well that the gentleman whose name I propose to this convention, should he direct me, would ask and request that, so far as his merits are concerned, they should be expressed with exceeding great modesty, for that is his character. I say here, as others have said before me, that I concede to the gentlemen named a great intellectual superiority over my candidate. I do not claim for General John F. Hartranft, of Pennsylvania, that he possesses great intellectuality, but I do claim for him that he knows enough to know that he does not know everything, and is willing to take and to follow good, sound, wholesome advice; and when an individual gets that far upon the road, he possesses decided merit, at least in my estimation. I can say this, gentlemen, in behalf of John F. Hartranft,—that his patriotism cannot be questioned; that his Republican principles cannot be questioned. His Republicanism was taught him under rebel fire. Before the echo of the first gun that fired on Fort Sumter had died away, John F. Hartranft was in the service of his country. He remained at the front, doing battle for his country, until material treason failed at Appomattox. His civil life has been a successful one. He has been an executive, reelected in the state of Pennsylvania. His character is that of a Christian gentleman. He possesses the requirements for an executive officer; and let me say here to you, that he has a patriotism as large as our land. It will cover every inch of territory in our land; and in our commonwealth his name is a synonyme of honesty. The people of Pennsylvania love him. You have pronounced in this convention over and over again, that Pennsylvania is a certain state. Let me say to the delegates here, that no single man upon our soil has done more to make her a pronounced Republican state than General John F. Hartranft. His administration has been economical. No word, no charge of corruption, was ever uttered successfully against his acts. Economy is his rule,—not that false economy that would send our representatives to foreign courts in nankeen pants and straw hats, but that good, wise economy of administration of government that is the evidence of statesmanship; and I say here, without detaining you further, that he is with us one of our chosen,—nay, our chosen leader. This nomination on the part of the Pennsylvania delegation was unsought by him. He never sought it. It was thrust on him by the Republican party of Pennsylvania; and I ask of you here to take his claims into due consideration, because we know he is worthy. He wants in nothing to complete a good and available and successful candidate of the Republican party.

ADJOURNMENT.

The PRESIDENT. It is not necessary to read the remaining states, as there are no other candidates.

Mr. CUMBACK, of Indiana. I move we adjourn till to-morrow morning at 10 o'clock, and that the vote be taken by the call of the states.

The PRESIDENT. The question is upon a motion that this convention adjourn until 10 o'clock to-morrow. The secretary will call the roll of states.

The roll-call was begun. Alabama voted 20 nays; Arkansas, 11 yeas and one nay. At this point,—

Mr. EDICK, of New York. I move as an amendment that we take an informal ballot, and after that, we take an adjournment until 10 o'clock to-morrow.

Another DELEGATE. The roll-call has commenced. That motion is out of order.

Mr. Frye, of Maine, inquired if the hall could be lighted.

The PRESIDENT. I desire to say, for the information of the convention, that I am informed that the gas-lights of this hall are in such condition that they cannot safely be lighted.

On motion, the convention then adjourned at 5:15 P. M. until 10 o'clock Friday morning.

THIRD DAY—FRIDAY, June 16, 1876.

At 10:30 A. M. the convention was called to order by the president, who requested unauthorized persons occupying seats set apart for delegates to retire, and announced that this rule would be absolutely enforced during the session of the day.

The proceedings of the morning were opened with prayer by the Rev. Mr. Morgan, of St. John's Episcopal Church, of Cincinnati, as follows:

OPENING PRAYER.

Almighty God, Father of all blessings, Ruler of the universe, to thee we come to ask for grace and mercy to rest upon this convention. We need thy help. We pray thee in mercy to interpose and vouchsafe unto us thy grace, as thou seest thy servants need at this time. We pray thee, O God, to look upon us graciously and bless us, gathered together in this council. We pray thee to bless the people of these United States: bless the fathers and mothers: bless our sons and our daughters. Bless, we pray thee, the chief magistrate of this nation. Bless, we pray thee, the senators and representatives of this people in congress assembled, and this national council. Vouchsafe unto them, we pray thee, the direction of thine own wisdom, that by their endeavors all things may be so ordered and settled upon the surest and best foundations, that truth and happiness, religion and piety, may be established among us for all generations. Save to us, we pray thee, the goodly heritage that thou hast bequeathed us by the hands of our fathers. Make strong and firm the hearts of the rulers; make patriotic and pious the hearts of the people of this land, we pray thee. Settle and establish our civil and religious institutions. Deliver us, we pray thee, from the blight of ignorance and superstition. Bring to naught the machinations of evil and designing men. We pray thee, O Lord, that truth and justice may be established in our land for all generations. These and all other mercies that we need, we humbly ask in the name and for the sake of thy Son and our Saviour Jesus Christ, who hath taught us to pray, and to say,—"Our Father which art in heaven, hallowed be thy name: thy kingdom come: thy will be done in earth, as it is in heaven: give us this day our daily bread: forgive us our trespasses as we forgive those who trespass against us: lead us not into temptation, but deliver us from evil;—for thine is the kingdom, the power, and the glory, forever and ever." Amen.

The PRESIDENT. Before proceeding to general business, the chair desires to call to the attention of the delegations from Alabama, from Florida, and from the District of Columbia, their privilege of naming a member of the National Committee for their respective districts, the order relative to the announcement of the committee having been passed prior to the settlement of the contests.

The chair has been requested to have the following announcements read:

The meeting of the National Executive Committee of the Union League of America will be held immediately after the final adjournment of the convention, at the head-quarters of the Illinois delegation, in the Burnet House.

WM. A. NEWELL, *Chairman.*

CINCINNATI, June 14, 1876.

To the President of the National Republican Convention:

DEAR SIR: The delegates to the National Republican Convention, and the friends in attendance, are very cordially invited to visit the annual exhibition of the School of Design of the Cincinnati University, at College Hall, on Walnut street, opposite the Gibson House.

The exhibition will be open on the 14th, 15th, 16th, and 17th inst. until 10 P. M.

Very respectfully,

ALEX. H. McGUFFEY,
GEORGE HOADLY,
RUFUS KING,
SAMUEL F. HUNT,
Committee on School of Design.

Also, the following:

JUNE 15, 1876.

To the Republican National Convention:

GENTLEMEN: I am requested by the Board of Directors of the House of Refuge of this city to extend a cordial invitation to the members of the convention to visit this institution, in a body or individually, and examine its various departments. Please designate a certain time, and every attention will be given visiting members.

Very respectfully,

E. C. KIMBALL, *Acting Secretary*

BALLOTING FOR PRESIDENT.

The PRESIDENT. The first business in order is the balloting for a candidate for the office of President of the United States. If it be the pleasure of the convention, the secretary will proceed to call the roll of states, and the chairman of each delegation will announce, as distinctly as possible, from his place, the choice of the delegation.

FIRST BALLOT.

At twenty minutes of 11, the balloting for President began, and proceeded as follows:

STATES.	Blaine.	Morton.	Conkling.	Bristow.	Hayes.	Hartranft.	Wheeler.	Jewell.
Alabama	10	....	....	7	2	....	....	1
Arkansas	....	12	....	....	....	....	....	....
California	9	....	1	2	....	....	....	....
Colorado	6	....	....	....	....	....	....	....
Connecticut	....	....	....	2	....	....	....	10
Delaware	6	....	....	....	....	....	....	....
Florida	1	4	3	....	....	....	....	....
Georgia	5	6	8	3	....	....	....	....
Illinois	38	....	....	3	1	....	....	....
Indiana	....	30	....	....	....	....	....	....
Iowa	22	....	....	....	....	....	....	....
Kansas	10	....	....	....	....	....	....	....
Kentucky	....	....	....	24	....	....	....	....
Louisiana	2	14	....	....	....	....	....	....
Maine	14	....	....	....	....	....	....	....
Maryland	16	....	....	....	....	....	....	....
Massachusetts	6	....	....	17	....	....	3	....
Michigan	8	....	1	9	4	....	....	....
Minnesota	10	....	....	....	....	....	....	....
Mississippi*	....	11	1	3	....	....	....	....
Missouri	14	12	1	2	1	....	....	....
Nebraska	6	....	....	....	....	....	....	....
Nevada	....	....	2	3	1	....	....	....
New Hampshire	7	....	....	3	....	....	....	....
New Jersey	13	....	....	....	5	....	....	....
New York	....	....	69	1	....	....	....	....
North Carolina*	9	2	7	1	....	....	....	....
Ohio	....	....	....	....	44	....	....	....
Oregon	6	....	....	....	....	....	....	....
Pennsylvania	....	....	....	....	....	58	....	....
Rhode Island	2	....	....	6	....	....	....	....
South Carolina	....	13	....	1	....	....	....	....
Texas	2	5	3	6	....	....	....	....
Tennessee	4	10	....	10	....	....	....	....
Vermont	1	....	....	8	1	....	....	....
Virginia	16	3	3	....	....	....	....	....
West Virginia	8	....	....	....	2	....	....	....
Wisconsin	20	....	....	....	....	....	....	....
Arizona	2	....	....	....	....	....	....	....
Dakota	2	....	....	....	....	....	....	....
Idaho	2	....	....	....	....	....	....	....
Montana	2	....	....	....	....	....	....	....
New Mexico	2	....	....	....	....	....	....	....
Utah	2	....	....	....	....	....	....	....
District of Columbia	....	2	....	....	....	....	....	....
Washington	2	....	....	....	....	....	....	....
Wyoming	....	....	....	2	....	....	....	....
Totals	285	124	99	113	61	58	3	11

* One absent.

During the call of the roll, persons in the galleries interfered considerably with the dispatch of business by applauding when the votes were announced. The delegates were annoyed by the cheers and applause, and rebuked it by hissing, which led the president to remark,—

The chair thinks he will take the responsibility of saying that there is an obvious impropriety in hissing, whatever may be said as to the propriety of cheering.

The votes of the successive states were, however, still greeted with manifestations, and the president again reminded those in the galleries that they were interfering with the transaction of the business of the convention.

A DELEGATE from Wisconsin. I would suggest that the chair notify the occupants of the gallery that business will be suspended unless order is preserved.

The PRESIDENT. It is very likely that the chair will reach that point in a very short time, unless there be a modification of the demonstrations in the galleries.

Mr. JAMES L. ALCORN, of Mississippi. We desire to change the vote of Mississippi, as announced.

The PRESIDENT. Under the rule, there can be no change at present.

Mr. BRUCE, of Mississippi. We desire to correct the vote. One of our delegates was absent when our state was called, but subsequently came in.

The PRESIDENT. The convention will please to come to order, as a very important point is involved in the pending proposition. The gentleman from Mississippi made the announcement of the vote as reported from the desk. Subsequently a member from Mississippi, who was reported as absent when the vote was taken in the delegation, came into the hall, and the proposition of the gentleman now is to correct the vote so as to include the vote of the gentleman who was absent when the delegation acted, and when the vote was announced. The chair desires to say that under the fourth rule adopted yesterday, this is laid down as the law: "And when any state has announced its vote, it shall so stand until the ballot is announced, unless in case of numerical error."

Another delegate from Mississippi took the floor to argue that the desired change in the vote should be made.

A Wisconsin DELEGATE. Let the chair rule on the proposition.

The Mississippi DELEGATE. The proposed change is strictly in order. The chairman of the Mississippi delegation was in error in the announcement of the vote. He certainly has or ought to have a right to correct an error made in the announcement of the vote.

The PRESIDENT. If the chairman of the delegation will rise and say that in the announcement of the vote he committed what is called a numerical error, the chair will hold that he has a right to correct it; but the chair rules that he has no right to change the vote so as to add one to the number of persons returned as voting.

Mr. BRUCE. I was in error in announcing the vote. It should have been 11 for Morton, 3 for Bristow, and 1 for Conkling. I also stated that one member was absent when we acted, but came in subsequently.

The PRESIDENT. Two propositions are involved. One is to correct an error made in announcing the vote, which he has a right to do, and the chair has opened the question for that purpose. Will the gentleman from Mississippi give me his attention and state how the vote would stand as corrected?

Mr. BRUCE. Eleven for Morton, 3 for Bristow, and 1 for Conkling.

The PRESIDENT. It is very important now to have everything correctly stated. The gentleman from Mississippi reports the vote of his state as standing 11 for Morton, Bristow 3, and Conkling 1. Now, upon the other point. Do you press the right of your absent delegate to vote?

Mr. BRUCE. I withdraw the request.

The PRESIDENT. The chair will announce the result of the ballot. The total number of votes cast was 754. Of these James G. Blaine received 285; Benjamin H. Bristow, 113; Roscoe Conkling, 99; John F. Hartranft, 58; Rutherford B. Hayes, 61; Marshall Jewell, 11; Oliver P. Morton, 124; William A. Wheeler, 3. No one having a majority of all the votes, there is no choice. The secretary will proceed with the next call.

Mr. H. H. BINGHAM, of Pennsylvania. *Mr. Chairman:* I move that this convention take a recess of fifteen minutes, to allow a consultation in various delegations.

Not agreed to.

SECOND BALLOT.

Alabama was twice called, but the delegation asked time for consultation.

Mr. WILLIAM ORTON, of New York. If it is in order, I suggest, whenever a state is not ready to respond to the call, that it be passed, and that the absentees be called at the end of the roll.

The PRESIDENT. That would create confusion, and is rather in antagonism with the spirit of the rules, which looks to the record of each vote in its order.

The convention then proceeded with the second ballot, with the following result:

STATES.	Blaine.	Morton.	Conkling.	Bristow.	Hayes.	Hartranft.	Washburne.	Wheeler.
Alabama	16			4				
Arkansas	1	11						
California	6		3		3			
Colorado	6							
Connecticut	2			9	1			
Delaware	6							
Florida	4	4						
Georgia	9	4	6	3				
Illinois	35			6	1			
Indiana		30						
Iowa	22							
Kansas	10							
Kentucky				24				
Louisiana *	3	12						
Maine	14							
Maryland	16							
Massachusetts	5			18				3
Michigan	8		1	9	4			
Minnesota	9						1	
Mississippi	1	6	3	6				
Missouri	15	11	1	2	1			
Nebraska	6							
Nevada			2			4		
New Hampshire	7			3				
New Jersey	12				6			
New York			69	1				
North Carolina *	8	2	3	1		5		
Ohio					44			
Oregon	6							
Pennsylvania	4					54		
Rhode Island	2			6				
South Carolina		13		1				
Texas	2	12	1	1				
Tennessee	8	8		8				
Vermont	1			8	1			
Virginia	14	4	4					
West Virginia	8				2			
Wisconsin	17	1		2				
Arizona	2							
Dakota	2							
Idaho	2							
Montana	1				1			
New Mexico	2							
Utah	2							
District of Columbia		2						
Washington	2							
Wyoming				2				
Totals	296	120	93	114	64	63	1	3

* One absent.

During the roll-call the following proceedings took place:

Some of the announcements of votes being greeted by hisses in the galleries,—

A DELEGATE from New York. I move that the sergeant-at-arms be instructed hereafter to remove any person hissing in the galleries.

The PRESIDENT. I think this difficulty will be very much obviated if the mature people in the gallery will consider for a moment how improper it is for those who are here purely by favor of the convention to be interfering with the business of the convention. The chair is very reluctant to interfere with the comfort and enjoyment of any one within this building, but it may become a necessary duty for the chair to clear the galleries, because the work of the convention must go on.

Subsequently the president remarked:

The chair has been informed that persons in the rear of the hall cannot hear the announcement of the votes. If there be no objection, a person will be stationed in the rear of the hall to reännounce the votes.

The suggestion was unanimously agreed to.

The vote of Pennsylvania being announced by the chairman of the delegation as 58 for Hartranft, Mr. J. Smith Futhey, of Chester, rising to his feet, said,—

"Mr. Chairman, I rise to a point of order. The vote for Pennsylvania was not correctly announced; myself and my colleague, representing the Sixth Congressional District, composed of the counties of Chester and Delaware, wish to cast our votes for James G. Blaine. We requested the chairman of the delegation to so announce our votes, but he refused, and we now ask and demand that our votes shall now be recorded for James G. Blaine."

Two other delegates from Pennsylvania made similar requests.

The PRESIDENT. A question of privilege of that sort must be settled before we pass to the next state.

Mr. CESSNA, of Pennsylvania. I ask the attention of the chair to Rule 3.

DELEGATE on the platform. Rule 6 covers the case.

The PRESIDENT. The chair will state the case. The chairman of the Pennsylvania delegation rises in his place and reports, as the vote of that state, fifty-eight votes for John F. Hartranft. The gentleman from the Westchester District, speaking for himself and his colleague of the Sixth Pennsylvania District, and the gentleman from Pittsburgh, Mr. Hampden, of the Twenty-second District, and Mr. Stewart, from the Twenty-first District, rise to a point of order, which is that the report of the vote made by the chairman of the delegation is not the report of the vote cast in the delegation, which, of course, raises a question of the very highest privilege. That point of order being raised, the chair rules that it is the right of any and of every member equally, to vote his sentiments in this convention.

Mr. McCORMICK, of Pennsylvania. I respectfully appeal from the decision of the chair.

The PRESIDENT. The gentleman from Pennsylvania appeals from the decision of the chair, and the question for the convention to determine is, Shall the decision of the chair be sustained?

The question was put, and the chair was sustained.

The PRESIDENT. The question of the right of these gentlemen having been settled, the chair holds, under the order of this body, that the four votes of the gentlemen shall be recorded as they elect they shall be.

Mr. CESSNA. My colleague, Mr. McCormick, asked to be heard before that vote was taken.

The PRESIDENT. I did not hear him.

Mr. McCORMICK. The trouble is, you did not want to hear me.

The PRESIDENT. I will say to my colleague from Pittsburgh that his imputation upon the chair is dishonoring to him.

Mr. R. W. THOMPSON, of Indiana (interrupting). I protest, in this convention, against the gentleman from Pennsylvania or the chair turning this convention into an arena for their personal controversies. Their personal controversies should be settled outside of this convention. We are here to transact the business of the Republican convention. We are here as the representatives of the greatest party in the world, and this convention is not to be turned into a theatre for the settlement of their personal controversies. When any gentleman in this convention chooses to hurl a personal insult into the face of one of his colleagues by telling him that he has dishonored himself, he abuses the privileges which we have confided to him. I protest against it in the name of the American people, and I demand that this convention shall be heard upon the question as to whether it affirms or disaffirms this opinion.

The PRESIDENT. Will the convention hear the chair for one moment. The chair has not the least desire in the world to interfere with the exercise by the convention, and by every member of the convention, of every right and every privilege which he possesses. I hope there is no gentleman within the limits of the United States who knows me, after some years of public service, who supposes that I would intentionally abuse the powers of this position, and that I would do any injustice to any gentleman of this convention. My colleague from Pittsburgh irritated me very much when he said that I did not wish to hear some appeal which he made. I say to the convention, as I said to him, that I did not hear the appeal.

Mr. THOMPSON. I do not object to that, sir. You told your colleague that he had dishonored himself.

The PRESIDENT. I am just coming to that point. The gentleman then said,—"You did not hear the appeal, because you did not wish to hear it." Now, I appeal to the gallant gentleman from Indiana whether it was very much out of place for a young man to retort in kind a remark of that sort. I withdraw the remark I made, however.

Mr. THOMPSON. I desire to say, sir, in response to that question, that it is out of place for the president of the convention to use it as an instrument to hurl back his anathemas at his colleagues.

Mr. HOAR, of Massachusetts. I raise the point of order, that while the roll-call is in order, and after the announcement of a vote, nothing of this kind is in order, nothing whatever can be done.

Mr. OLIVER, of Pennsylvania. [Cries of "sit down."] Gentlemen, you have given the chairman of this convention a chance. He here publicly— [confusion.] I wish to say something which concerns the chairman.

The PRESIDENT. I withdraw the remark.

Mr. OLIVER. Gentlemen, listen to me. I will not give you any trouble. [Cries of "Order!"]

Mr. OLIVER. The chair recognized me, and I have a right to make my statement. [Cries of "Order!"]

The PRESIDENT. The gentleman from Massachusetts rises to the point of order that the convention is in process of executing its own order and cannot be interrupted. It is a good point of order; but how are we to get out of the difficulty if a gentleman rises to announce his own vote? Perhaps it would be a good way to get rid of the difficulty, if, when an announcement is made, some gentleman interested therein should say that it is not a correct announcement, thus raising a question of privilege, and insisting upon his right to be fairly recorded.

A DELEGATE. The chair has declared the result.

Mr. CESSNA. Oh! no, we have no vote.

Mr. THORNBERG, of Tennessee. I move that the vote just taken to sustain the chair be reconsidered, for the purpose of allowing the gentleman from Pennsylvania to be heard.

Mr. HOAR. I move to lay that motion upon the table.

Mr. CESSNA. The gentleman has not the floor. Did not my friend from Tennessee yield me the floor?

Mr. THORNBERG. No, sir, I do not yield the floor. I move the previous question on my motion.

The PRESIDENT. The gentleman from Tennessee moves to reconsider the vote by which the chair was sustained.

Several gentlemen claimed the floor.

Mr. THORNBERG. I do not yield the floor. My motion is in order to reconsider the last vote, and then the Pennsylvania delegation on both sides should be heard.

A DELEGATE from Virginia. I rise to a point of order, that nothing is now in order but to call the roll.

Mr. SENER, of Virginia. Then the gentleman can yield his time to the gentleman from Pennsylvania.

Mr. THORNBERG. I yield five minutes of my time to Mr. Cessna.

A DELEGATE from Missouri. I raise the point that this whole thing is out of order.

The PRESIDENT That has been raised and overruled on the ground that, being a question of high personal privilege, it may be rightfully brought into the convention.

Mr. CESSNA. I trust I may come before this convention. All I ask is, that the convention may understand the position which the Pennsylvania delegation to-day occupies before this convention and before the country. I feel that my colleague in the chair made his decision without a proper understanding or examination of the rules, or he would not have made it in the way he has; therefore, I shall be compelled to vote for the motion of my friend from Tennessee, to reconsider the vote by which the appeal was laid upon the table. I ask the attention of my friend in the chair and of this convention to the second rule of this convention.

"Each state shall be entitled to double the number of its senators and representatives in congress, according to the last apportionment. Each territory and the District of Columbia shall be entitled to two votes. The votes of each delegation shall be reported by its chairman."

Now, the next rule provides that after the chairman of each delegation has reported, there shall be no change until the next ballot.

Mr. CESSNA. I beg now to read the authority. [Confusion.] I claim the right to read it to this convention.

The PRESIDENT. The gentleman is entitled to the floor. I hope the convention will come to order. This is a very important feature.

Mr. CESSNA. I am not here to cast any firebrands. I am here in the interest of peace and harmony in Pennsylvania, and in the interest of peace and harmony in this convention and throughout this broad land. No man will be more earnest for the final result of this convention than I will, if you will allow me to state my position. The convention which elected our delegates passed unanimously a resolution instructing us to vote for Hartranft, and cast the vote of Pennsylvania as a unit, as a majority of the delegation should direct it, and it was signed by Henry M. Hoyt, chairman of the state central committee, and Edward McPherson, president of this convention. Now, my fellow members, this delegation of ours met here and authorized our chairman to cast the vote of Pennsylvania as a unit for Hartranft; and we then passed a resolution that he should continue until he was called upon by twenty members of the convention to call us up for consultation, which has not been done. This was not reconsidered, and I pray my fellow-members not to bring the matter into the convention. We can settle it outside peaceably and harmoniously, and we will add strength to the nominee when he is chosen. We will raise the banner when we get him, and carry it from Erie to Delaware, from New York to Ohio, whether it be James G. Blaine or any other man.

Mr. STEWART, of Pennsylvania. I am a delegate here representing an independent congressional district, and while I acknowledge that I am under obligations here to our gallant governor, General John F. Hartranft, I have also a duty to perform to the convention which sent me here as a delegate. I have also to perform a duty to my constituents, who sent me to this convention to represent them, and I propose to do it, if this convention will allow me the simplest justice in the world. I have tried to fulfil my duty, as I have stated: on the first ballot I tried to fulfil my duty to Hartranft, and I was willing to have my vote cast for him. The second duty I tried to fulfil in the same way. What I consider my paramount duty is the duty I owe to my own constituents, whom I came here to represent. Those constituents sent me to this convention through the ordinary channels by which we get here, and I propose now, if this convention will award the simplest justice in the world, to represent those constituents in giving my vote, and my people are united on this subject. I propose to do that by casting my vote for James G. Blaine.

Mr. FUTHEY, of Pennsylvania. My colleague and myself represent the Sixth Congressional District of Pennsylvania, and we are here by virtue of an election held in our own district. We come here with credentials from our own district. We owe no allegiance to the state convention, and we recognize no right of that convention to say how we shall vote. We claim the right to represent our own constituents. The counties of Chester and Delaware are almost a unit for James G. Blaine, and, representing those counties, we should be false to our constituents and to ourselves if we voted for any one else. We ask that our votes shall be recorded in accordance with our views and the sentiments of our constituents. The sixth rule adopted by this convention says the chairman shall announce the number of votes for any candidate, or for or against any proposition. Our chairman did not announce our votes, and we have the right to demand, under that rule, that our votes shall be recorded.

Mr. HALE, of Maine. *Gentlemen:* Let me make a suggestion in the interest of the harmony of this convention. We should have little to do with differences arising in the Pennsylvania delegation, which we should not be called upon to settle here. I do not understand that a reflection is cast upon the chairman of the delegation in giving the vote as he did under the unit rule, but certain members of that delegation have asked that their votes be recorded as individual members of this convention. I do not believe that, when Pennsylvania retires to consider this question, the delegation from that state will insist that members shall have their votes declared contrary to their wishes; therefore I suggest that, by unanimous consent, while this roll-call proceeds, Pennsylvania be allowed to retire, and report to this convention in harmonious fashion, what are the actual wishes and votes of the individual members of the delegation. I, for one, am willing, on this proposition, to trust the old state of Pennsylvania. I ask that unanimous consent be given that the Pennsylvania delegation may retire.

Mr. THORNBERG. I object.

Mr. HALE. Then, Mr. President, I ask, in the interest of the expedition of the business of this convention, that the chair state the exact condition of the question; what is the condition of the appeal; is there to be any further action or debate upon it, or has it been sustained; and that the chair direct the secretary of the convention to announce the vote, and that then we proceed to what nine out of every ten men here earnestly desire, to close up our business in decent fashion, and go to the American people.

Mr. VAN ZANDT, of Rhode Island. We are unwilling in any way that this convention should interfere with or should suggest to any delegation in this convention whether they shall retire for consultation or otherwise. We desire to express the views of the little state of Rhode Island on this question.

The state of Pennsylvania can take care of herself. She is big enough and noble enough to do it; and if that convention passed resolutions instructing their delegates to cast a unit vote, and those gentlemen allowed themselves to be elected upon that platform, I care not whether the immediate constituencies represented by the gentlemen were unanimously in favor of the gentleman from Maine or any other gentleman, they are bound by the platform of their convention. I say they are bound by the platform of that convention; and not only that, but that platform, as I understand, was liberally qualified by the vote of the delegation of that great and noble state, who voted that at any time when twenty members—which is far less than a majority—wished to rescind that vote, it could be rescinded.

Now, sir, I have had some fifteen years' experience in parliamentary law, and I say that this convention, if it goes on in this way, will get to be a mob. The people of this great country, from their firesides and their homes, are looking toward us to-day,—for what? For propriety, decency, and order, and instead of that we have been converting ourselves into a sort of amateur bear-garden; and I implore my friends from Pennsylvania, whether they are for the one candidate or for the other, to allow this vote to be cast by their chairman under the platform of their convention, and under the rules which they have established for themselves, and then to proceed with the roll-call. If they desire to retire for consultation, let them, and God speed the candidate they vote for, and God speed the candidate of this convention.

Mr. OLIVER, of Pennsylvania. I will only take a few minutes of your time, gentlemen, and I think it will be for your interest, and will expedite business, if you will allow me quietly to state the case. You will undoubtedly have to make this decision. I will give you the story. The state convention of Pennsylvania met. It has been the rule in Pennsylvania that the state convention, and not the separate districts, should send the delegates to the national convention. The Republicans of Chester county, a district which now and then sets up a little for itself, and thinks it is a little in advance of the balance of our state, met in county convention and elected the gentleman who spoke before me, and his colleague, as delegates to the national convention. The state convention adopted those two delegates, and they are the only two delegates in the whole list of fifty-eight that were not elected by the state convention. John F. Hartranft was proposed for president: his friends had control of that convention. The Republican party of Pennsylvania, all of them, had control of that convention, because there was no opposition to him. A delegation was to be sent to Cincinnati favorable to him. These gentlemen, every one of them, pledged themselves to John F. Hartranft. The delegates met on Tuesday morning at head-quarters here. A resolution was passed there by the delegation that our chairman be instructed to cast the vote for the entire delegation. There was scarcely any objection to that. It was decided that a meeting might be held at any time, when twenty members would call it. They never called that meeting. They never asked for any change. Our chairman casts fifty-eight votes as he was instructed, not only by our delegation, but by the Republicans of Pennsylvania. Our chairman casts that vote. It was right; it was fair; it was in accordance with the rules of our party in our state; it was the wish of our people, and the wish of the majority of the delegation. The unit rule reads,—"And are hereby instructed to vote for John F. Hartranft,—to give him an earnest, constant, and united support; and upon all questions to be heard before or arising in the convention, to cast the vote of Pennsylvania as the majority of the delegation shall direct." The chairman of this convention was the chairman of the convention that passed that; and you [turning to the chairman] wrote the resolution yourself, sir.

The PRESIDENT. Not that resolution.

Mr. OLIVER. Yes, sir, you did. You wrote the resolution. We have the authority of your decision. If you will stultify yourself, you are not the man that Pennsylvania put forward as her chairman.

The PRESIDENT. The chair begs now to be heard. There is no doubt whatever that the first duty of this convention is to proceed with the roll-call. The first duty of the chair is to enforce the order of the convention, to direct the roll-call to proceed. Now, if the convention will recollect, the only question the chair decided was this: These parties claimed the right, in their individual capacity, to vote their particular sentiments. I, as chairman of this convention, know nothing whatever of any rules except the rules which you have laid down for my control. The chair therefore directs that the vote of Pennsylvania be recorded as fifty-four votes for John F. Hartranft and four votes for James G. Blaine, stating this, however, that if, at the end of the roll-call, it be the sense of the convention that the chair has made an erroneous ruling, or has done any one an injury or an injustice, it will then be competent for the convention to correct it, without any interruption of the roll-call.

The roll-call then proceeded, during which Mr. T. M. Pomeroy, of New York, took the chair, the president being called out in consultation with the Pennsylvania delegation.

After the roll-call, Mr. Thornberg moved the previous question upon the motion he made.

The CHAIR. The gentlemen will state his motion again.

Mr. THORNBERG. My motion was to reconsider the vote by which the convention sustained the chair in his ruling, that certain votes which were not cast by the chairman of the delegation should be taken and recorded.

The CHAIR. The question is upon the motion to reconsider, upon which the previous question is demanded.

The motion was lost.

Mr. HALE. I do not understand the motion.

The CHAIR. The motion is to reconsider the decision of the convention, by which the four votes of Pennsylvania were changed from Mr. Hartranft to Mr. Blaine.

Mr. HALE. How does the chair decide the vote?

The CHAIR. The previous question was demanded upon it. That was lost. The question is upon the motion to reconsider. Those in favor of the motion to reconsider will say "Aye,"—those opposed, "No." The nays appear to have it.

Calls were made for a division.

Mr. HALE. That is all right. We have no objection.

The CHAIR. A division is called for, which can only be had by a call of the roll. A call of the roll is asked. Is there a second? Kentucky seconds it. The clerk will call the roll, which is upon the motion to reconsider the vote by which the chair announced that the four votes from Pennsylvania could be changed.

Mr. Sener, of Virginia, inquired whether the vote on this question would settle the general question whether each delegation must vote as a unit.

The CHAIR. In answer to the gentleman, the chair will state that it is not in his power to decide what the effect of it will be. The motion is to reconsider the decision of the convention, by which the chair was sustained in changing those votes upon which the call of the roll is demanded, and no debate is now in order. Delegates will take their seats, and all persons not in their seats will be removed from the floor by the sergeant-at-arms. The chair recognizes nobody. No debate is in order; the call of the roll has already commenced. The chair is not entitled to recognize anybody, but by request he will again state the question, which is upon the motion to reconsider the vote of the convention in favor of the decision of the chair in allowing the change in the vote of the Pennsylvania delegation.

The clerk then called the roll, and the state delegations voted as follows:

States.	*Ay.*	*No.*	*States.*	*Ay.*	*No.*
Alabama	—	20	New York	56	12
Arkansas	10	2	North Carolina	12	7
California	5	7	Ohio	24	20
Colorado	—	6	Oregon	—	6
Connecticut	10	2	Pennsylvania	58	—
Delaware	—	6	Rhode Island	8	—
Florida	1	7	South Carolina	12	2
Georgia	17	5	Tennessee	8	16
Illinois	10	32	Texas	11	5
Indiana	30	—	Vermont	4	6
Iowa	—	22	Virginia	6	15
Kansas	—	10	West Virginia	2	8
Kentucky	23	1	Wisconsin	4	15
Louisiana	10	6	Arizona	—	2
Maine	—	14	Dakota	—	2
Maryland	—	16	District of Columbia	—	2
Massachusetts	5	11	Idaho	—	2
Michigan	21	1	Montana	—	2
Minnesota	2	8	New Mexico	—	2
Mississippi	8	8	Utah	—	2
Missouri	11	19	Washington	—	2
Nebraska	—	6	Wyoming	2	—
Nevada	6	—			
New Hampshire	—	9	Totals	381	359
New Jersey	5	13			

[During the roll-call the president resumed the chair.]

The PRESIDENT. The vote is reconsidered, and the question arises, Shall the decision of the chair be sustained?

Mr. INGERSOLL, of Illinois. I move to lay it on the table.

The PRESIDENT. There is no occasion for that. The question is directly on sustaining the appeal.

Mr. INGERSOLL, of Illinois. The simple question before this convention is, whether each delegate has a right to vote as he believes the people he represents wish him to vote, or whether he can be tied by packed caucuses, whether he can be tied by party machinery, and forced to vote against the sentiments of his constituents and against his own choice. I tell you that we cannot afford to go to this country upon the idea that a delegate from a state can be forced, against his will and against his conscience, to vote for a man that he does not believe his constituents want. It has been decided by a Republican convention for the United States, and it was decided in the case of Pennsylvania, that, notwithstanding an instruction to vote as a unit, the delegates had a right to vote as they pleased. What we want to find out is, who is the real choice of this convention; and what the convention wants to find out is, who is the real choice of the great Republican party of the United States. For one, I believe in allowing every delegate upon this floor the right to vote his choice, the right to represent his constituents, and I am utterly opposed to the gag law of caucus and party machinery.

Mr. THOMPSON, of Indiana. The simple question to be now decided by this convention is this: whether, after we have been sent here by our state conventions, under instructions from them, we have the individual right to violate those instructions; whether the voice of a sovereign state, declared through her state authorities, shall be defied by individuals under a claim of personal right. The Republican party of Pennsylvania has settled, in their state convention appointing their delegates to this convention, under a positive injunction, under irrevocable instructions, that they should cast their vote as a unit, not for themselves, but for the party in Pennsylvania. When they accepted their position as members of this convention, they became bound, by every consideration of justice, of right, of truth, and of honor, to obey those instructions; and I will not give my vote or my sanction to any system of rules or measures which shall disfranchise the people of Pennsylvania. I say, then, that if a gentleman accepts a position from a state convention under such instructions as these, it is his duty, if he cannot obey them, to retire, and let somebody else take his place.

Mr. HOTCHKISS, of New York. *Mr. Chairman and Gentlemen of this Convention:* The simple question presented to this convention, the practical question, is, whether there are law and order and discipline in the Republican party; whether, when this convention makes its nomination, each delegate here is bound by that nomination, or whether he may go home and violate the vote of the majority here. I hold to party discipline. An individual is born into society without his choice. When he joins a political party, he does it of his own free will. When he is born into society, he gives no pledges. When he joins a political party, he gives the pledge of his honor as a man. If he violates the law that you impose upon him, he is hung as a traitor, or ought to be; but if he violates the law that he himself has agreed to, he ought to be hung as a dastard.

Gentlemen of this convention, I represent, in part, the state of New York, the Republican state of New York. We make our own regulations there, and Pennsylvania does not interfere with them. Pennsylvania comes here with her regulations and her customs governing her representatives, and New York should not interfere with them; and it is for this convention to say whether other states should or not. Every state and every gentleman speaks here for himself. Now I beg this convention not to set the example, not to establish the precedent, that a state convention or a national convention, by its resolutions, does not bind every individual member of the party. If he does not like it, let him step out, but, as long as he belongs to that party, let him be governed by the laws of that party; and, when a delegate from Pennsylvania comes here, he comes here under the Pennsylvania constitution and Pennsylvania law. He is bound to obey that law; and I hope this convention will not excuse him. Practically, it amounts to nothing whether four votes go one way or four votes go another; but there is a principle that underlies this, which it would be dangerous to overthrow.

Mr. VAN ZANDT, of Rhode Island. I wish to say but one word, with the permission of the convention, and I wish they would allow me that particularly, because I believe I represent in a small way a small state here. I trust that we shall stick to our old rule, which has always guided the Republican party in all its former deliberations, and not vary from it. Do you know, Mr. President and gentlemen of the convention, the brink of the abyss you are standing upon when you sustain the chair? I look at it in this way,—that it would lead to the disintegration of the Republican party; for, if the convention in Pennsylvania instruct their delegates to vote as a unit, instruct them to stand upon the Republican platform and send them here as Republicans, and if those gentlemen can vary from these instructions in one respect they can in any other. I say, gentlemen of the convention, that applying that principle as correct, it may equally follow that any representatives in this convention who are dissatisfied with the choice of the convention can go home and bolt its nomination as individuals, and vote against those nominations. We are to be bound by certain rules and laws. Party lines hang loosely in this country at best, and they had better be tightened up here to-day, or the results will be disastrous with the great Republican party. I pray you, gentlemen,—and I would not have left my seat for any small or trivial reason,—I pray you not to open these great gates. The Republican convention of Pennsylvania instructed these gentlemen to vote for a certain candidate, and to vote as a unit. They have decided among themselves that when twenty of them desire to retire for consultation, the delegation will do so. It seems to me that is broad and liberal enough. These gentlemen who now desire to vote for another candidate understood those instructions when they accepted their position, and they are bound by them.

Mr. WOODFORD, of New York. *Mr. Chairman and Gentlemen of the Convention:* Thanks for the courtesy that permits me but a moment. I have no sympathy with the vote which that minority from Pennsylvania seeks to cast. I believe that any nomination that cannot carry the doubtful states is the burial of the Republican party in this canvass; but I believe that under the very existence alike of the nation and the Republican party, is the right of every man to cast his own vote. I want to say another thing. I love the Republican party with a love that pulses in every fibre of my being; but I love the Republican party for the ideas of the party, and not for the form and the deadness of its organization. I want to say another thing, for silence here were crime. As an honorable man I am bound, as honorable men you are bound, to abide the action of the convention; but should this or any convention make declaration of unworthy principles, or place thereon candidates whose lives and records do not represent what true Republicanism means, then let me to-day and here simply say, in words so plain that none may misunderstand, I am bound to my country and its welfare by a higher tie than that which binds me to the Republican party.

Mr. THATCHER, of Kansas. *Gentlemen:* The principle that is involved in this question is, whether the state of Pennsylvania shall make rules and laws for this convention, or whether this convention is supreme and shall make its own laws. This convention is a supreme body. No state, no caucus, has a right to make its laws and bring them in here and say that they shall bind this convention. We are supreme; we are original; we stand here representing the great Republican party of this nation, and neither Pennsylvania, nor New York, nor any other state, can come in here and bind us down with their caucus resolutions. More than that, as the speaker before me has said, the great principles of the Republican organization demand that each man shall have his vote himself, and not be bound up by some party or power that is behind him. We are not here to be handled like mere machines. We are not here to be driven in the traces. Talk about your discipline! I tell you the people of this country think there is a little too much discipline and a little too much machinery in our politics at the present time. The convention is supreme. It has the right, and it is its duty, its bounden duty, to let each delegate here represent the sentiments of his constituents, and not compel him to vote as any body shall dictate.

Mr. HALE. I only propose, Mr. President, to submit a bit of political history. In 1868, the Republican party assembled in convention in Chicago. There was unanimity of sentiment upon the question of the presidency. General Grant was nominated by every vote; but there was division upon the question of the vice-presidency, and then Pennsylvania presented one of her gifted sons for the second place in the American republic,—presented him under instructions from her state to present him, and stand by him, and vote for him. I was a delegate there myself, helping to represent the state of Maine, and the whole scene presents itself now before me, when Pennsylvania was called and her vote was cast as a unit for her war governor; but a delegate from Pittsburgh arose in his seat, and with earnestness and fervor upon his countenance and words of warning upon his lips, objected, and asserted the great principle of the individual right to be represented in that convention.

Mr. President, that appeal taken to the convention, raised then as now from the Keystone state, was sustained overwhelmingly, and the chairman was directed to cast the vote of the delegate for the individual of his choice. Now, I regret—no man can more profoundly regret—that these divisions have been brought in here. They have changed the current of this convention and endangered its turning aside, so that our attention is called from legitimate business to dissensions in state delegations. I promised, when I came up here, Mr. President, that I would only give this convention a bit of political history. We can go back on it if we choose; but if we do so, we do it by asserting that this convention nominates, not by a majority of its delegates, but by the votes of its states controlled in caucuses.

Mr. Thornberg moved the previous question. Agreed to.

The PRESIDENT. The question is, Shall the decision of the chair stand as the decision of the convention? The decision of the chair was, that the four gentlemen from Pennsylvania, who rose and declared their desire to cast their ballots for James G. Blaine, had a right, under the rules of the convention, so to do; and the chair directed their votes to be so recorded.

Mr. S. B. DUTCHER, of New York. Can I ask a question?

The PRESIDENT. Not except by consent.

[Cries of "No!" "No!"]

Mr. DUTCHER. Then I say this is a gag proceeding. I ask by what authority the delegates from Pennsylvania came to this convention, and what was the resolution of the convention sending them here?

The PRESIDENT. I reply that that is a question with which the chairman of this convention has nothing whatever to do, and has officially no knowledge of whatever. The Sixth Rule states,—"The vote of each state, territory, and the District of Columbia shall be announced by the chairman; and in case the votes of any state, territory, or the District of Columbia shall be divided, the chairman shall announce the number of votes cast for any candidate or for any proposition." The question is, Shall the decision of the chair stand as the judgment of the convention?

Mr. CUMBACK. I demand the vote by states.

The secretary then called the roll on the question of sustaining the decision of the chair, with the following result:

States.	*Ay.*	*No.*	*States.*	*Ay.*	*No.*
Alabama	20	—	New York	15	54
Arkansas	4	8	North Carolina	6	13
California	11	1	Ohio	14	30
Colorado	6	—	Oregon	6	—
Connecticut	3	9	Pennsylvania	1	57
Delaware	5	1	Rhode Island	1	7
Florida,	4	4	South Carolina	2	12
Georgia	9	13	Tennessee	19	5
Illinois	38	4	Texas	4	12
Indiana	1	29	Vermont	5	5
Iowa	22	—	Virginia	19	2
Kansas	10	—	West Virginia	10	—
Kentucky	1	23	Wisconsin	17	3
Louisiana	6	10	Arizona	2	—
Maine	14	—	Dakota	2	—
Maryland	16	—	District of Columbia	2	—
Massachusetts	15	7	Idaho	2	—
Michigan	3	19	Montana	2	—
Minnesota	7	3	New Mexico	2	—
Mississippi	9	6	Utah	2	—
Missouri	25	5	Washington	2	—
Nebraska	6	—	Wyoming	—	2
Nevada	—	6			
New Hampshire	10	—	Totals	395	353
New Jersey	15	3			

When Pennsylvania was called, the chairman, Mr. Cameron, read the following resolution, just adopted by the delegation from that state:

Resolved, That the Pennsylvania delegation sustain the action of its chairman in casting the vote of the delegation as a unit.

Mr. FUTHEY. I desire to cast my vote to sustain the chair.

The PRESIDENT. The chair so ruled before, and, until changed, that is the rule of the convention. One in the affirmative.

The roll-call was then completed.

The PRESIDENT. Upon sustaining the chair, the ayes are 395, and the noes 353. The decision of the chair is sustained. I therefore decide, as the judgment of this convention, under the Sixth Rule, that it is the right of every individual member thereof to vote his individual sentiments. Accepting the rule thus established by the convention for the second ballot for the presidency, the vote stands as follows: For James G. Blaine, 296; for Oliver P. Morton, 120; for Benjamin H. Bristow, 114; for Roscoe Conkling, 93; for Rutherford B. Hayes, 64; for John F. Hartranft, 63; for William A. Wheeler, 3; for Elihu B. Washburne, 1. No one having received a majority of all the votes, a third ballot is in order, and the clerk will call the roll of states.

THIRD BALLOT.

The roll was called, with the following result:

STATES.	Blaine.	Bristow.	Conkling.	Hartranft.	Hayes.	Morton.	Wheeler.	Washburne.
Alabama	15	4	1					
Arkansas	1					11		
California	6		3		3			
Colorado	6							
Connecticut	2	8			2			
Delaware	6							
Florida	2		3	3				
Georgia	9	3	6			4		
Illinois	35	6			1			
Indiana						30		
Iowa	22							
Kansas	10							
Kentucky		24						
Louisiana	5					11		
Maine	14							
Maryland	16							
Massachusetts	5	19					2	
Michigan	8	10			4			
Minnesota	8	1						1
Mississippi		7	2		2	5		
Missouri	15	3			1	11		
Nebraska	6							
Nevada		2	2	2				
New Hampshire	7	3						
New Jersey	12				6			
New York		1	69					
North Carolina	9	1	1	8				
Ohio					44			
Oregon	6							
Pennsylvania	3			55				
Rhode Island	2	6						
South Carolina		1				13		
Tennessee	7	8				9		

THIRD BALLOT—*continued.*

STATES.	Blaine.	Bristow.	Conkling.	Hartranft.	Hayes.	Morton.	Wheeler.	Washburne.
Texas	2	1	....	....	....	13	....	....
Vermont	1	8	....	....	1	....	....	....
Virginia	15	....	3	....	....	4	....	....
West Virginia	8	....	....	....	2	....	....	....
Wisconsin	16	3	....	....	....	1	....	....
Arizona	2	....	....	....	....	....	....	....
Dakota	2	....	....	....	....	....	....	....
District of Columbia	1	....	....	....	....	1	....	....
Idaho	2	....	....	....	....	....	....	....
Montana	1	....	....	....	1	....	....	....
New Mexico	2	....	....	....	....	....	....	....
Utah	2	....	....	....	....	....	....	....
Washington	2	....	....	....	....	....	....	....
Wyoming	....	2	....	....	....	....	....	....
Totals	293	121	90	68	67	113	2	1

The PRESIDENT. The vote stands as follows: 755 votes. Of these votes, James G. Blaine had 293; Benjamin H. Bristow had 121; Roscoe Conkling had 90; John F. Hartranft had 68; Rutherford B. Hayes had 67; Oliver P. Morton had 113; William A. Wheeler had 2; Elihu B. Washburne had 1. No one having received a majority of the votes cast, there is no nomination, and a fourth ballot is in order, and the secretary will call the roll.

FOURTH BALLOT.

The secretary called the roll of states, with the following result:

STATES.	Blaine.	Bristow.	Conkling.	Hartranft.	Hayes.	Morton.	Wheeler.	Washburne.
Alabama	16	4	....	....	....	....	....	....
Arkansas	1	....	....	....	....	11	....	....
California	6	....	3	....	3	....	....	....
Colorado	6	....	....	....	....	....	....	....
Connecticut	2	9	....	....	1	....	....	....
Delaware	6	....	....	....	....	....	....	....
Florida	2	....	2	4	....	....	....	....
Georgia	9	2	6	....	....	4	....	1

FOURTH BALLOT—*continued.*

STATES.	Blaine.	Bristow.	Conkling.	Hartranft.	Hayes.	Morton.	Wheeler.	Washburne.
Illinois	35	5			1			1
Indiana						30		
Iowa	21		1					
Kansas	10							
Kentucky		24						
Louisiana	5					11		
Maine	14							
Maryland	16							
Massachusetts	5	19					2	
Michigan	6	11			5			
Minnesota	8	1						1
Mississippi		7	2	1	1	4		
Missouri	18	3			1	8		
Nebraska	6							
Nevada		1	2	3				
New Hampshire	7	3						
New Jersey	12				6			
New York		2	68					
North Carolina	9			8	1	1		
Ohio					44			
Oregon	6							
Pennsylvania	3			55				
Rhode Island	2	6						
South Carolina		1				13		
Tennessee	7	10				7		
Texas	1	5				10		
Vermont		8			2			
Virginia	15					7		
West Virginia	8				2			
Wisconsin	16	3				1		
Arizona	2							
Dakota	2							
District of Columbia	1					1		
Idaho	2							
Montana	1				1			
New Mexico	2							
Utah	2							
Washington	2							
Wyoming		2						
Totals	292	126	84	71	68	108	2	3

The PRESIDENT. On this ballot, 754 votes were cast. Necessary to a choice, 378. James G. Blaine received 292 votes; Benjamin H.

Bristow, 126; Oliver P. Morton, 108 votes; Roscoe Conkling, 84 votes; John F. Hartranft, 71 votes; Rutherford B. Hayes, 68 votes; Elihu B. Washburne, 3 votes; William A. Wheeler, 2 votes. No one having received a majority of all the votes, there is no nomination. Another ballot will be taken, and the clerk will call the roll.

FIFTH BALLOT.

The secretary called the roll of states, the ballot resulting as follows:

States.	Blaine.	Bristow.	Conkling.	Hartranft.	Hayes.	Morton.	Wheeler.	Washburne.
Alabama	16	4	....	....	....	....	....	....
Arkansas	1	....	....	....	....	11	....	....
California	6	....	3	....	3	....	....	....
Colorado	6	....	....	....	....	....	....	....
Connecticut	2	8	....	....	2	....	....	....
Delaware	6	....	....	....	....	....	....	....
Florida	2	....	....	3	....	3	....	....
Georgia	8	2	6	....	....	5	....	1
Illinois	33	5	....	....	3	....	....	1
Indiana	....	....	....	....	....	30	....	....
Iowa	21	....	1	....	....	....	....	....
Kansas	10	....	....	....	....	....	....	....
Kentucky	....	24	....	....	....	....	....	....
Louisiana	5	....	....	....	....	11	....	....
Maine	14	....	....	....	....	....	....	....
Maryland	16	....	....	....	....	....	....	....
Massachusetts	5	19	....	....	....	....	2	....
Michigan	....	....	....	....	22	....	....	....
Minnesota	9	....	....	....	....	....	....	1
Mississippi	...	8	2	....	2	4	....	....
Missouri	20	3	....	....	2	5	....	....
Nebraska	6	....	....	....	....	....	....	....
Nevada	....	1	2	2	1	....	....	....
New Hampshire	7	3	....	....	....	....	....	....
New Jersey	12	....	....	....	6	....	....	....
New York	....	2	68	....	....	....	....	....
North Carolina	....	....	....	6	12	1	....	....
Ohio	....	....	....	....	44	....	....	....
Oregon	6	....	....	....	....	....	....	....
Pennsylvania	5	....	....	53	....	....	....	....
Rhode Island	2	6	....	....	....	....	....	....
South Carolina	5	3	....	....	1	5	....	....
Tennessee	7	10	....	....	....	7	....	....
Texas	3	3	....	1	1	8	....	....
Vermont	....	8	....	....	2	....	....	....
Virginia	16	....	....	3	....	3	....	....

FIFTH BALLOT—*continued.*

STATES.	Blaine.	Bristow.	Conkling.	Hartranft.	Hayes.	Morton.	Wheeler.	Washbarne.
West Virginia	7	....	....	1	2	....	....	....
Wisconsin	16	3	....	....	....	1	....	....
Arizona	2	....	....	....	....	....	....	....
Dakota	2	....	....	....	....	....	....	....
District of Columbia	1	....	....	....	....	1	....	....
Idaho	2	....	....	....	....	....	....	....
Montana	1	....	....	....	1	....	....	....
New Mexico	2	....	....	....	....	....	....	....
Utah	2	....	....	....	....	....	....	....
Washington	2	....	....	....	....	....	....	....
Wyoming	....	2	....	....	....	....	....	....
Totals	286	114	82	69	104	95	2	3

When Michigan was reached, Mr. W. A. Howard said,—

Mr. President: There is a man in this section of the country who has beaten in succession three Democratic candidates for President in his own state, and we want to give him a chance to beat another Democratic candidate for the Presidency in the broader field of the United States. Michigan therefore casts her twenty-two votes for Rutherford B. Hayes, of Ohio.

The president *pro tem.* (Mr. S. L. Woodford) announced the result of the ballot as follows:

Whole number of votes cast 755, one not voting. Of these, James G. Blaine has received 286; Benjamin H. Bristow, 114; Rutherford B. Hayes, 104; Oliver P. Morton, 95; Roscoe Conkling, 82; John F. Hartranft, 69; Elihu B. Washburne, 3; William A. Wheeler, 2. No choice. What is the pleasure of the convention? The clerk will proceed with the call of the roll by states.

When Alabama was called, there was no response.

The PRESIDENT. Shall time be given the Alabama delegation for consultation? [Cries of "Object."] It is the right of delegations to consult.

Mr. MADDEN, of New York. I think it is about time that the delegations from the different large states should retire to consult. Our delegation is so large and so spread out that it is impossible for us to consult.

The PRESIDENT. Does the gentleman move for a recess?

Mr. MADDEN. If the delegations have not a chance to consult here, they ought to be allowed to retire.

The PRESIDENT. What motion does the gentleman make?

Mr. MADDEN. The chair announced that the delegations should have time to consult before announcing their vote. I move for a recess.

Mr. CUMBACK. A point of order. The roll is calling now.

Mr. MADDEN. I move we take a recess for one hour.

Mr. CUMBACK. The roll is calling, and the motion is out of order.

The PRESIDENT. The point of order is made, that the roll-call having been commenced, a motion for an adjournment or recess is not in order. The chair decides that the point is well taken.

SIXTH BALLOT.

The roll-call was concluded as follows:

STATES.	Blaine.	Morton.	Conkling.	Bristow.	Hayes.	Hartranft.	Washburne.	Wheeler.
Alabama	15	....	....	4	1	....	....	....
Arkansas	1	11	....	....	....	....	....	....
California	6	....	2	....	4	....	....	....
Colorado	6	....	....	....	....	....	....	....
Connecticut	2	....	....	7	3	....	....	....
Delaware	6	....	....	....	....	....	....	....
Florida	4	4	....	....	....	....	....	....
Georgia	9	4	6	2	....	....	1	....
Illinois	32	....	....	5	3	....	2	....
Indiana	....	30	....	....	....	....	....	....
Iowa	21	....	....	....	1	....	....	....
Kansas	10	....	....	....	....	....	....	....
Kentucky	....	....	....	24	....	....	....	....
Louisiana	6	10	....	....	....	....	....	....
Maine	14	....	....	....	....	....	....	....
Maryland	16	....	....	....	....	....	....	....
Massachusetts	5	....	....	19	....	....	....	2
Michigan	....	....	....	....	22	....	....	....
Minnesota	9	....	....	....	....	....	1	....
Mississippi	1	5	2	4	4	....	....	....
Missouri	18	7	....	3	2	....	....	....
Nebraska	6	....	....	....	....	....	....	....
Nevada	....	....	2	2	1	1	....	....
New Hampshire	7	....	....	3	....	....	....	....
New Jersey	12	....	....	....	6	....	....	....
New York	....	....	68	2	....	....	....	....
North Carolina	12	1	....	....	1	5	....	....
Ohio	....	....	....	....	44	....	....	....
Oregon	6	....	....	....	....	....	....	....
Pennsylvania	14	....	....	....	....	44	....	....
Rhode Island	2	....	....	6	....	....	....	....
South Carolina	10	2	....	1	1	....	....	....
Texas	2	4	1	1	7	....	....	....
Tennessee	7	1	....	12	4	....	....	....
Vermont	....	....	....	8	2	....	....	....
Virginia	13	4	....	3	2	....	....	....
West Virginia	6	....	....	....	4	....	....	....

SIXTH BALLOT—*continued.*

STATES.	Blaine.	Morton.	Conkling.	Bristow.	Hayes.	Hartranft.	Washburne.	Wheeler.
Wisconsin	16	1	....	3	....	....	....	....
Arizona	2	....	....	....	....	....	....	....
Dakota	2	....	....	....	....	....	....	....
Idaho	2	....	....	....	....	....	....	....
Montana	1	....	....	....	1	....	....	....
New Mexico	2	....	....	....	....	....	....	....
Utah	2	....	....	....	....	....	....	....
District of Columbia	1	1	....	....	....	....	....	....
Washington	2	....	....	....	....	....	....	....
Wyoming	....	....	....	2	....	....	....	....
Totals	308	85	81	111	113	50	4	2

The president *pro tem.* (Mr. Woodford) announced the result of the ballot:

Total vote cast 754, two not voting. Of these, Mr. Blaine has received 308; Hayes, 113; Bristow, 111; Morton, 85; Conkling, 81; Hartranft, 50; Washburne, 4; Wheeler, 2. No choice.

SEVENTH BALLOT.

The secretary proceeded to call the roll.

A DELEGATE from Rhode Island. I move that we take a recess of ten minutes.

The PRESIDENT. The point of order is made that the calling of the roll having been commenced, the motion for a recess is not in order.

Mr. EDICK. I ask permission for the New York delegation to withdraw.

The PRESIDENT. If the New York delegation desires to withdraw, they can do so on their own motion, without addressing the chair.

Colorado having been called,—

Mr. ROGERS, of New York. I ask unanimous consent that the call be suspended until the delegations which desire to do so can retire and return.

Cries of "No!" "No!" and "Yes!" "Yes!"

The PRESIDENT. It requires unanimous consent to suspend the calling of the roll.

Several delegates made the motion.

Mr. AMBLER of Ohio. I move that a recess be taken for fifteen minutes, to allow the delegations time to consult.

The PRESIDENT. It is not in order to make that motion pending the roll-call.

Mr. AMBLER. I move to suspend the rules.

The PRESIDENT. Neither that motion nor any other is in order while the roll is being called.

Indiana having been called, Mr. Cumback ascended the platform and said,—

Mr. President and Gentlemen of the Convention: A very unpleasant duty is now imposed upon me, as chairman of the Indiana delegation, in withdrawing from the further consideration of this convention the name of the great statesman of Indiana. I express my own deep regret as well as that of every delegate from Indiana, and every alternate, and every citizen of Indiana who belongs to the Republican party. When I say he stands in the senate of the United States the peer of the noblest and best, I utter a truth that will not be disputed by any Republican in the United States of America. But we feel that the time has come for us not to ask any longer that our friends shall stand by us. We thank them for the noble support they have given us in this convention; and, in withdrawing his name, Indiana casts twenty-five votes for Rutherford B. Hayes, and five votes for Benjamin H. Bristow, of Kentucky.

When Kentucky was called, Mr. Harlan spoke as follows:

Mr. President and Gentlemen of the Convention: The Republicans of the state of Kentucky feel deeply grateful for the very cordial support which our distinguished fellow-citizen, Colonel Bristow, has received from the delegates of various states, both North and South. We feel especially grateful to those gallant men of Massachusetts and Vermont, and other states of New England, who, when it was circulated from one end of this land to the other that Benjamin H. Bristow was not to be President because he was born and reared in the South, came and said they did not believe it, but have done him and us the honor to say they believed that Bristow was true to the Republican party, and was to be trusted. Without detaining you any longer, I have come upon this stand for the purpose of withdrawing the name of Benjamin H. Bristow, and casting the entire vote of Kentucky for Rutherford B. Hayes.

Mr. Cumback (returning to the platform),—

Mr. President: As the name of Benjamin H. Bristow has been withdrawn, I am instructed to cast the other five votes from Indiana for Rutherford B. Hayes.

Mr. INGERSOLL, of Illinois. "I hold that under the Fourth Rule this change cannot be made. The provision of the rule is, that "when any state has announced its vote, it shall so stand, unless in case of numerical error."

Mr. EDICK, of New York. I raised a similar question some time ago, and it was ruled out of order. We insist on the same ruling now.

The PRESIDENT. A question of order is always in order. This is simply a question of order referring to the immediate proposition of the delegate from Indiana to change the vote.

Mr. EDICK. If the chairman remembers, on a similar proposition to change a vote, I was ruled out of order.

The PRESIDENT. To change a vote is a matter of the highest privilege, and is always in order. The gentleman from Illinois will make his point of order.

Mr. INGERSOLL. My point is, that it is against the rule to make a change of vote while the roll-call is proceeding.

The PRESIDENT. The delegate from Indiana rises to change the vote of his delegation, upon which the delegate from Illinois rises to a point of order, that under the Fourth Rule the change cannot be made. The provision of the rule is, that when any state has announced its vote, it shall so stand. The chair decides the point well taken.

When the state of New York was called, Mr. T. M. Pomeroy ascended the platform and said,—

To indicate that the state of New York is in favor of unity and victory, she casts sixty-one votes for Rutherford B. Hayes, and nine votes for James G. Blaine.

When Pennsylvania was called, Mr. J. D. Cameron said,—

I am instructed to withdraw the name of John F. Hartranft, and to cast twenty-eight votes for Rutherford B. Hayes, and thirty for James G. Blaine.

The ballot was concluded as follows:

STATES.	Blaine.	Bristow.	Hayes.
Alabama	17	3	....
Arkansas	11	....	1
California	6	....	6
Colorado	6	....	....
Connecticut	2	7	3
Delaware	6	....	....
Florida	8	....	....
Georgia	14	1	7
Illinois	35	5	2
Indiana	....	5	25
Iowa	22	....	....
Kansas	10	....	....
Kentucky	....	....	24
Louisiana	14	....	2
Maine	14	....	....
Maryland	16	....	....
Massachusetts	5	....	21
Michigan	....	....	22
Minnesota	9	....	1
Mississippi	....	....	16
Missouri	20	....	10
Nebraska	6	....	....
Nevada	....	....	6
New Hampshire	7	....	3

SEVENTH BALLOT—*continued.*

STATES.	Blaine.	Bristow.	Hayes.
New Jersey	12	....	6
New York	9	....	61
North Carolina	....	....	20
Ohio	....	....	44
Oregon	6	....	....
Pennsylvania	30	....	28
Rhode Island	2	....	6
South Carolina	7	....	7
Tennessee	6	....	18
Texas	1	....	15
Vermont	....	....	10
Virginia	14	....	8
West Virginia	6	....	4
Wisconsin	16	....	4
Arizona	2	....	....
Dakota	2	....	....
Idaho	2	....	....
Montana	....	....	2
New Mexico	2	....	....
Utah	2	....	....
District of Columbia	2	....	....
Washington	2	....	....
Wyoming	....	....	2
Totals	351	21	384

The president said,—

Gentlemen of the Convention: Rutherford B. Hayes, of the state of Ohio, having received a majority of all the votes cast, is hereby declared to be the nominee of this convention for the office of President of the United States; and the question is, Shall this nomination be made unanimous?

Mr. William P. Frye, of Maine, took the platform, and said:

Mr. President: I dare say that this immense and enthusiastic convention will pardon me if I say just one word of kindness and of thanks to the glorious supporters that our candidate, Mr. Blaine, has had here. No words of mine can express the thanks that Maine gives to you men who have stood by him as you have here to-day. God bless you forever and ever. Now, gentlemen, we recognize the fact that this convention in its wisdom has selected Governor Hayes as the standard-bearer in this next great contest for liberty, for justice, for humanity, and for civilization, and the state of Maine accepts and indorses fully and completely the choice which the convention has made. Our gallant chieftain, James G. Blaine, in September next, shall take the field in the state of Maine for the man you have selected, and we will sweep the state of Maine for Hayes by 20,000. And then, when we have finished Maine, we will go forward, under the leadership of Blaine, into the commonwealth of Massachusetts, and we will sweep her, with the help of her able men, by 60,000 majority.

Gentlemen, I will close by seconding the motion which has been made, that the nomination of Rutherford B. Hayes be made unanimous.

The motion was then carried, amid great acclamations.

Mr. J. F. LEWIS, of Virginia. I move that the chairman appoint a committee to wait upon Governor Hayes, and inform him of his unanimous nomination by this convention.

The PRESIDENT. How many?

Mr. LEWIS. Five.

The chair put the motion, and it was carried.

VICE-PRESIDENT.

The nomination of a Vice-President being in order,—

Mr. POLAND, of Vermont. I nominate the Hon. William A. Wheeler, of New York, on behalf of Vermont, for the Vice-Presidency.

Mr. E. R. Hoar, of Massachusetts, also nominated Marshall Jewell, of Connecticut, for that position.

Mr. T. C. Platt, of New York, nominated Stewart L. Woodford, of New York.

A member of the Kansas delegation here moved that the states be called alphabetically, each to nominate its candidate for the office of Vice-President. The motion was agreed to.

On the call of Kentucky, Mr. Harlan responded, and said,—

Mr. President and Gentlemen of the Convention: I am directed, by the unanimous vote of the Kentucky delegation in this convention, to present for the high office of Vice-President of the United States that distinguished Republican leader and statesman, General Joseph R. Hawley, of the state of Connecticut.

Mr. Seldon, of Mississippi, said, when his state was called,—

Mr. Chairman and Gentlemen of the Convention: I am requested by the Mississippi delegation to rise and second the nomination of one whom we believe will add strength and dignity to our ticket, especially in the South. It is very often the custom of conventions to pay but small attention to the nomination of the second man upon the ticket; but we have learned by bitter experience in our country that it is as important that a good sound man should be placed upon the second place as upon the first. It is my pleasure, coming away from the Gulf as we do, to second the nomination of one living near the Lakes; and it is with pride and pleasure that Mississippi seconds the nomination of Stewart L. Woodford.

Mr. PITNEY, of New Jersey. *Mr. Chairman and Gentlemen of the Convention:* I am directed, by the unanimous vote of the delegation from New Jersey, to present to this convention a name for the candidacy for the office of Vice-President of the United States. The name that I present is that of a man of spotless, untarnished reputation and character; a man whom the breath of slander has never dared to assail; one who, like Cæsar's wife, is in all respects above and beyond suspicion; a man who, during the dark days of the rebellion, devoted his whole time and energies in aiding the executive of his state in the great work of enlisting and equipping and forwarding to the front volunteers to aid in suppressing the rebellion; a man who has always served his state with great credit and ability, and, in a long course in the United States senate, has shown himself the peer of those who have stood by him there; a man who, in all times and in all circumstances, has proved himself to be a true Republican and a great statesman. The name I present is that of Frederick Theodore Frelinghuysen, of New Jersey.

Mr. James, of New York, briefly seconded the nomination of Mr. Wheeler for the office of Vice-President; and was followed by Mr. Russell, of Texas, who said:

Fellow-Citizens of the Convention: It is with great pleasure that I rise in this convention to make the nomination of that statesman and patriot from Connecticut—Marshall Jewell. There are other great names mentioned in connection with this position, fellow-citizens; but it is not disparaging to those other names to say that his is superior to any of them in all the qualities requisite to the second executive office of this nation. He is not unknown to the people of the United States. His dignity and cultured bearing at the court of the czar of Russia bears evidence of the highest type of American chivalry and lofty statesmanship. He has reformed the postal service of this country, and his mark is expressed all along the pathway he has made. He has held an honorable position in the cabinet of President Grant.

Mr. Wheeler's nomination having been seconded by the Pennsylvania delegation, the secretary proceeded to call the roll of states.

MR. WOODFORD WITHDRAWS.

When New York was called, Mr. Woodford took the platform and said:

Mr. Chairman and Gentlemen of the Convention: It has always been my belief that no citizen should ask office, or refuse to serve the public when called on to do so, provided his business and personal obligations are such as to justify the assumption of official duty.

But to-day I am fortunately freed from all such decision. The vote of my delegation has been polled. Without any suggestion of mine, my name was mentioned. The majority of my delegation do not desire to present my name. In this I am certain they show their great good sense, and I am grateful for the privilege of working in the ranks of the party. Let me heartily assure you that all that lies in my power, from now to the ratification by the people of the work you do this day, will be most cordially done. Permit me to withdraw my name from the nomination.

The large number of votes cast for Mr. Wheeler plainly indicated that he was the choice of the convention; and, after the vote of South Carolina, which made 366 votes for Mr. Wheeler, Mr. Kellogg, of Connecticut, withdrew the name of Marshall Jewell, and moved that the rules be suspended, and that William A. Wheeler, of New York, be nominated by acclamation.

The motion was carried, and Mr. Wheeler declared the nominee for Vice-President.

As far as the ballot proceeded, it stood as follows:

STATES.	Wheeler.	Woodford.	Jewell.	Hawley.	Frelinghuysen.
Alabama	17	....	3	....	....
Arkansas	5	5	....	....	2
California	....	12	....	....	....
Colorado	6	....	....	....	....
Connecticut	1	....	11	....	....
Delaware	6	....	....	....	....
Florida	....	8	....	....	....
Georgia	....	....	22	....	....
Illinois	42	....	....	....	....
Indiana	2	20	7	1	....
Iowa	22	....	....	....	....
Kansas	5	2	....	....	3
Kentucky	....	....	....	24	....
Louisiana	8	2	....	....	6
Maine	14	....	....	....	....
Maryland	....	....	16	....	....
Massachusetts	25	....	1	....	....
Michigan	22	....	....	....	....
Minnesota	10	....	....	....	....
Mississippi	1	15	....	....	....
Missouri	4	....	26	....	....
Nebraska	6	....	....	....	....
Nevada	....	6	....	....	....
New Hampshire	10	....	....	....	....
New Jersey	....	....	....	....	18
New York	70	....	....	....	....
North Carolina	20	....	....	....	....
Ohio	44	....	....	....	....
Oregon	6	....	....	....	....
Pennsylvania	....	....	....	....	58
Rhode Island	8	....	....	....	....
South Carolina	12	....	....	....	2

Mr. Lewis, of Virginia, offered a resolution, returning thanks to the president of the convention for the able and impartial manner in which he had discharged his arduous duties. The resolution was amended so as to include the secretaries, sergeant-at-arms, and other officers of the convention, and the citizens of Cincinnati for their hospitality and kindness.

The resolution was unanimously adopted.

Mr. Benjamin Eggleston, of Cincinnati, then returned thanks to the convention, on behalf of the Republicans of Ohio, for the nominating of Governor Rutherford B. Hayes for President.

AN ADDITION TO THE PLATFORM.

Mr. Smith, of New York, secretary of the committee on resolutions, offered the following, to be added to the platform:

We present as our candidates for President and Vice-President of the United States two distinguished statesmen, of eminent ability and character, and conspicuously fitted for those high offices, and we confidently appeal to the American people to intrust the administration of their public affairs to Rutherford B. Hayes and William A. Wheeler.

The resolution was adopted.

REPUBLICAN NATIONAL COMMITTEE.

The convention then proceeded to appoint members of the Republican National Committee, as follows:

Alabama	Jere Haralson.
Arkansas	Powell Clayton.
California	Geo. C. Gorham.
Colorado	Samuel H. Elbert.
Connecticut	Marshall Jewell.
Delaware	Samuel M. Harrington.
Florida	Wm. J. Purman.
Georgia	James G. Deveaux.
Illinois	James P. Root.
Indiana	Will Cumback.
Iowa	John Y. Stone.
Kansas	John A. Martin.
Kentucky	W. C. Goodloe.
Louisiana	P. B. S. Pinchback.
Maine	Wm. P. Frye.
Maryland	Chas. C. Fulton.
Massachusetts	John M. Forbes.
Michigan	Z. Chandler.
Minnesota	John T. Averill.
Mississippi	G. M. Buchanan.
Missouri	Chauncey I. Filley.
Nebraska	L. W. Osborn.
Nevada	John P. Jones.
New Hampshire	Wm. E. Chandler.
New Jersey	Geo. A. Halsey.
New York	A. B. Cornell.
North Carolina	Thos. B. Keogh.
Ohio	A. T. Wikoff.
Oregon	H. W. Scott.
Pennsylvania	Wm. H. Kemble.
Rhode Island	L. W. Aldridge.
South Carolina	John J. Patterson.
Tennessee	Wm. Rule.
Texas	E. J. Davis.
Vermont	M. S. Colburn.
Virginia	J. B. Sener.
West Virginia	John W. Mason.
Wisconsin	Elihu Enos.
Arizona	R. C. McCormick.
Dakota	Newton Edmunds.
Idaho	Thomas Donaldson.
Montana	Alex. H. Beattie.
New Mexico	Stephen B. Elkins.
Utah	John R. McBride.
District of Columbia	S. J. Bowen.
Washington	Orange Jacobs.
Wyoming	Jos. M. Carey.

The president read the following dispatch from Hon. James G. Blaine:

WASHINGTON, D. C.

To the Hon. Eugene Hale:

I hope you will find it convenient to stop in Columbus and bear my congratulations and sincere personal respects and regards to Governor Hayes. JAMES G. BLAINE.

Mr. W. A. Howard moved that a committee of one from each state be appointed by the chair, to wait on the candidates and give them formal notice of their nomination. This was agreed to; and the chairman stated that he would make the appointments in the evening at his hotel, which he did, as appears below.

This completed the work of the convention, and thereupon it adjourned.

In pursuance of authority conferred upon the undersigned by the Republican National Convention, he has appointed the following named persons, being one from each state and territory, as a committee, with the president of the convention, to inform Governor Hayes of his nomination for the office of President of the United States, and to request his acceptance of it, and of the resolutions adopted by the convention:

Alabama.........Willard Warner.
Arkansas.........Powell Clayton.
California........Alex. G. Abell.
Colorado...........J. B. Chaffee.
Connecticut...Joseph R. Hawley.
Delaware..........J. R. Lofland.
Florida...........S. B. Conover.
Georgia..........B. Chamberlain.
Illinois.........George S. Bangs.
Indiana..........Will Cumback.
Iowa...............Hiram Price.
Kansas...............J. P. Lowe.
Kentucky....William C. Goodloe.
Louisiana..........S. B. Packard.
Maine.............Eugene Hale.
Maryland...........W. G. Tuck.
Massachusetts........E. R. Hoar.
Michigan.....William A. Howard.
Minnesota....Alexander Ramsey.
Mississippi..........B. K. Bruce.
Missouri......Augustus St. Gem.
Nebraska..........N. R. Pinney.
Nevada..............J. P. Jones.
New Hampshire.....E. A. Straw.
New Jersey........W. A. Newell.
New York.........J. W. Husted.
North Carolina...Thomas Powers.
Ohio..............B. Eggleston.
Oregon..........J. C. Tolman.
Pennsylvania.....J. D. Cameron.
Rhode Island,...C. C. Van Zandt.
South Carolina....Jos. H. Rainey.
Tennessee..Jacob M. Thornberg.
Texas.........Edmund J. Davis.
Vermont.........Luke P. Poland.
Virginia..........John F. Lewis.
West Virginia..Joseph W. Davis.
Wisconsin......Elisha W. Keyes.
Arizona........R. C. McCormick.
Dakota.......Alexander Hughes.
District of Columbia..S. J. Bowen.
Idaho.........D. W. Thompson.
Montana..........W. F. Sanders.
New Mexico........S. B. Axtell.
Utah.........James B. McKean.
Washington......Orange Jacobs.
Wyoming...........J. M. Carey.

The committee will leave for Columbus at 1 : 30 P. M. to-day.

EDWARD McPHERSON,
President of the National Convention.

CINCINNATI, Ohio, June 17, 1876.

In accordance with the above notice, the committee, appointed to convey to Governor Hayes the official notification of his nomination, proceeded to Columbus from Cincinnati, headed by Mr. McPherson, the president of the convention. They proceeded to the executive chamber in the state house at 9 o'clock, where Governor Hayes received them. Mr. McPherson spoke as follows:

Governor Hayes: We have been deputed by the national convention of the Republican party, held at Cincinnati on the 14th of the present month, to inform you officially that you have been unanimously nominated by that convention for the office of President of the United States. The manner in which that action was taken, and the response to it from every portion of the country, attest the strength of the popular confidence in you, and the belief that your administration will be wise, courageous, and just. We say, sir, your administration, for we believe the people will confirm the action of the convention, and thus save the country from the control of the men and the operation of the principles and policy of the Democratic party. We have also been directed to ask your attention to the summary of Republican doctrine contained in the platform adopted by the convention; and discharging this agreeable duty we find cause for congratulation. In the harmonious action of the convention and the hearty response given by the people, we see the promise of assured success. Ohio, we know, trusts and honors you. Henceforth you belong to the whole country. Under circumstances so auspicious, we trust you will indicate your acceptance of the nomination.

Governor Hayes replied:

Sir: I have only to say, in response to your information, that I accept the nomination. Perhaps at the present time it would be improper for me to say more than this, although even now I should be glad to give some expression to the profound gratitude I feel for the confidence reposed in me by yourselves and those for whom you act. At a future time I shall take occasion to present my acceptance in writing, with my views upon the platform.

Subsequently, the following letter of acceptance was received from Governor Hayes:

COLUMBUS, Ohio, July 8, 1876.

Hon. Edward McPherson, Hon. William A. Howard, Hon. Joseph H. Rainey, and others, Committee of the Republican National Convention:

GENTLEMEN: In reply to your official communication of June 17, by which I am informed of my nomination for the office of President of the United States by the Republican National Convention at Cincinnati, I accept the nomination with gratitude, hoping that, under Providence, I shall be able, if elected, to execute the duties of the high office as a trust for the benefit of all the people.

I do not deem it necessary to enter upon any extended examination of the declaration of principles made by the convention. The resolutions are in accord with my views, and I heartily concur in the principles they announce. In several of the resolutions, however, questions are considered which are of such importance that I deem it proper briefly to express my convictions in regard to them. The fifth resolution adopted by the convention is of paramount interest. More than forty years ago a system of making appointments to office grew up, based upon the maxim "To the victors belong the spoils." The old rule, the true rule, that honesty, capacity, and fidelity constitute the only real qualifications for office, and that there is no other claim, gave place to the idea that party services were to be chiefly considered. All parties, in practice, have adopted this system. It has been essentially modified since its first introduction; it has not, however, been improved. At first, the President, either directly or through the heads of departments, made all the appointments. But gradually the appointing power, in many cases, passed into the control of members of congress. The offices in these cases have become not merely rewards for party services, but rewards for services to party leaders. This system destroys the independence of the separate departments of the government. It tends directly to extravagance and official incapacity; it is a temptation to dishonesty; it hinders and impairs that careful supervision and strict accountability by which alone faithful and efficient public service can be secured; it obstructs the prompt removal and sure punishment of the unworthy; in every way it degrades the civil service and the character of the government. It is felt, I am confident, by a large majority of the members of congress, to be an intolerable burden and an unwarrantable hindrance to the proper discharge of their legitimate duties. It ought to be abolished. The reform should be thorough, radical, and complete. We should return to the principles and practice of the founders of the government, supplying by legislation, when needed, that which was formerly the established custom. They neither expected nor desired from the public officers any partisan service. They meant that public officers should give their whole service to the government and to the people. They meant that the officer should be secure in his tenure as long as his personal character remained untarnished, and the performance of his duties satisfactory. If elected, I shall conduct the administration of the government upon these principles, and all constitutional powers vested in the executive will be employed to establish this reform.

The declaration of principles by the Cincinnati convention makes no announcement in favor of a single Presidential term. I do not assume to add to that declaration, but, believing that the restoration of the civil service to the system established by Washington, and followed by the early Presidents, can be best accomplished by an executive who is under no temptation to use the patronage of his office to promote his own reëlection, I desire to perform what I regard as a duty in stating now my inflexible purpose, if elected, not to be a candidate for election to a second term.

On the currency question I have frequently expressed my views in public, and I stand by my record on this subject. I regard all the laws of the United States relating to the payment of the public indebtedness, the legal tender notes included, as constituting a pledge and moral obligation of the government which must in good faith be kept. It is my conviction that the feeling of uncertainty, inseparable from an irredeemable paper currency, with its fluctuations of value, is one of the great obstacles to a revival of confidence and business, and to a return of prosperity. That uncertainty can be ended in but one way,—the resumption of specie payments. But the longer the instability of our money system is permitted to continue, the greater will be the injury inflicted upon our economical interests, and all classes of society. If elected, I shall approve every appropriate measure to accomplish the desired end, and shall oppose any step backward.

The resolution with respect to the public school system is one which should receive the hearty support of the American people. Agitation upon this subject is to be apprehended, until by constitutional amendment the schools are placed beyond all danger of sectarian control or interference. The Republican party is pledged to secure such an amendment.

The resolution of the convention on the subject of the permanent pacification of the country, and the complete protection of all its citizens in the free enjoyment of all of their constitutional rights, is timely and of great importance. The condition of the Southern states attracts the attention and commands the sympathy of the people of the whole Union. In their progressive recovery from the effects of the war, their first necessity is an intelligent and honest administration of government, which will protect all classes of citizens in their official and private rights. What the South most needs is "peace," and peace depends upon the supremacy of the law. There can be no enduring peace if the constitutional rights of any portion of the people are habitually disregarded. A division of political parties resting merely upon sectional lines is always unfortunate, and may be disastrous. The welfare of the South, alike with that of every other part of this country, depends upon the attractions it can offer to labor and immigration, and to capital. But laborers will not go, and capital will not be ventured, where the constitution and the laws are set at defiance, and distraction, apprehension, and alarm take the place of peace-loving and law-abiding social life. All parts of the constitution are sacred, and must be sacredly observed,—the parts that are new, no less than the parts that are old. The moral and national prosperity of the Southern states can be most effectually advanced by a hearty and generous recognition of the rights of all by all,—a recognition without reserve or exception. With such a recognition fully accorded, it will be practicable to promote, by the influence of all legitimate agencies of the general government, the efforts of the people of those states to obtain for themselves the blessings of honest and capable local government. If elected, I shall consider it not only my duty, but it will be my ardent desire, to labor for the attainment of this end. Let me assure my countrymen of the Southern states that if I shall be charged with the duty of organizing an administration, it will be one which will regard and cherish their truest interests,—the interests of the white and of the colored people both, and equally; and which will put forth its best efforts in behalf of a civil policy which will wipe out forever the distinction between North and South in our common country.

With a civil service organized upon a system which will secure purity, experience, efficiency, and economy, a strict regard for the public welfare solely in appointments, and the speedy, thorough, and unsparing prosecution and punishment of all public officers who betray official trusts; with a sound currency; with education, unsectarian and free to all; with simplicity and frugality in public and private affairs; and with a fraternal spirit of harmony pervading the people of all sections and classes, we may reasonably hope that the second century of our existence as a nation will, by the blessing of God, be preëminent as an era of good feeling, and a period of progress, prosperity, and happiness.

Very respectfully, your fellow-citizen,

R. B. HAYES.

MR. WHEELER'S LETTER OF ACCEPTANCE.

MALONE, July 15, 1876.

Hon. Edward McPherson, and others, of the Committee of the Republican National Convention:

GENTLEMEN: I received, on the 6th instant, your communication advising me that I had been unanimously nominated by the national convention of the Republican party, held at Cincinnati on the 14th ultimo, for the office of Vice-President of the United States, and requesting my acceptance of the same, and asking my attention to the summary of Republican doctrines contained in the platform adopted by the convention.

A nomination made with such unanimity implies a confidence on the part of the convention which inspires my profound gratitude. It is accepted with a sense of the responsibility which may follow. If elected, I shall endeavor to perform the duties of the office in the fear of the Supreme Ruler, and in the interest of the whole country.

To the summary of doctrines enunciated by the convention I give my cordial assent. The Republican party has intrenched in the organic law of our land the doctrine that liberty is the supreme, unchangeable law for every foot of American soil. It is the mission of that party to give full effect to this principle by "securing to every American citizen complete liberty and exact equality in the exercise of all civil, political, and public rights." This will be accomplished only when the American citizen, without regard to color, shall wear this panoply of citizenship as fully and as securely in the cane-brakes of Louisiana as on the banks of the St. Lawrence.

Upon the question of our Southern relations, my views were recently expressed as a member of the committee of the United States house of representatives upon Southern affairs. These views remain unchanged, and were thus expressed: We of the North delude ourselves in expecting that the masses of the South, so far behind in many of the attributes of enlightened improvement and civilization, are, in the brief period of ten or fifteen years, to be transformed into our model Northern communities. That can only come through a long course of patient waiting to which no one can now set certain bounds.

There will be a good deal of unavoidable friction which will call for forbearance, and which will have to be relieved by the temperate, fostering care of the government. One of the most potent if not indispensable agencies in this direction will be the devising of some system to aid in the education of the masses. The fact that there are whole counties in Louisiana in which there is not a solitary school-house is full of suggestion. We compelled these people to remain in the Union, and now duty and interest demand that we leave no just means untried to make them good, loyal citizens.

How to diminish the friction, how to stimulate the elevation of this portion of the country, are problems addressing themselves to our best and wisest statesmanship. The foundation for these efforts must be laid in satisfying the Southern people that they are to have equal, exact justice accorded to them. Give them to the fullest extent every blessing which the government confers upon the most favored. Give them no just cause for complaint, and then hold them, by every necessary means, to an exact, rigid observance of all their duties and obligations, under the constitution and its amendments, to secure to all within their borders manhood and citizenship, with every right thereto belonging.

The just obligations to public creditors created when the government was in the throes of threatened dissolution, and as an indispensable condition of its salvation, guaranteed by the lives and blood of thousands of its brave defenders, are to be kept with religious faith, as are all the pledges subsidiary thereto and confirmatory thereof.

In my judgment, the pledge of congress of Jan. 14, 1875, for the redemption of the notes of the United States in coin, is the plighted faith of the nation; and national honor, simple honesty, and justice to the people whose permanent welfare and prosperity are dependent upon true money as the basis of their pecuniary transactions, all demand the scrupulous observance of this pledge, and it is the duty of congress to supplement it with such legislation as shall be necessary for its strict fulfilment.

In our system of government, intelligence must give safety and value to the ballot;—hence the common schools of the land should be preserved in all their vigor, while in accordance with the spirit of the constitution, they and all their endowments should be secured by every possible and proper guaranty against every form of sectarian influence or control.

There should be the strictest economy in expenditures of government consistent with its effective administration, and all unnecessary offices should be abolished. Offices should be conferred only upon the basis of high character and particular fitness, and should be administered only as public trusts, and not for private advantage.

The foregoing are chief among the cardinal principles of the Republican party, and to carry them into full, practical effect is the work it now has in hand. To the completion of its great mission we address ourselves in hope and confidence, cheered and stimulated by the recollection of its past achievements,—remembering that, under God, it is to that party that we are indebted in this centennial year of our existence for a preserved, unbroken Union; for the fact that there is no master or slave throughout our broad domains; and that emancipated millions look upon the ensign of the republic as the symbol of the fulfilled declaration that all men are created free and equal, and the guaranty of their own equality, under the law, with the most highly favored citizen of the land.

To the intelligence and conscience of all who desire good government, good-will, good money, and universal prosperity, the Republican party, not unmindful of the imperfection and shortcomings of human organizations, yet with the honest purposes of its masses promptly to retrieve all errors and to summarily punish all offenders against the laws of the country, confidently submits its claims for the continued support of the American people.

Respectfully,

WILLIAM A. WHEELER.

APPENDIX.

ROLL OF

DELEGATES AND ALTERNATES

TO THE

Republican National Convention,

HELD AT

CINCINNATI, OHIO, JUNE 14, 15, & 16, 1876,

WITH POST-OFFICE ADDRESS OF EACH,

TOGETHER WITH A STATEMENT OF NUMBER OF DELEGATES TO WHICH EACH STATE WAS ENTITLED; NAMES OF OFFICERS OF THE NATIONAL, CONGRESSIONAL, AND STATE COMMITTEES; AND THE CALLS AND PLATFORMS OF ALL THE REPUBLICAN NATIONAL CONVENTIONS SINCE 1856.

Names and Post-Office Address of Delegates and Alternates to the Republican National Convention of 1876.

ALABAMA.

AT LARGE.

DELEGATES.	ALTERNATES.
Jeremiah Haralson	Janus Q. Smith
Willard Warner	Charles W. Buckley
Samuel F. Rice	George M. Duskin
Wm. H. Smith	George F. Sommerville

DISTRICTS.

DELEGATES.	ALTERNATES.
1—Morris D. Wickersham	
Frank H. Threatt	
2—Robert A. Knox	Patrick Robinson
Hershal D. Cashin	George W. Sewell
3—M. S. Patterson	James R. Treadwell
Robert T. Smith	J. A. C. Parker
4—James V. McDuffie	
Green S. W. Lewis	
5—Charles H. Miller	
William H. Nichols	
6—J. A. Cowdery	
William Miller	
7—Joseph W. Burke	
Robert A. Mosely	
8—J. R. Coffrey	
Thomas Masterson	

ARKANSAS.

Powell Clayton	Washington, D. C
S. W. Dorsey	Washington, D. C
John M. Peck	Washington, D. C
John McClure	Little Rock
M. W. Benjamin	Little Rock
Joseph Brooks	Little Rock
Henry M. Cooper	Little Rock
Asa Hodges	Little Rock
James Torrans	Little Rock
M. W. Gibbs	Little Rock
O. A. Hadley	Little Rock
O. P. Snyder	Pine Bluff
R. A. Dawson	Pine Bluff
J. F. Vaughn	Pine Bluff
J. H. Clendenning	Fort Smith
Wm. Keener	Yellville
H. A. Millen	Camden
R. A. Caldwell	Fayetteville
John H. Johnson	Augusta
W. P. Walsh	Hot Springs
J. N. Sarber	Clarksville
E. A. Fulton	Monticello
Frank Gallagher	Clarendon
C. C. Waters	Helena

CALIFORNIA.

AT LARGE.

DELEGATES.		ALTERNATES.	
Alexander G. Abell	San Francisco		
Charles F. Reed	Tolo co		
George S. Evans	San Joaquin co		
J. M. Peirce	San Diego co		

DISTRICTS.

DELEGATES.		ALTERNATES.	
1—Isaac Hecht	San Francisco		
John Martin	San Francisco		
2—L. H. Foote	Sacramento		
E. H. Dyer	Alameda		
3—A. P. Whitney	Sonora		
N. D. Rideout	Yuba		
4—Josiah Belden	Santa Clara		
M. E. Gonzales	Monterey		

COLORADO.

DELEGATES.		ALTERNATES.	
Jerome B. Chaffee	Denver	J. M. Paul	Fair Play.
J. B. Belford	Central City	W. H. Woods	Central City.
John L. Routt	Central City	Daniel Ransom	Boulder City.
W. B. Osborn	Greeley	A. B. Osborn	Laramie co.
Henry McAllister	Colorado Springs	H. R. Crosby	La Plata co.
George W. Morgan	Pueblo	T. C. Bowen	San Juan co.

CONNECTICUT.

AT LARGE.

DELEGATES.		ALTERNATES.	
Joseph R. Hawley	Hartford		
Stephen W. Kellogg	Waterbury		
Joseph Selden	Norwich		
John T. Rockwell	Winsted		

DISTRICTS.

1—Martin J. Sheldon	Suffield
Dwight Marcy	Rockville
2—Lynde Harrison	New Haven
John M. Douglass	Middletown
3—John A. Tibbits	New London
John M. Hall	Willimantic
4—Samuel Fessenden	Stanford
Wm. B. Rudd	Lakeville

DELAWARE.

Delegate	Residence	Alternate	Residence
Eli R. Sharp	Seaford, Sussex co	Jacob Moore	Georgetown, Sussex co.
David W. Moore	Laurel, Sussex co	Daniel I. Laybod	Georgetown, Sussex co.
J. H. Hoffecker	Smyrna, Kent co	John T. Jakes	Wyoming, Kent co.
J. R. Lofland	Milford, Kent co	John Dounhan	Canterbury, Kent co.
James Scott	Wilmington, Newcastle co	L. D. Cappin	Wilmington, Newcastle co.
R. G. Smith	Middletown, Newcastle co	J. H. Hoffecker, Jr	Wilmington, Newcastle co.

FLORIDA.

AT LARGE.

S. B. Conover
W. J. Purman
John G. Long
John R. Scott

DISTRICTS.

1—Manuel Gorin
Peter W. Bryant
2—Harrison Reed
J. W. Menard

GEORGIA.

AT LARGE.

DELEGATES.		ALTERNATES.	
Henry P. Farrow	Atlanta	William H. Smyth	Atlanta.
James Atkins	Savannah	Eugene R. Belcher	Augusta.
Henry M. Turner	Savannah	Benjamin Conley	Atlanta.
George Wallace	Macon	W. J. White	Augusta.

DISTRICTS.

DELEGATES.		ALTERNATES.	
1—John H. De Vaux	Savannah	W. M. Craft	Savannah.
J. T. Collins	Brunswick	Stephen T. Moore	Savannah.
2—Edward C. Wade	Quitman	Charles L. Bradwell	Thomasville.
Francis F. Putney	Albany	William H. Noble	Albany.
3—S. Wise Parker	Americus		
Elbert Head	Americus	Peter Griffin	Americus.
4—Randolph L. Mott	Columbus	Curtis Bell	Columbus.
Walter H. Johnson	West Point	John M. Ward	West Point.
5—George B. Chamberlin	Atlanta	L. W. Wimby	Atlanta.
Jones O. Winbish	Atlanta	George W. Ware	Atlanta.
6—Jefferson F. Long	Macon	George Wallace	Macon.
James B. De Vaux	Macon	W. W. Brown	Macon.
7—William L. Goodwin	Cartersville	W. H. Higinbotham	Rome.
J. N. Van Meter	Kingston	Jesse A. Glenn	Dalton.
8—Edwin Belcher	Augusta	J. W. Lyons	Augusta.
C. H. Prince	Augusta	John Heard	Greensboro.
9—Isham S. Fannin	Augusta	Jefferson J. Findley	Gainesville.
Madison Davis	Athens	Richard S. Taylor	Athens.

ILLINOIS.

AT LARGE.

Joseph Robbins....Quincy....H. H. Spencer....Cairo.
Robert G. Ingersoll....Peoria....Cairo D. Trimble....Ottawa.
Green B. Raum....Golconda....R. W. McClaughry....Joliet.
George S. Bangs....Chicago....E. B Warner....Sterling.

DISTRICTS.

1—Sydney Smith....Chicago....Geo. M. How....Chicago.
George M. Bogue....Chicago....L. C. Clark....Chicago.
2—John McArthur....Chicago....U. R. Hawley....Chicago.
S. K. Dow....Chicago....E. B. Sherman....Chicago.
3—F. W. Palmer....Chicago....H. F. Waite....Waukegan.
Charles B. Farwell....Chicago....A. L. Chetlain....Chicago.
4—William Coffin....Batavia....W. H. Watson....Aurora.
E. E. Ayers....Harvard....G. A. Pffrangle....Aurora.
5—R. L. Burchell....Erie....S. D. Atkins....Freeport.
Alexander Walker....Stillman's Valley....I. C. Smith....Galena.
6—A. R. Mock....Cambridge....A. S. Comstock....Cambridge.
Joel W. Hopkins....Granville....A. G. Scott....
7—Jeremiah Evarts....Yorkville....James Hastings....Minooka.
George N. Chittenden....Joliet....E. Henderson....Mendota.
8—Joseph F. Culver....Pontiac....Charles Holt....Kankakee.
A. Buck....Kankakee....J. J. Cassells....El Paso.
9—Thomas A. Boyd....Lewiston....George V. Dietrich....Galesburg.
Enoch Emery....Peoria....Miles A. Fuller....Toulon.
10—D. G. Tunnicliff....Carthage....
David McDill....Biggsville....Edgar L. Larkin....New Windsor.
11—J. M. Davis....Carrolton....Daniel Wilcox....Quincy.
George W. Ware....Jerseyville....I. N. Allen....Mt. Sterling.

ILLINOIS—CONTINUED.

DELEGATES.	DISTRICTS.	ALERNATES.	
12—William Prescott	Springfield	Horace Chapin	Jacksonville.
N. W. Branson	Petersburg	L. H. Tichenon	Springfield.
13—C. R. Cummings	Pekin	James Tuttle	Atlanta.
R. B. Latham	Lincoln	B. F. Funk	Bloomington.
14—D. D. Evans	Danville	J. C. Walker	Tuscola.
L. J. Bond	Monticello	James H. Clark	Mattoon.
15—Benson Wood	Effingham	Geo. D. Chaffee	Shelbyville.
Thomas J. Golden	Marshall	W. O. Pinnell	Paris.
16—James S. Martin	Salem	Rufus E. Cope	Flora.
George S. McCord	Greenville	I. M. Truett	Hillsboro.
17—John I. Rinaker	Carlinville	James R. Miller	Collinsville.
H. S. Baker	Alton	John M. Pearson	Godfrey.
18—William McAdams	Chester	J. M. Neeley	Duquoin.
Isaac Clements	Carbondale	George W. McKeag	Cairo.
19—C. D. Ham	Mt. Vernon	Robert Bell	Mt. Carmel.
W. A. Robinson	Fairfield	Thomas W. Scott	Fairfield.

INDIANA.

AT LARGE.

Richard W. Thompson	Terre Haute	Isaac Jenkinson	Richmond.
Will Cumback	Greensburgh	Charles H. Mason	Cannelton.
James N. Tyner	Peru	Henry A. Matison	Evansville.
Thomas M. Browne	Winchester	David C. Branham	Madison.

DISTRICTS.

1—William Heilman	Evansville	Robert Nichols	Evansville.
R. T. Kercheval	Rockport	Jas. C. Denny	

2—Laz Noble..........Vincennes....S. M. Smith..........Washington.
N. R. Peckinpaugh..........Leavenworth....A. W. Springer..........Sullivan.
3—J. H. McCampbell..........Charleston....John P. Clark..........Brownstown.
Simeon Stansifer..........Columbus....James B. Hicks..........Salem.
4—J. H. Tripp..........North Vernon....A. D. Vanarsdel..........Madison.
William J. Baird..........Vevay....John B. Coles..........Rising Sun.
5—R. M. Haworth..........Liberty....Asahel Stone..........Winchester.
John Schwartz..........Lawrenceburg....Chester Meeker..........Connersville.
6—Simon T. Powell..........New Castle....S. P. Oyler..........Franklin.
Asbury Steele..........Marion....W. R. Hough..........Greenfield.
7—L. M. Campbell..........Danville....G. H. Williamson..........Green Castle.
J. C. S. Harrison..........Indianapolis....G. W. Grubbs..........Martinsville.
8—Amzi L. Munson..........Mitchell....Charles Cruft..........Terre Haute.
William K. Edwards..........Terre Haute....J. A. Y. Cummings..........Brazil.
9—M. H. Bunnell..........Lebanon....P. S. Kennedy..........Crawfordsville.
Henry Taylor..........La Fayette....Samuel H. Doyle..........Frankfort.
10—E. S. Merrifield..........Valparaiso....A. B. Wade..........Rensselaer.
Edwin Nicar..........South Bend....C. D. Wood..........Winamac.
11—K. G. Shryock..........Rochester....C. C. Cowgill..........Wabash.
J. R. Gray..........Noblesville....S. D. Taylor..........Tipton.
12—George Arnold..........Bluffton....J. W. Baker..........Columbia City.
A. W. Delong..........Huntington....William M. Twibill..........Hartford City.
13—B. L. Davenport..........Goshen....John P. Jones..........La Grange.
James S. Frazer..........Warsaw....John W. Irwin..........Elkhart.

IOWA.

AT LARGE.

Hiram Price..........Davenport....Samuel P. Merrill..........Polk.
James F. Wilson..........Fairfield....C. F. Clarkson..........Grundy.
John Y. Stone..........Mills....Alexander Clark..........Muscatine.
Geo. D. Perkins..........Woodbury....A. W. Thomas..........Allamakee.

IOWA—CONTINUED.

DELEGATES.	DISTRICTS.	ALTERNATES.	
1—Frank Hatton	Burlington	Geo. A. Henry	Van Buren co.
Samuel M. Clarke	Keokuk	Geo. W. McAdam	Henry co.
2—Wm. T. Shaw	Anamosa	Jerome Caskshaddan	Muscatine co.
E. S. Bailey	Clinton	B. F. Thomas	Jackson co.
3—W. G. Donnan	Buchanan co.	Samuel Murdock	Clayton co.
A. F. Tipton	Clayton co.	Joseph Hobson	Fayette co.
4—S. W. Mackenzie	Franklin co.	A. A. Noyes	Cerro Gordo co.
J. H. Brush	Mitchell co.	John Mabin	Black Hawk co.
5—S. F. Cooper		E. C. McMillan	Marshall co.
E. T. Johnson	Benton co.	Leander Clark	Tama co.
6—R. L. Tilden	Wapello co.	Val Mendal	Monroe co.
S. G. Smith	Jasper co.	C. Mastellar	Marion co.
7—J. J. Steadman	Clarke co.	J. J. Hutchings	Madison co.
R. C. Webb	Polk co.	J. O. Parish	Decatur co.
8—John T. Baldwin	Pottawattamie co.	G. W. Beymer	Union co.
M. L. Brooks	Taylor co.	N. Hanna	Montgomery co.
9—A. C. Call	Kossuth co.	L. G. Coffin	Webster co.
J. D. Hunter	Hamilton co.	E. J. Hartshorn	Palo Alto co.

KANSAS.

David P. Lowe	Fort Scott	E. A. Wasser	Girard, Crawford co.
F. M. Shaw	Paola, Miami co.	John T. Lanter	Garnett, Anderson co.
T. Dwight Thacher	Lawrence, Douglas co.	G. W. Higginbotham	Manhattan, Riley co.
A. L. Redden	Eldorado, Butler co.	James Burgess	Topeka, Shawnee co.
O. H. Sheldon	Burlingame, Osage co.	C. L. Hubbs	Kinsley, Eldorado co.
Cyrus Leland, Jr.	Troy, Doniphan co.	D. H. Baker	Salina, Saline co.

Delegate	Residence	Alternate	Residence
A. J. Banta	Beloit, Mitchell co.	G. W. Shriner	Washington, Washington co.
Albert H. Horton	Atchison, Atchison co.	John K. Wright	Junction City, Davis co.
T. C. Sears	Ottawa, Franklin co.	R. B. Taylor	Wyandotte, Wyandotte co.
William Martindale	Madison, Greenwood co.	R. W. P. Muse	Newton, Harvey co.

KENTUCKY.

AT LARGE.

Delegate	Residence	Alternate	Residence
J. M. Harlan	Louisville	John B. Bowman	Lexington.
W. H. Wadsworth	Maysville	W. J. Berry	Hartford.
W. C. Goodloe	Lexington	J. C. Jackson	Lexington.
Robert Boyd	London	James Bell	Lancaster.

DISTRICTS.

District	Delegate	Residence	Alternate	Residence
1	J. T. Long	Princeton	Edwin Farley	Paducah.
	J. R. Puryear	Paducah	J. T. Long	Eddyville.
2	E. H. Murray	Louisville	E. C. Hubbard	Hartford.
	E. R. Weer, Sr.	Greenville	C. J. Pratt	Madisonville.
3	E. L. Motley	Bowling Green	W. G. Hunter	Burksville.
	E. G. Sebree	Trenton	J. N. Henry	Glasgow.
4	W. H. Hays	Springfield	O. P. Ross	Elizabethtown.
	T. E. Burns	Lebanon	H. Scott	Hardinsburg.
5	James Speed	Louisville	W. Krippenstaple	Louisville.
	Madison Minnis	Louisville	W. H. Ward	Louisville.
6	J. J. Landram	Warsaw	Wm. Blackburn	Covington.
	J. W. Finnell	Covington	C. P. Wilcox	Covington.
7	T. O. Shackelford	Shelbyville	Thomas Todd	Shelbyville.
	Gabriel Burdett	Nicholasville	E. W. Hammond	Paris.
8	A. R. Burnam	Richmond	W. H. Lucas	Danville.
	T. Z. Morrow	Somerset	Wm. Berkle	Lancaster.

KENTUCKY—CONTINUED.

DELEGATES.	DISTRICTS.	ALTERNATES.	
9—J. H. Wilson	London	J. H. Wilson	Barboursville.
H. C. Rainey	Mt. Sterling	A. J. Auxier	Piketon.
10—W. W. Culbertson		N. Cooper	
Reuben Gudgell		D. W. Steele	

LOUISIANA.

AT LARGE.

DELEGATES.	DISTRICTS.	ALTERNATES.	
William P. Kellogg	New Orleans		
S. B. Packard	New Orleans		
P. B. S. Pinchback	New Orleans		
W. G. Brown	New Orleans		

DISTRICTS.

DELEGATES.	DISTRICTS.	ALTERNATES.	
1—C. J. Adolphe			
W. F. Loan			
2—H. Dumas		Y. H. Campbell	Orleans Parish.
R. H. Chadbourne		W. R. Chapman	Jefferson Parish.
3—Chester B. Darrall		George Drury	Assumption Parish.
Pierre Landry		Samuel Wakefield	Iberia Parish.
4—George L. Smith			
J. Y. Kelso			
5—David Young		W. J. Q. Baker	Ouachita Parish.
G. B. Hamlet		J. Ross Stewart	Tensas Parish.
6—C. E. Nash		E. L. Weber	West Feliciana Parish.
J. H. Burch		J. E. Breaux	Point Coupee Parish.

MAINE.

AT LARGE.

Delegate	Residence	Alternate	Residence
Nelson Dingley, Jr.	Lewiston	Charles Hamlin	Presque Isle.
Josiah H. Drummond	Portland	Jos. H. West	Franklin.
John L. Stevens	Augusta	W. H. Rounds	Richmond.
Frank Cobb	Rockland	Thomas Tarbox	Biddeford.

DISTRICTS.

District	Delegate	Residence	Alternate	Residence
1	John B. Brown	Portland	Stanley T. Pullen	Portland.
	James M. Stone	Kennebunk	Frederic Robie	Portland.
2	W. P. Frye	Lewiston	J. W. Wakefield	
	Enoch Foster, Jr.	Bethel	Nelson Dingley	
3	R. B. Shepherd	Skowhegan	W. H. Bigelow	Readfield.
	Edwin Flye	New Castle	Henry H. Lovell	Waldoboro.
4	Chas. A. Boutelle	Bangor	Henry R. Downes	Presque Isle.
	Josiah B. Mayo	Foxcroft	J. L. Crosby	
5	Eugene Hale	Ellsworth	John S. Case	Rockland.
	S. L. Milliken	Belfast	Ambrose White	Bucksport.

MARYLAND.

AT LARGE.

Delegate	Residence
Joseph B. Pugh	Port Deposit, Cecil co
John L. Thomas, Jr.	Baltimore, Baltimore co
C. C. Fulton	Baltimore, Baltimore co
Edward Wilkins	Chestertown, Kent co

DISTRICTS.

District	Delegate	Residence	Alternate	Residence
1	E. G. Waters	Cambridge	J. C. Mullikin	
	William Perkins	Cambridge	Joseph Godfrey	

MARYLAND—Continued.

DELEGATES.	DISTRICTS.	ALTERNATES.	
2—John T. Ensor	Towsontown, Baltimore co	J. J. Weaver	
W. A. McKillup	Westminster	H. C. Longnecker	Towsontown.
3—Robert Turner	Baltimore	N. C. Groome	Baltimore.
Peter Thompson	Baltimore	Jacob Seaton	Baltimore.
4—Samuel M. Shoemaker	Baltimore	J. McCurley, Jr.	Baltimore.
Samuel Chase	Baltimore	W. J. Gray	Baltimore.
5—W. G. Tuck	Annapolis	N. R. Henderson	Ellicott's Mills.
J. A. Gary	Baltimore city	W. W. Dannenhauer	
6—F. M. Darby	Hagerstown	William Moodie	
L. H. Steiner	Frederick	J. A. Crockett	

MASSACHUSETTS.

AT LARGE.

E. R. Hoar			
Richard H. Dana, Jr.			
Paul A. Chadbourne			
John M. Forbes			

DISTRICTS.

1—Wm. T. Davis	Plymouth		
Robert T. Davis	Fall River		
2—John E. Sanford			
Edward L. Pierce			
3—Henry D. Hyde			
J. Felt Osgood			
4—Alpheus Hardy	Boston		
C. R. McLean			

Delegate	Residence	Alternate	Residence
5—James M. Shute	Somerville		
James F. Dwinal	Winchester		
6—George B. Loring	Salem		
Henry Carter	Bradford		
7—Wm. A. Russell	Lawrence	E. C. Whitney	Marlboro.
C. H. Waters	Groton	C. A. Stott	Lowell.
8—James F. Clark			
James R. Lowell			
9—A. J. Bartholomew	Worcester		
Geo. F. Hoar			
10—James F. Moore			
William Whiting			
11—Edward Learned	Pittsfield		
S. R. Phillips	Springfield		

MICHIGAN.

AT LARGE.

Delegate	Residence	Alternate	Residence
H. P. Baldwin	Detroit	E. J. Penniman	Plymouth.
Wm. A. Howard	Grand Rapids	John P. Hoyt	Vassar.
J. J. Woodman	Paw Paw	W. J. Baxter	Jonesville.
D. L. Filer	Ludington	C. E. Holland	Houghton.

DISTRICTS.

Delegate	Residence	Alternate	Residence
1—W. G. Thompson	Detroit	Alfred Russell	Detroit.
Herman Keifer	Detroit	Otto Kirchner	Detroit.
2—Rice A. Beal	Ann Arbor	H. A. Conant	Monroe.
Charles Rynd	Adrian	Jno. A. Armstrong	Hillsdale.
3—W. H. Withington	Jackson	S. V. Irwin	Albion.
E. S. Lacey	Charlotte	Adam Elliott	Hickory Corners, Barry co.
4—N. A. Hamilton	St. Joseph, Berrien co	R. R. Pealer	Three Rivers.
Geo. Hannahs	South Haven	L. C. Chapin	Kalamazoo.

MICHIGAN—Continued.

DELEGATES.	DISTRICTS.	ALTERNATES.	
5—A. B. Watson	Grand Rapids	Geo. W. Webber	Ionia.
B. D. Pritchard	Allegan	Chauncey Davis	Muskegon.
6—Wm. L. Smith	Flint	Josiah Turner	Owosso.
W. S. George	Lansing	Peter Dow	Pontiac.
7—J. C. Waterbury	Lexington	Townsend North	Vassar.
S. J. Tomlinson	Lapeer	Jeremiah Jenks	Rock Falls, Huron co.
8—Theodore F. Shepard	Bay City	H. M. Hinds	Greenville.
H. H. Hoyt	East Saginaw	B. F. Smith	Alabaster.
9—W. H. C. Mitchell	Traverse City	W. M. Dunham	Manistee.
John C. Merriam	Negaunee	A. B. Milton	Mackinac.

MINNESOTA.

AT LARGE.

Alexander Ramsey	St. Paul	Theodore Sander	St. Paul.

DISTRICTS.

1—J. B. Wakefield	Faribault		
M. C. Fosness	Winona	C. C. Crane	Mower.
W. G. Ward	Waseca	Wm. Thomas	Blue Earth.
2—John T. Ames	Northfield, Rice co	C. A. Baker	Dakotah co.
Albert Knight	Nicollet	P. J. Temple	Brown co.
L. Boegen	New Ulm, Brown co	H. E. Lewis	Carver, Carver co.
3—R. B. Langdon	Hennepin	T. A. Perrine	Wright.
N. P. Clark	Stearns	John L. Merriam	Ramsey.
D. M. Sabin	Washington	George W. Bennidict	Benton.

MISSISSIPPI.

AT LARGE.

Delegate	Residence	Alternate	Residence
2 B. K. Bruce		R. M. Tindal	
Adelbert Ames		H. R. Pease	
J. L. Alcorn			
R. C. Powers			

DISTRICTS.

Delegate	Residence	Alternate	Residence
1—J. M. Bynum	Corinth	W. D. Frazee	Okolona.
F. H. Little	Aberdeen	J. L. Stafford	
2—George M. Buchanan	Holly Springs	J. H. Pierce	Oxford.
J. T. Settle	Sardis	S. R. Bland	
3—Jason Niles	Kosciusko	D. P. Coffee	
T. J. White	Macon	M. H. Tuttle	Carrolton.
4—H. W. Warren	Jackson	R. J. Ross	Canton.
J. J. Spellman	Jackson	R. J. Simmons	Panola.
5—Jas. A. Hoskins	Brookhaven		
M. Shaughnessey	Jackson		
6—C. W. Clarke	Greenville	W. Muller	
J. D. Cessor	Fayetteville	W. W. Edwards	Vicksburg.

MISSOURI.

AT LARGE.

Delegate	Residence	Alternate	Residence
B. F. Loan		S. H. Boyd	
R. T. Van Horn		F. A. Jones	
G. A. Finkelnburg		John B. Henderson	
James T. Smith		J. H. Storer	

MISSOURI—Continued.

DELEGATES.	DISTRICTS.	ALTERNATES.
1—Hugo Auler		
George Bain		
2—Chauncey I. Filley		
M. A. Rosenblatt		
3—William H. Cornell		
John H. Pohlmar		
4—Augustus St. Gem		
John A. Weber		
5—Amos P. Foster		
W. J. Wallace		
6—H. E. Havens		
A. L. Cahn		
7—Milo Blair		
Mack J. Leaming		
8—D. S. Twitchell		
A. U. Holcombe		
9—A. E. Wyatt		
Charles G. Comstock		
10—M. A. Lowe		
J. P. Jones		
11—A. F. Denny		
M. L. De Mott		
12—J. Sands		
S. W. Birch		
13—Theodore Breuere		
T. J. C. Fagg		

NEBRASKA.

Delegate	Residence	Alternate	Residence
N. R. Pinney	Nebraska city, Otoe co		
R. G. Brown	Sutton, Clay co		
L. W. Osborne	Blair, Washington co		
Albinus Nance	Osceola, Polk co		
H. S. Kaley	Red Cloud, Webster co		
C. F. Bayha	West Point, Cumming co		

NEVADA.

AT LARGE.

Delegate	Residence	Alternate	Residence
John. P. Jones	Gold Hill	E. A. Sherman	
C. N. Harris		C. E. De Long	
Frank Bell		R. S. Messick	
R. S. Clapp		Joseph Munckton	
Thomas Wren		R. H. Rand	
A. A. Curtis			

NEW HAMPSHIRE.

AT LARGE.

Delegate	Residence	Alternate	Residence
Daniel Hall	Dover		
Nathaniel White	Concord		
C. H. Burns	Wilton		
Ira Colby, Jr.	Claremont		

DISTRICTS.

Delegate	Residence	Alternate	Residence
1—Alonzo Nute	Farmington	Samuel Adams	Portsmouth.
Geo. W. Marston	Portsmouth	Charles M. Murphy	Dover.

NEW HAMPSHIRE—CONTINUED.

DELEGATES.	DISTRICTS.	ALTERNATES.	
2—E. A. Straw	Manchester	J. H. Gallinger	Concord.
Jesse Gault	Hooksett	Gilman C. Scripture	Nashua.
3—Benjamin F. Whidden	Lancaster	Tileston A. Barker	Keene.
Thomas C. Rand	Keene	G. A. Greeley	Lebanon.

NEW JERSEY.

AT LARGE.

Wm. J. Sewell	Camden	Wm. Bettle	Camden.
Frederick A. Potts	Pittstown, Hunterdon co	John W. Griggs	Paterson.
George A. Halsey	Newark	E. L. Dobbins	Newark.
Garret A. Hobart	Paterson	Benjamin G. Clark	Jersey City.

DISTRICTS.

1—Richard S. Leaming	Dennisville, Cape May co	F. F. Patterson	Woodbury.
Wm. E. Potter	Bridgeton	Benj. Acton	Salem.
2—Frederick W. Roebling	Trenton	George D. Horner	Tom's River.
James N. Stratton	Mt. Holly	Joseph Carr	Mt. Holly.
3—Wm. A. Newell	Allentown	Jonathan Edgar	Summit.
Wm. J. Magie	Elizabeth	John A. Howland	Long Branch.
4—John I. Blair	Blairstown	Charles A. Skillman	Lambertville.
Isaiah N. Dilts	Somerville	O. P. Armstrong	Lafayette.
5—Henry C. Pitney	Morristown	Geo. Richards	Dover.
J. Wyman Jones	Englewood	Cornelius H. Blauvelt	Hackensack.
6—John L. Blake	Orange	Samuel Morrow	Newark.
S. V. C. Van Rensselaer	Newark	James W. Grover	Newark.
7—L. H. Kendrick	Hoboken	John F. Jenney	Jersey City.
M. T. Newbold	Jersey City	Henry F. White	Jersey City.

NEW YORK.

AT LARGE.

Alonzo B. Cornell..........................New York....Edwin A. Merritt..........................Potsdam.
Henry Highland Garnett..........................Ithaca..........................
Theodore M. Pomeroy..........................Auburn....George B. Sloane..........................Oswego.
James M. Matthews..........................Buffalo....Albert C. Judson..........................Albany.

DISTRICTS.

1—L. Bradford Prince..........................Flushing....George T. Hewlett..........................Woodsburgh.
George William Curtis.........West New Brighton....James Otis..........................Belleport.
2—Abiel A. Low..........................Brooklyn....Andrew J. Perry..........................Brooklyn.
Silas B. Dutcher..........................Brooklyn....William A. Rowan..........................Brooklyn.
3—Stewart L. Woodford..........................Brooklyn....Timothy C. Cronin..........................Brooklyn.
Benjamin D. Silliman..........................Brooklyn....Benjamin W. Wilson..........................Brooklyn.
4—Jacob Worth..........................Brooklyn....Benjamin Estes..........................Brooklyn.
David Williams..........................Brooklyn....John Mitchell..........................Brooklyn.
5—William Orton..........................New York....Pierre C. Van Wyck..........................New York.
Abraham Lent..........................New York....Charles V. Lewis..........................New York.
6—Benjamin K. Phelps..........................New York....Nathan H. Hall..........................New York.
Abram J. Dittenhoefer..........................New York....John C. Limbeck..........................New York.
7—De Witt C. Wheeler..........................New York....Bernard Rourke..........................New York.
Thomas Murphy..........................New York....Joseph C. Pinckney..........................New York.
8—George F. Merklee..........................New York....Hugh Gardner..........................New York.
John D. Lawson..........................New York....Isaac Dayton..........................New York.
9—Marshall O. Roberts..........................New York....Henry G. Leaske..........................New York.
Joel W. Mason..........................New York....Richard H. Greene..........................New York.
10—Clarence A. Seward..........................New York....Isaac H. Bailey..........................New York.
Rufus B. Cowing..........................New York....Charles E. L. Holmes..........................New York.
11—Edwin D. Morgan..........................New York....Salem H. Wales..........................New York.
George Opdyke..........................New York....Charles A. Peabody, Jr..........................New York.

NEW YORK—CONTINUED.

DISTRICTS.	DELEGATES.		ALTERNATES.	
12	William H. Robertson	Katonah	Amherst Wight	Portchester.
	James W. Husted	Peekskill	T. Astley Atkins	Yonkers.
13	John H. Ketcham	Dover Plains	Abiah W. Palmer	Amenia.
	Jacob W. Hoysradt	Hudson	John T. Hogeboom	Ghent.
14	Edward M. Madden	Middletown	George H. Clark	Newburgh.
	John W. Ferdon	Sparkill	C. V. R. Luddington	Monticello.
15	William S. Kenyon	Kingston	Jacob Lefever	New Paltz.
	Joshua Fiero, Jr.	Catskill	James Harroway	Richmondville.
16	Charles E. Smith	Albany	Alfred Le Roy	Cohoes.
	John F. Smyth	Albany	Nathan D. Wendell	Albany.
17	Isaac V. Baker, Jr.	Comstock's Landing	A. Dallas Wait	Fort Edward.
	Gilbert Robertson, Jr.	Troy	John A. Quackenboss	Troy.
18	George Cahoon	Ausable Forks	Nathan Lapham	Peru.
	Franklin W. Tobey	Port Henry	Robert Waddell	Johnsburg.
19	Wells S. Dickinson	Bangor	Leslie W. Russell	Canton.
	Henry R. James	Ogdensburg	E. D. Brooks	Potsdam.
20	James M. Marvin	Saratoga Springs	John B. Clute	Schenectady.
	Stephen Sanford	Amsterdam	Chauncey Argensinger	Johnstown.
21	Hugh G. Crozier	Smithville	Albert F. Gladding	Norwich.
	Samuel S. Edick	Cooperstown	David Wilbur	Milford.
22	Amos V. Smiley	Lowville	James W. Walton	Prospect.
	James C. Feeter	Little Falls	John C. Knowlton	Watertown.
23	Charles M. Dennison	Whitestown	William Lewis	Steuben.
	Arthur B. Johnson	Utica	Edward Evans	Rome.
24	John C. Churchill	Oswego	George M. Case	Fulton.
	Benjamin R. Wendell	Cazenovia	Garrett A. Forbes	Canastota.
25	George N. Crouse	Syracuse	J. C. Carmichael	Cortlandville.
	Frank Hiscock	Syracuse	Asel F. Wilcox	De Witt.

26—John H. Camp..........Lyons....T. G. Yeomans..........Walworth.
William B. Woodin..........Auburn....William A. Halsey..........Port Byron.
27—Hathorn Burt..........Mount Morris....Reynold M. Peck..........West Bloomfield.
John S. Sheppard..........Penn Yan....James B. Gardner..........Hopewell.
28—Thomas C. Platt..........Owego....Charles W. Clauharty..........Havana.
Giles W. Hotchkiss..........Binghamton....Anson W. Knettles..........South Lansing.
29—William M. Smith..........Angelica....Orrin T. Stacy..........Rushford.
Harlow Hakes..........Hornellsville....Charles H. Thomson..........Corning.
30—Charles E. Fitch..........Rochester....John Van Voorhees..........Rochester.
Henry A. Glidden..........Albion....Edwin L. Pitts..........Medina.
31—Wolcott J. Humphrey..........Warsaw....Willard A. Cobb..........Lockport.
William Pool..........Niagara Falls....Holden T. Miller..........Byron.
32—Philip Becker..........Buffalo....Frederick H. James..........Lancaster.
Sherman S. Rogers..........Buffalo....Charles M. King..........Buffalo.
33—Walter L. Sessions..........Panama....John Manley..........Little Valley.
Alonzo Hawley..........Hillsdale....Winfield S. Cameron..........Jamestown.

NORTH CAROLINA.

AT LARGE.

Thomas Powers..........Newbern....J. W. Alberton..........Hertford.
James H. Harris..........Raleigh....W. D. Jones..........Wake Forest.
William H. Wheeler..........Salem ...Rufus Barringer..........Charlotte.
Virgil S. Lusk..........Asheville....George W. Logan..........Rutherfordton.

DISTRICTS.

1—Paleman John..........Elizabeth City....John R. Page..........Edenton.
J. J. Martin..........Williamston....George McDonald..........Camden.
2—W. P. Mabson..........Tarboro....Joseph Dixon..........Snow Hill.
E. R. Page..........Kinston..........
3—James Heaton..........Wilmington..........
....

NORTH CAROLINA—Continued.

DELEGATES.	DISTRICTS.	ALTERNATES.	
4—William A. Smith	Princeton	John A. McDonald	Raleigh.
Richard C. Badger	Raleigh	Washington Dake	Durham.
5—Thomas M. Owen	Greensboro	Thomas B. Keogh	Greensboro.
Robert M. Douglas	Greensboro	J. W. Bean	Franklinsville.
6—J. R. Nocho	Charlotte	T. D. McAlpine	Charlotte.
R. M. Norment	Lumberton	A. F. Dockray	Mangum.
7—J. J. Mott			
T. M. Cooper			
8—John G. Heap	Bakersville	T. P. Axley	Henderson.
Pinckney Rollins	Asheville	J. B. Eaves	Rutherfordton.

OHIO.

AT LARGE.

Benjamin F. Wade	Jefferson	Charles H. Grosvenor	Athens.
Edward F. Noyes,	Cincinnati	Clark Waggoner	Toledo.
J. Warren Keifer	Springfield	Lewis Wei Zel	Cincinnati.
William H. Upson	Akron	Samuel Craighead	Dayton.

DISTRICTS.

1—Benjamin Eggleston	Cincinnati	Lawrence Spath	Cincinnati.
Christian Moerlein	Cincinnati	M. B. Hagans	Cincinnati.
2—Henry Kessler	Cincinnati	E. P. Ransom	Cincinnati.
L. C. Weir	Cincinnati	William M. Yeatman	Cincinnati.
3—H. L. Morey	Hamilton	Mills Gardner	Washington C. H.
Frank Browning	Wilmington	Watts McMurchy	Batavia.
4—William D. Bickham	Dayton	C. Folkern	Eaton.
B. Collins	Greenville	John Little	Xenia.
5—James L. Price	Van Wert	J. L. H. Long	Ottawa.
James Irvine	Lima	Brice Hilton	Brunersburg.

6—N. M. Howard....Toledo....Alexander Reed....Toledo.
Earl W. Merry....Bowling Green....D. B. Ainger....Bryan.
7—Samuel H. Hurst....Chillicothe....Chambers Baird....Ripley.
John A. Smith....Hillsborough....Smith Grimes....West Union.
8—H. W. Smith....London....Milton Steen....De Graff.
A. R. Byrkett....Troy....John Howell....Springfield.
9—T. C. Jones....Delaware....W. G. Beatty....Cardington.
Hylas Sabin....Richwood....S. E. De Wolf....Marion.
10—R. P. Buckland....Fremont....Frank Sawyer....Norwalk.
J. B. Rothchild....Findlay....James A. Blair....Tiffin.
11—H. C. Jones....McArthur....Elias Nigh....Ironton.
S. H. Bright....Logan....H. A. Towne....Portsmouth.
12—L. J. Critchfield....Columbus....A. J. Ashbrook....Somerset.
John Groce....Circleville....Peter Bope....Lancaster.
13—E. L. Lybarger....Coshocton....Elmer J. Rambo....Dresden.
J. L. McIlvaine....New Philadelphia....W. R. Shields....Newcomerstown.
14—D. W. Wilson....Belleville....J. C. Cook....Nevada.
H. C. Carhart....Galion....T. B. Cunningham....Millersburg.
15—V. B. Horton....Pomeroy....William T. Hunter....Woodsfield.
Jewett Palmer....Marietta....George W. Baker....Athens.
16—J. T. Updegraff....Mount Pleasant....J. D. Taylor....Cambridge.
John Lemmox....Caldwell....W. B. Hearn....Cadiz.
17—C. Aultman....Canton....J. H. Taylor....Carrollton.
J. A. Ambler....Salem....George Brook....Ellsworth.
18—A. S. McClure....Wooster....J. H. Greene....Medina.
Geo. T. Perkins....S. S. Warner....Wellington.
19—H. B. Perkins....Warren....S. A. Northway....Jefferson.
George H. Ford....Burton....Aaron Wilcox....Painesville.
20—Edwin C. Cowles....Cleveland....W. S. Streater....Cleveland.
Julius C. Schenck....Cleveland....Julius C. Schenck....Cleveland.

OREGON.

AT LARGE.

DELEGATES.		ALTERNATES.	
J. C. Tolman	Ashland		
J. B. David	Portland		
B. C. Van Houghton	Eugene City		
J. H. Foster	Albany		
H. K. Hines	Dallas		
H. W. Scott	Portland		

PENNSYLVANIA.

AT LARGE.

DELEGATES.		ALTERNATES.	
J. D. Cameron	Harrisburg	David Aiken	Pittsburgh.
Wm. R. Leeds	Philadelphia	Henry Harly	Titusville.
Henry M. Hoyt	Wilkesbarre	John N. Purviance	Butler.
R. W. Mackey	Philadelphia		

DISTRICTS.

DELEGATES.		ALTERNATES.	
Henry H. Bingham	Philadelphia	John O'Donnell	Philadelphia.
Wm. J. Pollock	Philadelphia	H. C. Selby	Philadelphia.
John L. Hill	Philadelphia	A. C. Roberts	Philadelphia.
Morton McMichael	Philadelphia	Geo. S. Jones	Philadelphia.
Geo. W. Fairman	Philadelphia	Thomas Smith	Philadelphia.
M. Hall Stanton	Philadelphia	John B. Sepler	Philadelphia.
Wm. B. Mann	Philadelphia	Geo. D. Whelen	Philadelphia.
Wm. H. Kemble	Philadelphia	E. H. Jeffries	Philadelphia.
J. M. Byram	Philadelphia	James Whitaker	Philadelphia.
Joseph Johnson	Philadelphia	James S. Tull	Philadelphia.
H. T. Darlington	Doyleston	J. Paul Knight	Feasterville.
Alan Wood, Jr.	Conshohocken	John Wood	Conshohocken.

G. E. Darlington	Media	Isaac W. Vanlear	Wallace, Chester co.
J. Smith Futhey	West Chester	W. H. Osborn	Media.
W. S. McManus	Reading	J. K. Sterrett	Reading.
E. E. Griesemer	Reading	L. H. Smith	Reading.
B. F. Eshelman	Lancaster	B. F. Eshelman	Lancaster.
Henry S. Eberly	Lancaster	A. Craig	Columbia.
H. J. Reeder	Easton	R. Clay Hammersly	Allentown.
E. B. Young	Allentown	B. E. Schuman	
Charles Albright	Mauch Chunk	J. Lantz	Stroudsburg.
D. A. Beckley	Bloomsburg	Edgar Pinchot	Milford.
J. B. Van Bergen	Scranton	J. B. Van Bergen	Kingston.
H. W. Palmer	Wilkesbarre	L. C. Darte	Carbondale.
Lin Bartholomew	Pottsville	Wallace Guss	Tamaqua.
Daniel P. Miller	Pinegrove		
Samuel F. Barr	Harrisburg	E. Wilvert	Sunbury.
J. W. Grove	Lebanon	W. H. Oram	Shamokin.
J. E. Carmalt	Montrose	A. P. Stevens	Great Bend.
Wm. T. Davis	Towanda	George J. Bentley	Honesdale.
John R. Bowen	Wellsboro	W. M. Dietrick	Williamsport.
Lucius Rogers	Smethport	J. C. Johnson	Emporium.
John Cessna	Bedford	Benj. L. Hewitt	Holidaysburg.
Edward Scull	Somerset	R. A. Clark	Altoona.
John Stewart	Chambersburg	W. H. Woods	Huntingdon.
John Wister	Duncannon	Franklin Schoch	Silinsgrove.
Chas. H. Mullen	Mt. Holly Springs	A. Koser	Mechanicsburg.
Ed. McPherson	Gettysburg	G. Ed. Hersh	York.
H. T. Harvey	Lock Haven	J. H. Hagerty	Ridgway.
T. H. Murray	Clearfield	John B. Linn	Harrisburg.
D. S. Atkinson	Greensburg	C. W. Baker	
Andrew Stewart	Uniontown	William Parshall	
C. L. Magee	Pittsburgh	C. W. Bachelor	Pittsburgh.
J. H. Hampton	Pittsburgh	J. A. McDevit	Pittsburgh.

PENNSYLVANIA—Continued.

DELEGATES.	DISTRICTS.	ALTERNATES.	
H. W. Oliver, Jr.	Pittsburgh.	Walton Woolsey	Allegheny.
J. A. Chambers	Pittsburgh.	Hugh McNeill	Allegheny.
M. S. Quay	Beaver.	F. S. Reeder	New Brighton.
W. S. Moore	Washington.	John W. Donan	
R. Ruloffson	Strattanville.	E. L. Davis	
Simon Truby	Brush Valley.	Jos. Henderson	
L. G. Linn	Butler.	C. A. Sullivan	Butler.
Henry C. Bloss	Titusville.	Geo. S. McMullen	Conneautville.
Thomas M. Walker	Erie.	W. S. Brown	Erie.
E. W. Smiley	Franklin.	E. W. Smiley	Franklin.

RHODE ISLAND.

DELEGATES.	DISTRICTS.	ALTERNATES.	
Charles C. Van Zandt	Newport.	Edward W. Lawton	Newport.
Charles Nourse	Woonsocket.	Lyman A. Cook	Woonsocket.
Nelson W. Aldrich	Providence.	Edward R. Dawley	Providence.
Gorham P. Pomeroy	Providence.	Abraham Payne	Providence.
Edward L. Freeman	Central Falls.	James Davis	Pawtucket.
Henry Howard	Providence.	Thomas W. Chase	Providence.
Isaac F. Williams	Bristol.	Lewis B. Smith	Nayatt.
James M. Pendleton	Westerly.	Nathaniel P. S. Thomas	Providence.

SOUTH CAROLINA.

AT LARGE.

DELEGATES.	DISTRICTS.	ALTERNATES.	
Robert B. Elliott	Columbia.	Benj. F. Whittemore	Darlington C. H.
Daniel H. Chamberlain	Columbia.	A. O. Jones	Charleston.
Richard H. Gleaves	Beaufort.	Warren Minton	Charleston.
John J. Patterson	Columbia.	Charles M. Wilder	Columbia.

DISTRICTS.

Delegate	Residence	Alternate	Residence
1—Stephen A. Swails	Kingstree	Thomas B. Johnston	Sumter.
Joseph H. Rainey	Georgetown	Henry J. Maxwell	Bennettsville.
2—Henry G. Worthington	Charleston	A. B. Knowlton	Orangeburg.
Wm. J. McKinlay	Charleston	R. H. Cain	Charleston.
3—Henry C. Corwin	Newberry	A. W. Curtis	Columbia.
Wm. B. Nash	Columbia	T. N. Tolbert	Abbeville C. H.
4—A. S. Wallace	Yorkville	C. C. Macoy	Chester.
John Winsmith	Spartanburg C. H		
5—Robert Smalls	Beaufort	Wm. M. Thomas	Summerville.
Lawrence Cain	Edgefield C. H	Fred. A. Palmer	Aiken.

TENNESSEE.

AT LARGE.

Delegate	Residence	Alternate	Residence
J. M. Thornburg	Knox co	G. W. Levere	
J. C. Napier	Davidson co	A. M. Hughes	
David A. Nunn	Haywood co	W. W. Murray	
J. T. Wilder	Hamilton co	Abe Smith	

DISTRICTS.

Delegate	Residence	Alternate	Residence
1—R. R. Butler	Johnson co	Charles P. Tonery	
T. H. Reeves	Washington co	W. P. Gillenwaters	
2—E. C. Camp	Knox co	J. M. Meek	New Market.
William Rule	Knox co	J. C. Tate	Clinton co.
3—A. G. Sharp		H. S. Chamberlain	
T. L. Cate	Bradley co	Samuel Parker	White co.
4—James Peacock		C. M. Johnson	
W. L. Waters		J. H. Harding	
5—J. A. Warder	Bedford co	W. T. Nicks	Lincoln.
W. Y. Elliott	Rutherford co	Jefferson Brown	

TENNESSEE—CONTINUED.

DELEGATES.	DISTRICTS.	ALTERNATES.	
6—H. H. Harrison	Davidson co.	Sanford Griffin	
J. H. Burres		P. J. O'Rourke	
7—M. T. Weir		D. B. Cliffe	
G. W. Blackburn		Commodore Perry	
8—S. W. Hawkins		R. H. Thorn	
E. G. Ridgeley		T. C. Muse	
9—A. A. Freeman		W. M. Hall	
J. W. Boyd		H. A. Gibson	
10—Edward Shaw		John T. Lattin	
William M. Randolph		R. H. Patterson	

TEXAS.

AT LARGE.

Delegate		Alternate	
Edmund J. Davis	Austin	W. A. Price	Galveston.
S. H. Russell	Harrison	J. H. Washington	Grimes.
A. Zadek	Nevarro	Nathan Patton	Walker.
A. B. Norton	Dallas	J. J. Hamilton	Travis.

DISTRICTS.

Delegate		Alternate	
1—L. W. Cooper	Houston	S. D. Wood	Smith.
S. T. Newton	Bexar	E. B. Dwyer	Houston.
2—A. G. Malloy	Marion	S. T. Carter	Fairview.
F. W. Minor	Lamar	Wm. Lewis	Marion.
3—I. L. L. McCall	Parker	J. R. Burns	Collin.
L. W. Williams	Grayson	Daniel Webster	Grayson.
4—R. Allen	Harris	John Armstrong	
J. R. Burns	McLennan	C. F. Moore	Bryan, Brazos co.
5—N. W. Cuney	Galveston	W. H. Holland	Wharton.
S. A. Hackworth	Brenham		
6—J. P. Newcomb	San Antonio	Ridge Paschal	Corpus Christi.
Wm. Billings	Victoria	Frank Green	Columbus.

VERMONT.

AT LARGE.

Luke P. Poland........................St. Johnsbury....Bliss N. Davis ....Danville.
Wheelock G. Veazie........................Rutland....Pitt W. Hyde..........................Castleton.
George Howe........................Brattleboro....W. W. Lynde..........................Marlboro.
Geo. H. Bigelow........................Burlington....Philip K. Gleed ....Morristown.

DISTRICTS.

1—Mason S. Colburn, Manchester (P. O., Factory Point)....J. Halsey Cushmam......................Bennington.
Fred. E. Woodbridge..................Vergennes....James M. Slade......................Middlebury.
2—Warren C. French..................Woodstock....Wm. H. Walker..........................Ludlow.
Roswell Farnham......................Bradford....John W. Rowell..................West Randolph.
3—Silas P. Carpenter......................Richford....D. D. Wead ....Sheldon.
John L. Mason......................Richmond....Walter D. Crane..........................Newport.

VIRGINIA.

AT LARGE.

W. H. H. Stowell..................Washington, D. C....J. W. Woltz......................Fredericksburg.
John F. Lewis........................Linnwood....W. C. Wickham..........................Richmond.
Richard H. Carter.......Salem Fauquier, Fauquier Cape....Edgar Allen..........................Farmville.
W. N. Stevens........................Stony Creek....C. J. Malord..........................Richmond.

DISTRICTS.

1—J. B. Sener......................Fredericksburg....L. R. Stewart..........................Warsaw.
P. J. Carter..........................Franktown....E. W. Massey......................West Point.
2—J. F. Dezendorf..........................Norfolk....Wm. Stevens......................Stony Creek.
J. M. Dawson......................Williamsburg....M. McDivitt..........................Norfolk.
3—O. H. Russell..........................Richmond....J. R. Popham..........................Richmond.
P. W. Poindexter......................Louisa C. H....J. Crump..........................

VIRGINIA—CONTINUED.

DISTRICTS.

	DELEGATES.		ALTERNATES.	
4	W. L. Fernald	Burkeville	G. S. Richardson	Petersburg
	Ross Hamilton	Boydton	J. R. Hooper	Farmville.
5	D. S. Lewis	Danville	J. B. Stovall	Meadsville.
	J. B. Dehaven	Rocky Mount	J. F. Hannibas	Meadsville.
6	J. H. Rives	Lynchburg	S. Patterson	Lynchburg.
	Geo. V. Case	Liberty	L. F. Loux	Fincastle.
7	J. W. Porter	Charlotteville	R. J. Shelton	Staunton.
	Joseph Harrison	Greenville	E. Terry	Charlottesville.
8	Wm. Miller	Winchester	F. L. Van Auken	Alexandria.
	O. Blanchard	Herndon	R. Bundy	Berryville.
9	Jacob Wagner	Wytheville	W. F. Slater	Wytheville.
	W. S. Oakey	Salem	J. M. Rose	Abingdon.

WEST VIRGINIA.

AT LARGE.

Delegate		Alternate	
Thomas H. Logan	Wheeling	Geo. W. Brown	Grafton.
Waitman L. Willey	Morgantown	Richard Burk	Union, Monroe co.
James W. Davis	Lewisburg		
R. W. Simmons	Parkersburg		

DISTRICTS.

	Delegate		Alternate	
1	W. E. Stephenson	Parkersburg		
	N. Goff, Jr.	Clarsksburg		
2	John E. Schley	Shepherdstown	E. S. Troxell	Martinsburg.
	E. W. S. Moore	Fairmount	A. M. Pomedstone	Buckhanon.
3	Z. D. Ramsdall	Ceredo, Wayne co.	G. F. Taylor	Braxton C. H.
	Eugene Dana	Boon C. H.	C. W. Willard	

WISCONSIN.

AT LARGE.

Delegate	Residence	Alternate	Residence
David Atwood	Madison, Dane co.	Llywelyn Breeze	Portage City, Columbia co.
Philetus Sawyer	Oshkosh, Winnebago co.	Jno. T. Kingston	Necedah, Juneau co.
3 James H. Howe	Kenosha, Kenosha co.	J. S. Crane	Burlington, Racine co.
Mark Douglass	Melrose, Jackson co.	E. M. Rogers	Viroqua, Vernon co.

DISTRICTS.

Delegate	Residence	Alternate	Residence
1—Elihu Enos	Waukesha, Waukesha co.	James Aram	Delavan, Walworth co.
James Bintliff	Janesville, Rock co.	A. L. Phillips	Racine, Racine co.
2—Elisha W. Keyes	Madison, Dane co.	George B. Burrows	Madison, Dane co.
James T. Lewis	Columbus, Columbia co.	Geo. W. Burchard	Fort Atkinson, Jefferson co.
3—Wm. H. Brisbane	Arena, Iowa co.	A. Ludlow	Monroe, Green co.
Ephraim Bowen	Brodhead, Green co.	J. C. Holloway	Lancaster, Grant co.
4—Edward Sanderson	Milwaukee, Milwaukee co.	E. S. Turner	Ozaukee, Ozaukee co.
Irving M. Bean	Milwaukee, Milwaukee co.	Fred. C. Winkler	Milwaukee, Milwaukee co.
5—Cal. E. Lewis	Beaver Dam, Dodge co.	Geo. F. Wheeler	Waupun, Dodge co.
J. H. Mead	Sheboygan, Sheboygan co.	Geo. Marsh	Sheboygan, Sheboygan co.
6—R. L. D. Potter	Wautoma	Wm. J. Fisk	Fort Howard.
George Grimmer	Kewaunee, Kewaunee co.	A. J. Reid	Appleton, Outagamie co.
7—E. O. Rudd	Rudd's Mills, Monroe co.	J. G. Callahan	Eau Claire, Eau Claire co.
John Comstock	Hudson, St. Croix co.	A. W. Newman	Trempealeau, Trempealeau co.
8—Geo. C. Ginty	Chippewa Falls, Chippewa co.	F. M. Washburne	Elroy, Juneau co.
Myron H. McCord	Jenny, Lincoln co.	R. W. Button	Angelica, Shawano co.

TERRITORIES.

ARIZONA.

DELEGATES.		ALTERNATES.	
R. C. McCormick	Tucson		
De Forest Porter			

DAKOTA.

DELEGATES.		ALTERNATES.	
Alex. Hughes	Elk Point, Union co.	G. P. Flannery	Bismarck, Burleigh co.
A. McHench	Fargo, Cass co.	Geo. H. Hand	Yankton, Yankton co.

DISTRICT OF COLUMBIA.

DELEGATES.		ALTERNATES.	
Sayles J. Bowen		C. Crusor	
A. M. Green		Andrew Gleason	

IDAHO.

DELEGATES.		ALTERNATES.	
D. P. Thompson	Boise City	Thomas Donaldson	Boise City.
Austin Savage	Boise City	J. A. Pinney	Boise City.

MONTANA.

DELEGATES.		ALTERNATES.	
W. F. Sanders	Helena	B. H. Tatem	Helena.
R. O. Hickman	Virginia City		

NEW MEXICO.

Delegate	Residence	Alternate	Residence
S. B. Axtel			
William Breeden			

UTAH.

Delegate	Residence	Alternate	Residence
James B. McKean		John R. McBride	
George A. Black		John W. Graham	

WASHINGTON.

Delegate	Residence	Alternate	Residence
Elwood Evans	Olympia		
Thomas T. Miner	Port Townsend	J. B. George	Walla Walla.

WYOMING.

Delegate	Residence	Alternate	Residence
J. M. Carey	Cheyenne, Laramie co.	F. Wolcott	Cheyenne, Laramie co.
Wm. Hinton	Evanston, Uinta co.	J. W. Meldrum	Laramie City, Albany co.

Number of Delegates to which each State and Territory was entitled, under the call of the National Committee.

States.	
Alabama	20
Arkansas	12
California	12
Colorado	6
Connecticut	12
Delaware	6
Florida	8
Georgia	22
Illinois	42
Indiana	30
Iowa	22
Kansas	10
Kentucky	24
Louisiana	16
Maine	14
Maryland	16
Massachusetts	26
Michigan	22
Minnesota	10
Mississippi	16
Missouri	30
Nebraska	6
Nevada	6
New Hampshire	10
New Jersey	18
New York	70
North Carolina	20
Ohio	44
Oregon	6
Pennsylvania	58
Rhode Island	8
South Carolina	14
Tennessee	24
Texas	16
Vermont	10
Virginia	22
West Virginia	10
Wisconsin	20

Territories.	
Arizona	2
Dakota	2
District of Columbia	2
Idaho	2
Montana	2
New Mexico	2
Utah	2
Washington	2
Wyoming	2
Total	756

Number of Electors, ...369

Majority of Electoral Votes, ...185

REPUBLICAN NATIONAL CONVENTIONS.

CALLS AND PLATFORMS.

Call for the Convention at Philadelphia, 1856.

The people of the United States, without regard to past political differences or divisions, who are opposed to the repeal of the Missouri compromise, to the policy of the present administration, to the extension of slavery into the territories, in favor of the admission of Kansas as a free state, and of restoring the action of the federal government to the principles of Washington and Jefferson, are invited by the National Committee, appointed by the Pittsburgh Convention of the 22d of February, 1856, to send from each state three delegates from every congressional district, and six delegates at large, to meet in Philadelphia, on the seventeenth day of June next, for the purpose of recommending candidates to be supported for the offices of President and Vice-President of the United States.

E. D. MORGAN, N. Y.	FRANCIS P. BLAIR, Md.
JOHN M. NILES, Conn.	DAVID WILMOT, Penn.
A. P. STONE, Ohio.	WILLIAM M. CHASE, R. I.
JOHN Z. GOODRICH, Mass.	GEO. RYE, Va.
ABNER R. HALLOWELL, Me.	E. S. LELAND, Ill.
CHARLES DICKEY, Mich.	GEO. G. FOGG, N. H.
A. J. STEVENS, Iowa.	CORNELIUS COLE, Cal.
LAWRENCE BRAINERD, Vt.	WILLIAM GROSE, Ind.
WYMAN SPOONER, Wis.	C. M. K. PAULISON, N. J.
E. D. WILLIAMS, Del.	JOHN G. FEE, Ky.
JAMES REDPATH, Mo.	LOUIS CLEPHANE, D. C.

National Committee.

WASHINGTON, March 29, 1856.

PLATFORM ADOPTED AT PHILADELPHIA, 1856.

This convention of delegates, assembled in pursuance of a call addressed to the people of the United States, without regard to past political differences or divisions, who are opposed to the repeal of the Missouri compromise, to the policy of the present administration, to the extension of slavery into free territory, in favor of admitting Kansas as a free state, of restoring the action of the federal government to the principles of Washington and Jefferson, and who purpose to unite in presenting candidates for the offices of President and Vice-President, do resolve as follows:

1. That the maintenance of the principles promulgated in the Declaration of Independence and embodied in the federal constitution is essential to the preservation of our republican institutions, and that the federal constitution, the rights of the states, and the union of the states, shall be preserved; that, with our republican fathers, we hold it to be a self-evident truth, that all men are endowed with the inalienable rights to life, liberty, and the pursuit of happiness, and that the primary object and ulterior design of our federal government were to secure these rights to all persons within its exclusive jurisdiction; that, as our republican fathers, when they had abolished slavery in all our national territory, ordained that no person should be deprived of life, liberty, or property without due process of law, it becomes our duty to maintain this provision of the constitution, against all attempts to violate it for the purpose of establishing slavery in the United States, by positive legislation prohibiting its existence or extension therein; that we deny the authority of congress, of a territorial legislature, of any individual or association of individuals, to give legal existence to slavery in any territory of the United States while the present constitution shall be maintained.

2. That the constitution confers upon congress sovereign power over the territories of the United States for their government, and that in the exercise of this power it is both the right and the duty of congress to prohibit in the territories those twin relics of barbarism,—polygamy and slavery.

3. That, while the constitution of the United States was ordained and established by the people "in order to form a more perfect union, establish justice, insure domestic tranquillity, provide for the common defence, promote the general welfare, and secure the blessings of liberty," and contains ample provisions for the protection of the life, liberty, and property of every citizen, the dearest constitutional rights of the people of Kansas have been fraudulently and violently taken from them; their territory has been invaded by an armed force; spurious and pre-

tended legislative, judicial, and executive officers have been set over them, by whose usurped authority, sustained by the military power of the government, tyrannical and unconstitutional laws have been enacted and enforced; the right of the people to keep and bear arms has been infringed; test-oaths of an extraordinary and entangling nature have been imposed as a condition of exercising the right of suffrage and holding office; the right of an accused person to a speedy and public trial by an impartial jury has been denied; the right of the people to be secure in their persons, houses, papers, and effects, against unreasonable searches and seizures, has been violated; they have been deprived of life, liberty, and property without due process of law; the freedom of speech and of the press has been abridged; the right to choose their representatives has been made of no effect; murders, robberies, and arsons have been instigated and encouraged, and the offenders have been allowed to go unpunished; that all these things have been done with the knowledge, sanction, and procurement of the present administration,—and that for this high crime against the constitution, the Union, and humanity, we arraign the administration, the President, his advisers, agents, supporters, apologists, and accessories, either *before* or *after* the fact, before the country, and before the world; and that it is our fixed purpose to bring the actual perpetrators of these atrocious outrages and their accomplices to a sure and condign punishment hereafter.

4. That Kansas should be immediately admitted as a state of the Union, with her present free constitution, as at once the most effectual way of securing to her citizens the enjoyment of the rights and privileges to which they are entitled, and of ending the civil strife now raging in her territory.

5. That the highwayman's plea, that "might makes right," embodied in the Ostend circular, was in every respect unworthy of American diplomacy, and would bring shame and dishonor upon any government or people that gave it their sanction.

6. That a railroad to the Pacific ocean by the most central and practicable route is imperatively demanded by the interests of the whole country, and that the federal government ought to render immediate and efficient aid in its construction; and, as an auxiliary thereto, to the immediate construction of an emigrant route on the line of the railroad.

7. That appropriations by congress for the improvement of rivers and harbors of a national character, required for the accommodation and security of our existing commerce, are authorized by the constitution and justified by the obligation of government to protect the lives and property of its citizens.

8. That we invite the affiliation and coöperation of freemen of all parties, however differing from us in other respects, in

support of the principles herein declared; and, believing that the spirit of our institutions, as well as the constitution of our country, guarantees liberty of conscience and equality of rights among citizens, we oppose all legislation impairing their security.

Call for the Convention at Chicago, 1860.

A National Republican Convention will meet at Chicago, on Wednesday, the 13th day of June next, at 12 o'clock, noon, for the nomination of candidates to be supported for President and Vice-President at the next election.

The Republican electors of the several states, the members of the People's party of Pennsylvania, and of the Opposition party of New Jersey, and all others who are willing to coöperate with them in support of the candidates who shall there be nominated, and who are opposed to the policy of the present administration; to federal corruption and usurpation; to the extension of slavery into the territories; to the new and dangerous political doctrine, that the constitution, of its own force, carries slavery into all the territories of the United States; to the reopening of the African slave trade; to any inequality of rights among citizens; and who are in favor of the immediate admission of Kansas into the Union under the constitution recently adopted by its people; of restoring the federal administration to a system of rigid economy, and to the principles of Washington and Jefferson; of maintaining inviolate the rights of the states, and defending the soil of every state and territory from lawless invasion; and of preserving the integrity of this Union and the supremacy of the constitution, and laws passed in pursuance thereof, against the conspiracy of the leaders of a sectional party to resist the majority principle as established in this government at the expense of its existence, are invited to send from each state two delegates from every congressional district and four delegates at large to the convention.

EDWIN D. MORGAN, N. Y.
JOSEPH BARTLETT, Me.
GEORGE G. FOGG, N. H.
LAWRENCE BRAINERD, Vt.
JOHN T. GOODRICH, Mass.
WM. M. CHASE, R. I.
GIDEON WELLES, Conn.
THOMAS WILLIAMS, Penn.
GEORGE HARRIS, Md.
ALFRED CALDWELL, Va.
THOMAS SPOONER, Ohio.
CASSIUS M. CLAY, Ky.
JAMES RITCHIE, Ind.
NORMAN B. JUDD, Ill.
ZACHARIAH CHANDLER, Mich.
JOHN H. TWEEDY, Wis.
ALEXANDER H. RAMSEY, Minn.
ANDREW J. STEVENS, Iowa.
ASA S. JONES, Mo.
MARTIN F. CONWAY, Kan.
LEWIS CLEPHANE, D. C.

Platform Adopted at Chicago, 1860.

Resolved, That we, the delegated representatives of the Republican electors of the United States, in convention assembled, in discharge of the duty we owe to our constituents and our country, unite in the following declarations:

1. That the history of the nation during the last four years has fully established the propriety and necessity of the organization and perpetuation of the Republican party, and that the causes which called it into existence are permanent in their nature, and now, more than ever before, demand its peaceful and constitutional triumph.

2. That the maintenance of the principles promulgated in the Declaration of Independence and embodied in the federal constitution,—"that all men are created equal; that they are endowed by their Creator with certain inalienable rights; that among these are life, liberty, and the pursuit of happiness; that to secure these rights governments are instituted among men, deriving their just powers from the consent of the governed,"—is essential to the preservation of our republican institutions; and that the federal constitution, the rights of the states, and the union of the states must and shall be preserved.

3. That to the union of the states this nation owes its unprecedented increase in population, its surprising development of material resources, its rapid augmentation of wealth, its happiness at home, and its honor abroad: and we hold in abhorrence all schemes for disunion, come from whatever source they may: and we congratulate the country that no Republican member of congress has uttered or countenanced the threats of disunion so often made by Democratic members without rebuke, and with applause from their political associates: and we denounce those threats of disunion in case of a popular overthrow of their ascendency, as denying the vital principles of a free government, and as an avowal of contemplated treason, which it is the imperative duty of an indignant people sternly to rebuke and forever silence.

4. That the maintenance inviolate of the rights of the states, and especially the right of each state to order and control its own domestic institutions according to its own judgment exclusively, is essential to that balance of power on which the perfection and endurance of our political fabric depends: and we denounce the lawless invasion by armed force of the soil of any state or territory, no matter under what pretext, as among the gravest of crimes.

5. That the present Democratic administration has far exceeded our worst apprehensions, in its measureless subserviency to the exactions of a sectional interest, as especially evinced

in its desperate exertions to force the infamous Lecompton constitution upon the protesting people of Kansas; in construing the personal relation between master and servant to involve an unqualified property in persons; in its attempted enforcement everywhere, on land and sea, through the intervention of congress and of the federal courts, of the extreme pretensions of a purely local interest; and in its general and unvarying abuse of the power entrusted to it by a confiding people.

6. That the people justly view with alarm the reckless extravagance which pervades every department of the federal government. That a return to rigid economy and accountability is indispensable to arrest the systematic plunder of the public treasury by favored partisans, while the recent startling developments of frauds and corruptions at the federal metropolis show that an entire change of administration is imperatively demanded.

7. That the new dogma, that the constitution, of its own force, carries slavery into any or all of the territories of the United States, is a dangerous political heresy, at variance with the explicit provisions of that instrument itself, with contemporaneous exposition, and with legislative and judicial precedent; is revolutionary in its tendency, and subversive of the peace and harmony of the country.

8. That the normal condition of all the territory of the United States is that of freedom; that, as our republican fathers, when they had abolished slavery in all our national territory, ordained that no person should be deprived of life, liberty, or property without due process of law, it becomes our duty, by legislation, whenever such legislation is necessary, to maintain this provision of the constitution against all attempts to violate it; and we deny the authority of congress, of a territorial legislature, or of any individuals, to give legal existence to slavery in any territory of the United States.

9. That we brand the recent reopening of the African slave trade, under the cover of our national flag, aided by perversions of judicial power, as a crime against humanity, and a burning shame to our country and age; and we call upon congress to take prompt and efficient measures for the total and final suppression of that execrable traffic.

10. That in the recent vetoes, by their federal governors, of the acts of the legislatures of Kansas and Nebraska, prohibiting slavery in those territories, we find a practical illustration of the boasted democratic principle of non-intervention and popular sovereignty, embodied in the Kansas-Nebraska bill, and a demonstration of the deception and fraud involved therein.

11. That Kansas should, of right, be immediately admitted as a state under the constitution recently formed and adopted by her people and accepted by the house of representatives.

12. That while providing revenue for the support of the general government by duties upon imports, sound policy requires such an adjustment of these imposts as to encourage the development of the industrial interest of the whole country; and we commend that policy of national exchanges which secures to the workingmen liberal wages, to agriculture remunerating prices, to mechanics and manufacturers an adequate reward for their skill, labor, and enterprise, and to the nation commercial prosperity and independence.

13. That we protest against any sale or alienation to others of the public lands held by actual settlers, and against any view of the free homestead policy which regards the settlers as paupers or suppliants for public bounty; and we demand the passage by congress of the complete and satisfactory homestead measure which has already passed the house.

14. That the Republican party is opposed to any change in our naturalization laws, or any state legislation, by which the rights of citizenship hitherto accorded to immigrants from foreign lands shall be abridged or impaired; and in favor of giving a full and efficient protection to the rights of all classes of citizens, whether native or naturalized, both at home and abroad.

15. That appropriations by congress for river and harbor improvements of a national character, required for the accommodation and security of an existing commerce, are authorized by the constitution, and justified by the obligation of government to protect the lives and property of its citizens.

16. That a railroad to the Pacific ccean is imperatively demanded by the interests of the whole country; that the federal government ought to render immediate and efficient aid in its construction; and that, as preliminary thereto, a daily overland mail should be promptly established.

17. Finally, having thus set forth our distinctive principles and views, we invite the coöperation of all citizens, however differing on other questions, who substantially agree with us in their affirmance and support.

Call for the Convention at Baltimore, 1864.

The undersigned, who, by original appointment, or subsequent designation to fill vacancies, constitute the executive committee created by the national convention held at Chicago on the 16th day of May, 1860, do hereby call upon all qualified voters who desire the unconditional maintenance of the Union, the supremacy of the constitution, and the complete suppression of the existing rebellion, with the cause thereof, by vigorous war and all apt and efficient means, to send delegates to a convention to assemble at Baltimore, on Tuesday, the 7th day of June, 1864, at 12 o'clock, noon, for the purpose of presenting candidates for the offices of President and Vice-President of the United States. Each state having a representation in congress will be entitled to as many delegates as shall be equal to twice the number of electors to which such state is entitled in the electoral college of the United States.

EDWIN D. MORGAN, N. Y., *Chairman.*
CHARLES J. GILMAN, Me.
E. H. ROLLINS, N. H.
L. BRAINERD, Vt.
J. Z. GOODRICH, Mass.
THOMAS G. TURNER, R. I.
GIDEON WELLES, Conn.
DENNING DUER, N. J.
EDWARD McPHERSON, Penn.
N. B. SMITHERS, Del.
J. F. WAGNER, Md.
THOMAS SPOONER, Ohio.
H. S. LANE, Ind.
SAMUEL L. CASEY, Ky.
E. PECK, Ill.
HERBERT M. HOXIE, Iowa.
AUSTIN BLAIR, Mich.
CARL SCHURZ, Wis.
W. D. WASHBURN, Minn.
CORNELIUS COLE, Cal.
WM. A. PHILLIPS, Kan.
O. H. IRISH, Neb.
JOS. GERHARDT, D. C.

WASHINGTON, Feb. 22, 1864.

PLATFORM ADOPTED AT BALTIMORE, 1864.

1. *Resolved*, That it is the highest duty of every American citizen to maintain against all their enemies the integrity of the Union and the paramount authority of the constitution and laws of the United States; and that, laying aside all differences of political opinion, we pledge ourselves, as Union men, animated by a common sentiment, and aiming at a common object, to do everything in our power to aid the government in quelling, by force of arms, the rebellion now raging against its authority, and in bringing to the punishment due to their crimes the rebels and traitors arrayed against it.

2. *Resolved*, That we approve the determination of the government of the United States not to compromise with the rebels, or to offer them any terms of peace, except such as may be based upon an unconditional surrender of their hostility, and a return to their just allegiance to the constitution and laws of the United States, and that we call upon the government to maintain this position, and to prosecute the war with the utmost possible vigor to the complete suppression of the rebellion, in full reliance upon the self-sacrificing patriotism, the heroic valor,

and the undying devotion of the American people to their country and its free institutions.

3. *Resolved*, That as slavery was the cause and now constitutes the strength of this rebellion, and as it must be, always and everywhere, hostile to the principles of Republican government, justice and the national safety demand its utter and complete extirpation from the soil of the republic; and that, while we uphold and maintain the acts and proclamations by which the government in its own defence has aimed a death-blow at this gigantic evil, we are in favor, furthermore, of such an amendment to the constitution, to be made by the people in conformity with its provisions, as shall terminate and forever prohibit the existence of slavery within the limits or the jurisdiction of the United States.

4. *Resolved*, That the thanks of the American people are due to the soldiers and sailors of the army and navy who have perilled their lives in defence of their country and in vindication of the honor of its flag; that the nation owes to them some permanent recognition of their patriotism and their valor, and ample and permanent provision for those of their survivors who have received disabling and honorable wounds in the service of the country; and that the memories of those who have fallen in its defence shall be held in grateful and everlasting remembrance.

5. *Resolved*, That we approve and applaud the practical wisdom, the unselfish patriotism, and the unswerving fidelity to the constitution and the principles of American liberty with which Abraham Lincoln has discharged, under circumstances of unparalleled difficulty, the great duties and responsibilities of the presidential office; that we approve and endorse, as demanded by the emergency and essential to the preservation of the nation, and as within the provisions of the constitution, the measures and acts which he has adopted to defend the nation against its open and secret foes; that we approve, especially, the Proclamation of Emancipation, and the employment as Union soldiers of men heretofore held in slavery; and that we have full confidence in his determination to carry these and all other constitutional measures essential to the salvation of the country into full and complete effect.

6. *Resolved*, That we deem it essential to the general welfare that harmony should prevail in the national councils; and we regard as worthy of public confidence and official trust those only who cordially indorse the principles proclaimed in these resolutions, and which should characterize the administration of the government.

7. *Resolved*, That the government owes to all men employed in its armies, without regard to distinction of color, the full

protection of the laws of war, and that any violation of these laws, or of the usages of civilized nations in time of war, by the rebels now in arms, should be made the subject of prompt and full redress.

8. *Resolved*, That foreign immigration, which in the past has added so much to the wealth, development of resources, and increase of power to this nation,—the asylum of the oppressed of all nations,—should be fostered and encouraged by a liberal and just policy.

9. *Resolved*, That we are in favor of a speedy construction of the railroad to the Pacific coast.

10. *Resolved*, That the national faith, pledged for the redemption of the public debt, must be kept inviolate, and that for this purpose we recommend economy and rigid responsibility in the public expenditures, and a vigorous and just system of taxation; and that it is the duty of every loyal state to sustain the credit and promote the use of the national currency.

11. *Resolved*, That we approve the position taken by the government, that the people of the United States can never regard with indifference the attempt of any European power to overthrow by force or to supplant by fraud the institutions of any republican government on the Western Continent; and that they will view with extreme jealousy, as menacing to the peace and independence of their own country, the efforts of any such power to obtain new footholds for monarchical governments, sustained by foreign military force, in near proximity to the United States.

Call for the Convention at Chicago, 1868.

The undersigned, constituting the national committee designated by the convention held at Baltimore on the 7th of June, 1864, do appoint that a convention of the Union Republican party be held at the city of Chicago, on Wednesday, the 20th day of May next, at 12 o'clock M., for the purpose of nominating candidates for the offices of President and Vice-President of the United States.

Each state in the United States is authorized to be represented in said convention by a number of delegates equal to twice the number of senators and representatives to which each state is entitled in the national congress.

We invite the coöperation of all citizens who rejoice that our great civil war has happily terminated in the discomfiture of rebellion; who would hold fast the unity and integrity of the republic, and maintain its paramount right to defend to the utmost its existence, whether imperilled by a secret conspiracy or armed force; of an economical administration of the public expenditures; of the complete extirpation of the principles and policy of slavery, and of the speedy reorganization of those states whose governments were destroyed by the rebellion, and the permanent restoration to their proper practical relations with the United States, in accordance with the true principles of a republican government.

JNO. D. DEFREES, Ind., *Secretary.*	MARCUS L. WARD, N. J., *Chairman.*
J. B. CLARK, N. H.	S. F. HERSEY, Me.
A. B. GARDNER, Vt.	WM. CLAFLIN, Mass.
S. A. PURVIANCE, Penn.	J. S. FOWLER, Tenn.
B. C. COOK, Ill.	MARSH GIDDINGS, Mich.
D. B. STUBBS, Iowa.	A. W. CAMPBELL, W. Va.
H. C. HOFFMAN, Md.	N. B. SMITHERS, Del.
W. J. COWING, Va.	W. A. PILE, Mo.
C. L. ROBINSON, Fla.	S. JUDD, Wis.
HORACE GREELEY, N. Y.	H. H. STARKWEATHER, Ct.
B. R. COWEN, Ohio.	WM. WINDOM, Minn.
N. EDMUNDS, Da.	D. R. GOODLOE, N. C.
THOS. G. TURNER, R. I.	SAMUEL CRAWFORD, Kan.
S. J. BOWEN, D. C.	J. P. CHAFFEE, Col.

Platform Adopted at Chicago, 1868.

The National Union Republican party of the United States, assembled in national convention, in the city of Chicago, on the 20th day of May, 1868, make the following declaration of principles:

1. We congratulate the country on the assured success of the reconstruction policy of congress, as evinced by the adoption, in a majority of the states lately in rebellion, of constitutions securing equal civil and political rights to all, and regard it as the duty of the government to sustain those constitutions, and to prevent the people of such states from being remitted to a state of anarchy or military rule.

2. The guaranty by congress of equal suffrage to all loyal men at the South was demanded by every consideration of public safety, of gratitude, and of justice, and must be maintained; while the question of suffrage in all the loyal states properly belongs to the people of those states.

3. We denounce all forms of repudiation as a national crime; and national honor requires the payment of the public indebtedness in the utmost good faith to all creditors at home and

abroad, not only according to the letter but the spirit of the laws under which it was contracted.

4. It is due to the labor of the nation that taxation should be equalized, and reduced as rapidly as national faith will permit.

5. The national debt, contracted as it has been for the preservation of the Union for all time to come, should be extended over a fair period for redemption; and it is the duty of congress to reduce the rate of interest thereon whenever it can honestly be done.

6. That the best policy to diminish our burden of debt is to so improve our credit that capitalists will seek to loan us money at lower rates of interest than we now pay, and must continue to pay so long as repudiation, partial or total, open or covert, is threatened or suspected.

7. The government of the United States should be administered with the strictest economy; and the corruptions which have been so shamefully nursed and fostered by Andrew Johnson call loudly for radical reform.

8. We profoundly deplore the untimely and tragic death of Abraham Lincoln, and regret the accession of Andrew Johnson to the presidency, who has acted treacherously to the people who elected him and the cause he was pledged to support; has usurped high legislative and judicial functions; has refused to execute the laws; has used his high office to induce other officers to ignore and violate the laws; has employed his executive powers to render insecure the property, peace, liberty, and life of the citizen; has abused the pardoning power; has denounced the national legislature as unconstitutional; has persistently and corruptly resisted, by every means in his power, every proper attempt at the reconstruction of the states lately in rebellion; has perverted the public patronage into an engine of wholesale corruption; and has been justly impeached for high crimes and misdemeanors, and properly pronounced guilty thereof by the votes of thirty-five senators.

9. The doctrine of Great Britain and other European powers, that because a man is once a subject he is always so, must be resisted at every hazard by the United States, as a relic of the feudal times, not authorized by the law of nations, and at war with our national honor and independence. Naturalized citizens are entitled to be protected in all their rights of citizenship, as though they were native born; and no citizen of the United States, native or naturalized, must be liable to arrest and imprisonment by any foreign power, for acts done or words spoken in this country; and if so arrested and imprisoned, it is the duty of the government to interfere in his behalf.

10. Of all who were faithful in the trials of the late war, there were none entitled to more especial honor than the brave

soldiers and seamen who endured the hardships of campaign and cruise, and imperilled their lives in the service of the country. The bounties and pensions provided by law for these brave defenders of the nation are obligations never to be forgotten. The widows and orphans of the gallant dead are the wards of the people,—a sacred legacy bequeathed to the nation's protecting care.

11. We highly commend the spirit of magnanimity and forgiveness with which the men who have served the rebellion, but now frankly and honestly coöperate with us in restoring the peace of the country and reconstructing the Southern state governments upon the basis of impartial justice and equal rights, are received back into the communion of the loyal people; and we favor the removal of the disqualifications and restrictions imposed upon the late rebels in the same measure as the spirit of disloyalty will die out, and as may be consistent with the safety of the loyal people.

12. We recognize the great principles laid down in the immortal Declaration of Independence as the true foundation of Democratic government; and we hail with gladness every effort towards making these principles a living reality on every inch of American soil.

13. Foreign immigration, which in the past has added so much to the wealth, development of resources, and increase of power to this nation,—the asylum of the oppressed of all nations,—should be fostered and encouraged by a liberal and just policy.

14. This convention declares its sympathy with all the oppressed peoples which are struggling for their rights.

Call for the Convention at Philadelphia, 1872.

The undersigned, constituting the National Committee designated by the convention held at Chicago on the 20th of May, 1868, hereby call a convention of the Union Republican party, at the city of Philadelphia, on Wednesday, the 5th day of June next, at 12 o'clock, noon, for the purpose of nominating candidates for the offices of President and Vice-President of the United States.

Each state is authorized to be represented in the convention by delegates equal to twice the number of senators and representatives to which it will be entitled in the next national congress, and each organized territory is authorized to send two delegates.

In calling this convention, the committee remind the country that the promises of the Union Republican Convention of 1868 have been fulfilled. The states lately in rebellion have been restored to their former relations to the government. The laws of the country have been faithfully executed, public faith has been preserved, and the national credit firmly established. Governmental economy has been illustrated by the reduction at the same time of the public debt and of taxation ; and the funding of the national debt at a lower rate of interest has been successfully inaugurated. The rights of naturalized citizens have been protected by treaties, and immigration encouraged by liberal provisions. The defenders of the Union have been gratefully remembered, and the rights and interests of labor recognized. Laws have been enacted, and are being enforced, for the protection of persons and property in all sections. Equal suffrage has been engrafted on the national constitution, the privileges and immunities of American citizenship have become a part of the organic law, and a liberal policy has been adopted toward all who engaged in the rebellion. Complications in foreign relations have been adjusted in the interest of peace throughout the world, while the national honor has been maintained. Corruption has been exposed, offenders punished, responsibility enforced, safeguards established, and now, as heretofore, the Republican party stands pledged to correct all abuses and carry out all reforms necessary to maintain the purity and efficiency of the public service. To continue and firmly establish its fundamental principles, we invite the coöperation of all the citizens of the United States.

WM. E. CHANDLER, N. H., *Secretary*.
JOHN A. PETERS, Me.
LUKE P. POLAND, Vt.
L. B. FRIEZE, R. I.
H. H. STARKWEATHER, Ct.
JAMES GOPSILL, N. J.
WM. H. KEMBLE, Penn.
HOWARD M. JENKINS, Del.
B. R. COWEN, Ohio.
JOHN COBURN, Ind.
C. B. FARWELL, Ill.
ZACH. CHANDLER, Mich.
J. T. AVERILL, Minn.
DAVID ATWOOD, Wis.
GEORGE W. McCRARY, Iowa.
C. C. FULTON, Md.
FRANKLIN STEARNS, Va.
JOHN R. HUBBARD, W. Va.
WILLIAM SLOAN, N. C.

WILLIAM CLAFLIN, Mass., *Chairman*.
THOMAS W. OSBORN, Fla.
L. C. CARPENTER, S. C.
JOHN H. CALDWELL, Ga.
JAMES P. STOW, Ala.
M. H. SOUTHWORTH, La.
A. C. FISK, Miss.
S. C. POMEROY, Kan.
B. F. RICE, Ark.
JOHN B. CLARK, Mo.
A. A. BURTON, Ky.
HORACE MAYNARD, Tenn.
E. B. TAYLOR, Neb.
JAMES W. NYE, Nev.
H. W. CORBETT, Or.
GEORGE C. GORHAM, Cal.
JOHN B. CHAFFEE, Col.
W. A. BURLEIGH, Da.
SAYLES J. BOWEN, D. C.

WASHINGTON, D. C., Jan. 11, 1872.

Platform Adopted at Philadelphia, 1872.

The Republican party of the United States, assembled in national convention in the city of Philadelphia, on the 5th and 6th days of June, 1872, again declares its faith, appeals to its history, and announces its position upon the questions before the country.

1. During eleven years of supremacy, it has accepted with grand courage the solemn duties of the time. It suppressed a gigantic rebellion, emancipated four millions of slaves, decreed the equal citizenship of all, and established universal suffrage. Exhibiting unparalleled magnanimity, it criminally punished no man for political offences, and warmly welcomed all who proved loyalty by obeying the laws, and dealing justly with their neighbors. It has steadily decreased with a firm hand the resultant disorders of a great war, and initiated a wise and humane policy towards the Indians. The Pacific Railroad and similar vast enterprises have been generously aided and successfully conducted, the public lands freely given to actual settlers, immigration protected and encouraged, and a full acknowledgment of the naturalized citizen's rights secured from European powers. A uniform national currency has been provided, repudiation frowned down, the national credit sustained under the most extraordinary burdens, and new bonds negotiated at lower rates. The revenues have been carefully collected and honestly applied. Despite large annual reductions of the rates of taxation, the public debt has been reduced during General Grant's presidency at the rate of a hundred millions a year, great financial crises have been avoided, and peace and plenty prevail throughout the land. Menacing foreign difficulties have been peacefully and honorably composed, and the honor and power of the nation kept in high respect throughout the world. This glorious record of the past is the party's best pledge for the future. We believe the people will not entrust the government to any party or combination of men composed chiefly of those who have resisted every step of this beneficent progress.

2. The recent amendments to the national constitution should be cordially sustained because they are right,—not merely tolerated because they are laws,—and should be carried out according to their spirit by appropriate legislation, the enforcement of which can safely be entrusted only to the party that secured those amendments.

3. Complete liberty and exact equality in the enjoyment of all civil, political, and public rights should be established and effectually maintained throughout the Union by efficient and appropriate state and federal legislation. Neither the law nor its administration should admit any discrimination in respect

of citizens by reason of race, creed, color, or previous condition of servitude.

4. The national government should seek to maintain honorable peace with all nations, protecting its citizens everywhere, and sympathizing with all peoples who strive for greater liberty.

5. Any system of the civil service, under which the subordinate positions of the government are considered rewards for mere party zeal, is fatally demoralizing, and we therefore favor a reform of the system by laws which shall abolish the evils of patronage, and make honesty, efficiency, and fidelity the essential qualifications for public positions, without practically creating a life-tenure of office.

6. We are opposed to further grants of the public lands to corporations and monopolies, and demand that the national domain be set apart for free homes for the people.

7. The annual revenue, after paying current expenditures, pensions, and the interest on the public debt, should furnish a moderate balance for the reduction of the principal, and that revenue, except so much as may be derived from a tax upon tobacco and liquors, should be raised by duties upon importations, the details of which should be so adjusted as to aid in securing remunerative wages to labor, and to promote the industries, prosperity, and growth of the whole country.

8. We hold in undying honor the soldiers and sailors whose valor saved the Union. Their pensions are a sacred debt of the nation, and the widows and orphans of those who died for their country are entitled to the care of a generous and grateful people. We favor such additional legislation as will extend the bounty of the government to all our soldiers and sailors who were honorably discharged, and who, in the line of duty, became disabled, without regard to the length of service or the cause of such discharge.

9. The doctrine of Great Britain and other European powers concerning allegiance—"once a subject always a subject"—having at last, through the efforts of the Republican party, been abandoned, and the American idea of the individual's right to transfer allegiance having been accepted by European nations, it is the duty of our government to guard with jealous care the rights of adopted citizens against the assumption of unauthorized claims by their former governments; and we urge continued careful encouragement and protection of voluntary immigration.

10. The franking privilege ought to be abolished, and the way prepared for a speedy reduction in the rates of postage.

11. Among the questions which press for attention is that which concerns the relations of capital and labor; and the

Republican party recognizes the duty of so shaping legislation as to secure full protection and the amplest field for capital,— and for labor, the creator of capital, the largest opportunities and a just share of the mutual profits of these two great servants of civilization.

12. We hold that congress and the President have only fulfilled an imperative duty in their measures for the suppression of violent and treasonable organizations in certain lately rebellious regions, and for the protection of the ballot-box, and therefore they are entitled to the thanks of the nation.

13. We denounce repudiation of the public debt, in any form or disguise, as a national crime. We witness with pride the reduction of the principal of the debt, and of the rates of interest upon the balance, and confidently expect that our excellent national currency will be perfected by a speedy resumption of specie payment.

14. The Republican party is mindful of its obligations to the loyal women of America for their noble devotion to the cause of freedom. Their admission to wider fields of usefulness is viewed with satisfaction, and the honest demand of any class of citizens for additional rights should be treated with respectful consideration.

15. We heartily approve the action of congress in extending amnesty to those lately in rebellion, and rejoice in the growth of peace and fraternal feeling throughout the land.

16. The Republican party proposes to respect the rights reserved by the people to themselves, as carefully as the powers delegated by them to the state and to the federal government. It disapproves of the resort to unconstitutional laws for the purpose of removing evil, by interference with rights not surrendered by the people to either the state or national government.

17. It is the duty of the general government to adopt such measures as may tend to encourage and restore American commerce and shipbuilding.

18. We believe that the modest patriotism, the earnest purpose, the sound judgment, the practical wisdom, the incorruptible integrity, and the illustrious services of Ulysses S. Grant have commended him to the heart of the American people, and with him at our head we start to-day upon a new march to victory.

19. Henry Wilson, nominated for the Vice-Presidency, known to the whole land from the early days of the great struggle for liberty as an indefatigable laborer in all campaigns, an incorruptible legislator, and a representative man of American institutions, is worthy to associate with our great leader, and share the honors which we pledge our best efforts to bestow upon them.

Call for the Convention at Cincinnati, 1876.

The next Union Republican National Convention, for the nomination of candidates for President and Vice-President of the United States, will be held in the city of Cincinnati, on Wednesday, the fourteenth day of June, 1876, at 12 o'clock, noon, and will consist of delegates from each state equal to twice the number of its senators and representatives in congress, and of two delegates from each organized territory and the District of Columbia.

In calling the conventions for the election of delegates, the committees of the several states are recommended to invite all Republican electors, and all other voters, without regard to past political differences or previous party affiliations, who are opposed to reviving sectional issues, and desire to promote friendly feeling and permanent harmony throughout the country by maintaining and enforcing all the constitutional rights of every citizen, including the full and free exercise of the right of suffrage without intimidation and without fraud; who are in favor of the continued prosecution and punishment of all official dishonesty, and of an economical administration of the government by honest, faithful, and capable officers; who are in favor of making such reforms in government as experience may from time to time suggest; who are opposed to impairing the credit of the nation by depreciating any of its obligations, and in favor of sustaining in every way the national faith and financial honor; who hold that the common-school system is the nursery of American liberty, and should be maintained absolutely free from sectarian control; who believe that, for the promotion of these ends, the direction of the government should continue to be confided to those who adhere to the principles of 1776, and support them as incorporated in the constitution and the laws; and who are in favor of recognizing and strengthening the fundamental principle of national unity in this centennial anniversary of the birth of the republic.

E. D. MORGAN, *Chairman.* WM. E. CHANDLER, *Secretary.*

Republican National Committee.

WASHINGTON, Jan. 13, 1876.

[FOR PLATFORM OF 1876, SEE PROCEEDINGS ANTE PAGE 55.]

REPUBLICAN NATIONAL COMMITTEE,

1876.

JERE HARALSON........Selma, Alabama (M. C., Washington, D. C.)
POWELL CLAYTON, Little Rock, Arkansas (M. C., Washington, D. C.)
GEO. C. GORHAM, San Francisco, California (Secretary U. S. Senate, Washington, D. C.)
SAM'L H. ELBERT...........Colorado (address Washington, D. C.)
MARSHALL JEWELL..........................Hartford, Connecticut.
SAM'L M. HARRINGTON...... ....Wilmington, Delaware.
WM. J. PURMAN....Tallahassee, Florida (M. C., Washington, D. C.)
JAMES G. DEVEAUX..............................Macon, Georgia.
JAMES P. ROOT................................Chicago, Illinois.
WILL CUMBACK...........................Greensburg, Indiana.
JOHN Y. STONE................................Glenwood, Iowa.
JOHN A. MARTIN..............................Atchison, Kansas.
WM. CASSIUS GOODLOE.......................Lexington, Kentucky.
P. B. S. PINCHBACK.......................New Orleans, Louisiana.
WM. P. FRYE..........Lewiston, Maine (M. C., Washington, D. C.)
C. C. FULTON............................Baltimore, Maryland.
JOHN M. FORBES ...., ...Boston, Massachusetts.
ZACH. CHANDLER.....Detroit, Michigan (address Washington, D. C.)
JOHN T. AVERILL............................St. Paul, Minnesota.
G. M. BUCHANAN........................Holly Springs, Mississippi.
C. I. FILLEY................................St. Louis, Missouri.
L. W. OSBORN....................................Blair, Nebraska.
JOHN P. JONES........Gold Hill, Nevada (M. C., Washington, D. C.)
WM. E. CHANDLER.......................Concord, New Hampshire.
GEO. A. HALSEY............................Newark, New Jersey.
ALONZO B. CORNELL...........................New York, N. Y.
THO'S B. KEOGH......................Greensboro', North Carolina.
EDWARD F. NOYES*.............................Cincinnati, Ohio.
H. W. SCOTT..................................Portland, Oregon.
WM. H. KEMBLE.......................Philadelphia, Pennsylvania.
NELSON W. ALDRIDGE...................Providence, Rhode Island.
JOHN J. PATTERSON, Columbia, South Carolina (M. C., Washington, D. C.)
WM. RULE..............................Knoxville, Tennessee.
E. J. DAVIS......................................Austin, Texas.
M. S. COLBURN............................Factory Point, Vermont.
J. B. SENER...........................Fredericksburg, Virginia.
JOHN W. MASON...........................Grafton, West Virginia.

---

* Appointed by State Committee in place of A. T. Wikoff resigned.

ELIHU ENOS................................Waukesha, Wisconsin.
R. C. MCCORMICK, Tucson, Arizona (address 5th Avenue Hotel, New York city.)
NEWTON EDMUNDS..............................Yankton, Dakota.
S. J. BOWEN,....................Washington, District of Columbia.
THO'S DONALDSON, Boisé City, Idaho (address Centennial Committee, Philadelphia, Pa.)
ALEX. H. BEATTIE.............................Helena, Montana.
STEPHEN B. ELKINS, Santa Fe, New Mexico (M. C., Washington, D. C.)
JOHN R. MCBRIDE...........................Salt Lake City, Utah.
ORANGE JACOBS......................Seattle, Washington Territory.
JOS. M. CAREY..............................Cheyenne, Wyoming.

EXECUTIVE COMMITTEE, 1876.

Z. CHANDLER...*Chairman.*
R. C. MCCORMICK....................................*Secretary.*
A. B. CORNELL.......................................New York.
JOHN M. FORBES...Boston.
MARSHALL JEWELL.................................Hartford, Conn.
GEORGE A. HALSEY..................................Newark, N. J.
WM. H. KEMBLE....................................Philadelphia.
WM. E. CHANDLER.................................Concord, N. H.
CHARLES C. FULTON...................................Baltimore.
EDWARD F. NOYES....................................Cincinnati.
W. CUMBACK.....................................Greensburg, Ind.
JAMES P. ROOT..Chicago.
C. I. FILLEY..St. Louis.
GEO. C. GORHAM......................San Francisco (Washington).
JOHN T. AVERILL...................................St. Paul, Minn.
JOHN J. PATTERSON.................Columbia, S. C. (Washington).
JOHN Y. STONE...................................Glenwood, Iowa.
ELIHU ENOS.......................................Waukesha, Wis.

HEAD-QUARTERS :—*Fifth Avenue Hotel, New York City.*

WESTERN HEAD-QUARTERS :—*Chicago.*

REPUBLICAN CONGRESSIONAL COMMITTEE,

1876.

CHARLES HAYS....................................Alabama.
S. W. DORSEY....................................Arkansas.
A. A. SARGENT....................................California.
JNO. T. WAIT....................................Connecticut.
S. B. CONOVER....................................Florida.
JNO. A. LOGAN....................................Illinois.
M. C. HUNTER....................................Indiana.
JAMES WILSON....................................Iowa.
WM. A. PHILLIPS....................................Kansas.
JNO. D. WHITE....................................Kentucky.
J. R. WEST....................................Louisiana.
EUGENE HALE....................................Maine.
HENRY L. PIERCE....................................Massachusetts.
JAY A. HUBBELL....................................Michigan.
H. B. STRAIT....................................Minnesota.
J. L. ALCORN....................................Mississippi.
P. W. HITCHCOCK....................................Nebraska.
WM. WOODBURN....................................Nevada.
A. H. CRAGIN....................................New Hampshire.
C. H. SINNICKSON....................................New Jersey.
THO'S C. PLATT....................................New York.
JNO. A. HYMAN....................................North Carolina.
CHAS. FOSTER....................................Ohio.
JNO. H. MITCHELL....................................Oregon.
SIMON CAMERON....................................Pennsylvania.
L. W. BALLOU....................................Rhode Island.
A. S. WALLACE....................................South Carolina.
JACOB M. THORNBURG....................................Tennessee.
MORGAN HAMILTON....................................Texas.
C. H. JOYCE....................................Vermont.
WM. H. H. STOWELL....................................Virginia.
J. M. RUSK....................................Wisconsin.
J. P. KIDDER....................................Dakota.
S. B. ELKINS....................................New Mexico.
ORANGE JACOBS....................................Washington Territory.

EXECUTIVE COMMITTEE.

SIMON CAMERON, *Chairman.*
A. H. CRAGIN.
JOHN A. LOGAN.
J. R. WEST.
S. W. DORSEY.
THOMAS C. PLATT.
JAY A. HUBBELL.
J. M. RUSK.
C. H. SINNICKSON.

Committee on Finance.

Messrs. RUSK, PLATT, and WEST.

Committee on Printing.

Messrs. DORSEY, HUBBELL, and SINNICKSON.

J. M. EDMUNDS, *Secretary;* JACOB TOME, *Treasurer;* E. T. GETCHELL, *Chief Clerk.*

HEAD-QUARTERS:—1,006 *F Street N. W., Washington, D. C.*

NAMES AND POST-OFFICE ADDRESSES

OF

CHAIRMEN AND SECRETARIES

OF

REPUBLICAN STATE COMMITTEES.

ALABAMA........*Chairman*—Charles E. Mayer, Montgomery.
Secretary—Henry Turner, Montgomery.

ARKANSAS.......*Chairman*—S. W..Dorsey, Helena
(U. S. S., Washington, D. C.)
Secretary—James Torrans, Little Rock.

CALIFORNIA......*Chairman*—A. G. Abell, San Francisco.
Secretary—M. D. Boruck, San Francisco.

COLORADO.......*Chairman*—J. C. Wilson, Colorado Springs.
Secretary—W. R. Beattie, Denver.

CONNECTICUT....*Chairman*—Lynde Harrison, New Haven.
Secretary—Edward B. Bennett, Hartford.

DELAWARE.......*Chairman*—Henry F. Pickels, Wilmington.
Secretary— ——— ———

FLORIDA.........*Chairman*—Dennis Egan, Tallahassee.
Secretary—H. S. Harmon, Gainesville.

GEORGIA.........*Chairman*—John E. Bryant, Savannah.
Secretary—S. A. Darnell, Atlanta.

ILLINOIS.........*Chairman*—A. C. Babcock, Chicago.
Secretary—Daniel Shepard, Chicago.

INDIANA..........*Chairman*—Geo. W. Friedley, Indianapolis.
Secretary—D. S. Alexander, Indianapolis.

IOWA............*Chairman*—Henry C. Leighton, Oskaloosa.
Secretary— ——— ———

KANSAS..........*Chairman*—John Guthrie, Topeka.
Secretary—J. Jay Buck, Topeka.

KENTUCKY.......*Chairman State Com.*—W. J. Landrum, Lancaster.
Secretary—Frank P. Schmitt, Louisville.
Chairman Executive Com.—R. M. Kelly, Louisville.
Secretary—Thomas S. Speed, Louisville.

LOUISIANA.......*Chairman*—S. B. Packard, New Orleans.
Secretary—Charles Hill, New Orleans.

MAINE...........*Chairman*—James G. Blaine, Augusta.
Secretary—Zimri A. Smith, Portland.

MARYLAND.......*Chairman*—John L. Thomas, Jr., 128 West Balt. street, Baltimore.
Secretary—Albert Small, Baltimore.

MASSACHUSETTS..*Chairman*—Alanson W. Beard, Boston.
Secretaries—Geo. S. Merrill, Cadwallader Curry.
Head-quarters, 383 Washington street, Boston.

MICHIGAN........*Chairman*—S. D. Bingham, Lansing.
Secretary—S. S. Olds, Lansing.

MINNESOTA......*Chairman*—D. M. Sabin, Stillwater.
Secretary—J. C. Braden, Litchfield.

MISSISSIPPI.......*Chairman*—Wm. M. Hancock, Quitman.
Secretary—J. L. Lake, Jr., Jackson.

MISSOURI........*Chairman*—George H. Shields, St. Louis.
Secretary—D. C. Coleman.

NEBRASKA.......*Chairman*—J. W. Dawes, Crete, Saline Co.
Secretary—G. L. Brown, Omaha.

NEVADA.........*Chairman*—Isaac L. Requa, Virginia City.
Secretary—Geo. A. King, Virginia City.

NEW HAMPSHIRE..*Chairman*—Daniel Hall, Dover.
Secretary—B. F. Prescott, Concord.

NEW JERSEY......*Chairman*—Joseph Coult, 766 Broad st., Newark.
Secretary—John Y. Foster, Newark.

NEW YORK.......*Chairman*—A. B. Cornell, 5th Avenue Hotel, New York.
Secretary—Henry A. Glidden, 5th Avenue Hotel, New York.

NORTH CAROLINA. *Chairman*—Thomas B. Keogh, Greensboro'.
Secretary—F. M. Sorrell, Raleigh.

OHIO .... *Chairman*—A. T. Wikoff, Columbus.
Secretary—J. C. Donaldson, Columbus.

OREGON.......... *Chairman*—George A. Steele, Portland.
Secretary— ——— ———

PENNSYLVANIA ... *Chairman*—Henry M. Hoyt, Wilkesbarre.
Secretary— A. Wilson Norris, Harrisburg.
Head-quarters, 1303 Chestnut street, Philadelphia.

RHODE ISLAND ... *Chairman*—Charles R. Brayton, Providence.
Secretary—N. P. S. Thomas, Providence.

SOUTH CAROLINA. *Chairman*—R. B. Elliott, Columbia.
Secretary—James Kennedy, Columbia.

TENNESSEE....... *Chairman*—D. B. Cliffe, Nashville.
Secretary—G. N. Tillman, Shelbyville.

TEXAS........... *Chairman*—Edmund J. Davis, Austin.
Secretary—N. W. Cuney, Galveston.

VERMONT........ *Chairman*—George W. Grandey, Vergennes.
Secretary—George Nichols, Northfield.

VIRGINIA .... *Chairman*—C. P. Ramsdell, Petersburg.
Secretary—J. D. Brady, Portsmouth.
Chairman Executive Committee—S. E. Chamberlain, Petersburg.

WEST VIRGINIA... *Chairman*—O. G. Scofield, Parkersburg.
Secretary—George W. Brown, Grafton.
Chairman Executive Committee—J. W. Mason, Grafton.

WISCONSIN....... *Chairman*—E. W. Keyes, Madison.
Secretary—Frank Leland, Delavan.

ARIZONA .... *Chairman*—A. P. K. Safford, Tucson.
Secretary—Levi Bashford, Prescott.

DAKOTA .... *Chairman*—George H. Hand, Yankton.
Secretary—L. D. F. Poore, Springfield.

IDAHO........... *Chairman*—L. F. Carter, Boisé City.
Secretary—J. S. Gray, Boisé City.

MONTANA........ *Chairman*—Wesley W. Jones, Deer Lodge.
Secretary—E. S. Stackpole, Deer Lodge.

NEW MEXICO.....*Chairman*—Wm. Breeden, Santa Fe.
Secretary—W. W. Griffin, Santa Fe.

UTAH...........*Chairman*—John R. McBride, Salt Lake City.
Secretary— ——— ———

WASHINGTON.....*Chairman*—Thomas T. Minor, Port Townsend.
Secretary—W. McMicken, Olympia.

WYOMING........*Chairman*—E. P. Snow, Cheyenne.
Secretary— ——— ———

DISTRICT OF COLUMBIA..*Chairman*—Geo. Holmes, Washington.
Secretary—J. L. N. Bowen, Washington.

www.ingramcontent.com/pod-product-compliance
Lightning Source LLC
LaVergne TN
LVHW011232110826
845150LV00006B/1612
9781425514563